CARMELITE STUDIES

CONTEMPORARY PSYCHOLOGY
AND
CARMEL

John Sullivan, OCD
Editor

ICS Publications
Washington, DC
1982

ICS Publications
2131 Lincoln Road, NE
Washington, DC 20002

Carmelite Studies is a series of the Institute of Carmelite Studies. Its editor, Fr John Sullivan, prepares each volume after receiving editorial advice and assistance from the members of the I.C.S. Sales may be arranged through ICS Publications, but *no* subscriptions are possible due to the cycle of publication and fluctuations in monetary value.

Library of Congress Cataloging in Publication Data
Main entry under title:

Contemporary psychology and Carmel.

    Carmelite Studies; 2
    Includes bibliographical references.
    Contents: Christian freedom and the nights of St. John of the Cross / David Centner — Teresa, a self-actualized woman / J. Ruth Aldrich — Toward a contemporary model of spiritual direction / Kevin Culligan — [etc.]
    1. Spiritual life—Catholic authors—Addresses, essays, lectures. 2. John of the Cross, Saint, 1542–1591—Addresses, essays, lectures. 3. Teresa, of Avila, Saint, 1515–1582—Addresses, essays, lectures. 4. Mary, Blessed Virgin, Saint—Addresses, essays, lectures. 5. Carmelites—Addresses, essays, lectures. I. Sullivan, John, 1942–   . II. Series.
BX2350.2.C6137   255'.73   82-1091
ISBN 0-935216-00-6   AACR2

TABLE OF CONTENTS

ACKNOWLEDGEMENTS

We wish to express appreciation to the following publishers for permission to print articles:

Libreria Editrice Vaticana for first translation rights to the article "Quaestio de Fide apud S. Joannem a Cruce," *Collectanea Theologica*, 21 (1950), 418-68. © Libreria Editrice Vaticana, Vatican City, 1982.

Ephemerides Carmeliticae for the reprinting of the article "Toward A Contemporary Model of Spiritual Direction: A Comparative Study of Saint John of the Cross and Carl R. Rogers," 31 (1980), 29-90.

ABBREVIATIONS

For citations of the major works of either St John of the Cross or St Teresa of Jesus we will continue to use the following abbreviations adopted in Vol. I of *Carmelite Studies*:

ST JOHN OF THE CROSS

A = The Ascent of Mount Carmel   In A and N the first number
N = The Dark Night   indicates the book
C = The Spiritual Canticle
F = The Living Flame of Love

ST TERESA OF JESUS

L = The Book of Her Life
W = The Way of Perfection
C = The Interior Castle   In C the first number indicates the Dwelling
F = Book of the Foundations

INTRODUCTION

For this second volume of *Carmelite Studies* we are going to follow some advice of St Teresa carried in the Introduction to the first volume of our series, that is, "it is we who are the beginners now [and] let them continually strive to be beginners too." We are bringing together studies by persons who, in recent years, have reaped the fruits of long hours of research on Carmelite authors so as to obtain for their findings the highest level of academic recognition. Now active in their respective fields of specialization, almost every one of them crowned his or her academic career with a doctoral dissertation on a Carmelite topic.

The first part of this volume, as a result, presents articles by a cluster of young American authors who have done theses on either St Teresa or St John of the Cross. What further characterizes all of these works is their common approach of mining the teachings of the two Carmelite mystics in a particularly fascinating way: they use the findings of such established twentieth-century psychologists as Rollo May, Abraham Maslow, Carl Rogers and Carl Jung and apply them to Teresa and John's descriptions of spiritual development. The overall effort discernible in their four articles is one of contextualization for our times and our quest after modern approaches to interiority, even as they pay tribute to the perennial wisdom of both Carmelite saints. We hope that our presentation of this set of studies will encourage still others to seek out links between currents of contemporary thought and the always fascinating testimonies of the mystics.

Due to the length of "Contemporary Psychology and Carmel," the second part contains just two articles. By dealing with a Marian theme the second one mines a vein of Carmelite spirituality long held in esteem by the Order, namely, devotion to Mary the Queen Beauty of Carmel. The first article, for its illustrious author and interesting background, obviously deserves a more detailed introduction.

Last year the first doctoral thesis of Pope John Paul II, submitted by him as a young priest to Rome's Angelicum University in 1948, was published in English under the title *Faith According to St John of the Cross* (San Francisco: Ignatius Press, 1981). As indicated by the translator-editor, Fr Jordan Aumann, OP, the young Polish Fr Wojtyła did this thesis under the direction of leading theologians in the Eternal City and then composed a shorter summary of it for the Warsaw theological journal called *Collectanea Theologica* after he returned to his homeland. That summary article was written in Latin, as was the thesis, and both have remained inaccessible to an English-language reading audience — along with so many other works of this great admirer of John of the Cross — until his election to the papacy. *Carmelite Studies* appreciates this chance to make the summary of "Papa Wojtyła's" thesis available to our readers in the fine translation of Fr Christopher Latimer, a member of the Institute of Carmelite Studies and also Editor-in-Chief of *Spiritual Life* Magazine. Thanks go too, to the Libreria Editrice Vaticana for its kind authorization to publish this translation for the first time. Karol Wojtyła's thoughts of thirty years ago are of primary importance for us today, with the way the Church he now leads needs to lean on the sustaining power of faith more than ever. The same faith that St John of the Cross relied on for light in the "dark night" is necessary for us to see through our own night of nuclear fears, structured and random violence, financial uncertainty, devious political maneuverings, unjust oppression of human rights in all forms, and other social ills around the world. While the world of Pope John Paul II is no longer the same one he knew when he first wrote this summary, one can still hope that we will face it with a serenity like his own for having read his words on the "saint of the dark night." To ensure that our text maintains some of the flavor of the Pope's article of 1950, we will give the direct quotes from St John of the Cross placed in the footnotes by Fr Wojtyła according to the original Spanish version then current.

One final word about *Carmelite Studies* itself. The sales

records of our first volume have been most gratifying (5,000 copies sold by the end of eleven months), and they have encouraged the Institute of Carmelite Studies to carry on with a fair amount of optimism. Future volumes are already taking shape and we hope we will succeed at accomplishing our self-assigned task of enriching our readers' spiritual growth in the process. Look for many articles in the near future on St Teresa, in connection with the Fourth Centenary of her death.

John Sullivan, OCD
Editor

CONTEMPORARY PSYCHOLOGY AND CARMEL

CHRISTIAN FREEDOM AND THE NIGHTS OF ST JOHN OF THE CROSS

David Centner, O.C.D.

Father David Centner did his theological studies in Rome at the Teresianum. He obtained the Doctorate in Sacred Theology there by presenting a thesis on the theme of this article.

INTRODUCTION

*L*ibertad! *Uhuru!* Freedom Now! Later generations might well call our age an age of liberation. The aspirations of men and women for freedom and their experience of personal and social alienation from it can be termed leitmotifs of the complex social developments of the past few generations. Liberation and alienation are pervasive themes in art and literature, in national and international politics; and their influence can be felt in the ferment which is changing the life of such basic social units as the family and Church. Freedom has become an important theme in theologies which are not content merely to examine its abstract nature but which seek to foster programs of pastoral liberation by Gospel values.

One must know what freedom is in order to begin the task of realizing it. But freedom is never fully known. It is a transcendental value which exceeds every category of discursive knowl-

edge. Though a given in human experience it is looked for as
something to come. It is a mystery, a problem which encroaches
on its own data and, like so many other basic values, tends to
be defined in terms of itself. As Karl Rahner says: "The ground
of freedom is the abyss of mystery which can never be conceived
as something not yet known but knowable in the future . . ."[1]
It is an *a priori* category of experience which must be examined
theologically through the use of a transcendental method.[2] For
many idealist schools of philosophy and the theologies and
political ideologies derived from them, freedom is not an attribute of persons at all but an *a priori* structure of reality.[3] Empiricist philosophies tend to explain away freedom entirely.[4]
Because it is a transcendental value, freedom is not amenable
to direct examination by the natural sciences, though they may
help to elucidate it and foster the conditions of its realization.
The humanist psychologist Carl Rogers could hardly make this
fact clearer when he states:

> For some time I have been perplexed over the living paradox
> which exists in psychotherapy between freedom and deter-
> minism. In the therapeutic relationship some of the most com-
> pelling subjective experiences are those in which the client feels
> within himself the power of naked choice. . . . Yet as we enter
> this field of psychotherapy with objective research methods, we
> are, like any other scientist, committed to a complete deter-
> minism.[5]

Still, the problem of freedom goes beyond the age-old question of the existence of a free will. Determinism is not the central problem. Rollo May states:

> Indeed, the central core of modern man's "neurosis," it may be
> fairly said, is the undermining of his experience of himself as
> responsible, the sapping of his will and ability to make decisions.
> The lack of will is much more than merely an ethical problem:
> the modern individual so often has the conviction that even if he
> *did* exert his "will" — or whatever illusion passes for it — his ac-

tions wouldn't do any good anyway. It is this inner experience
of impotence, this contradiction in will, which constitutes our
critical problem.[6]

E. W. Trueman Dicken went straight to the heart of the problem when he wrote:

> We commonly speak as if freedom of the will depended simply
> upon our power to choose between a right and a wrong course
> of action, unmindful of the fact that we cannot strictly be said to
> be "free" to will anything which we cannot accomplish. We may
> indeed wish it, but there is no freedom of choice where there is
> no possibility of realizing what we wish.[7]

It is this crisis of the entire person which distinguishes the
present problem of freedom from earlier disputes regarding free
will. The question we face today is not whether the will is free
but whether we are, or even can be, free. If a person is so psychologically out of touch with himself that he cannot effectively
will anything, or if in his individuation he is so cut off from the
world of people and things that any choice that may be possible
for him has no bearing on his goals as a human person, he is
not free. He is *alienated*. He lives in dissociation from himself,
the world, and others. He loses something of his "self" and
becomes the instrument of his circumstances while trying to
make an instrument of those — including himself — from whom
he has become dissociated.[8]

If we may extrapolate from our contemporaries' experience
of non-freedom in alienation we may arrive at some positive
understanding of that transcendental value we call freedom: it
is at least the achievement of a selfhood and an existence which
is lived by an individual, through personal choices, for the sake
of his own purpose, goal, or end in life.[9] And indeed, as Karl
Rahner has stated in one of his many works touching on
freedom, it is neither "freedom of choice" nor an interior stoic
"freedom of attitude" like that exalted by Sartre and which is
more truly called fatalism.

Freedom is first of all "freedom of being." It is not merely the quality of an act as such as it is sometimes performed, but a transcendental qualification of being human. . . . Primarily . . . freedom is not concerned with this is or that which it might do or not do. . . . Freedom is never a mere choice between individual objects, but *it is the self-realization of man who makes a choice,* and only within this freedom in which man is capable of realizing himself is he also free as regards the material of his self-realization. He can do or not do this or that with respect to is own inescapable self-realization.[10]

But to say that man will be free when he has realized himself and that he is free insofar as he is realizing himself is still not to say what freedom is. "What we shall later be has not yet come to light."[11] In the final analysis, a proper understanding of freedom can only be derived from theological reflection on man's end as revealed in Jesus who stated: "If you live according to my teaching . . . then you will know the truth, and the truth will set you free."[12] Theology, for its part, cannot ignore the contemporary issue of freedom and alienation. Nor has it.[13] Yet much of its attention has been directed toward the social and political implications of christian freedom with a near neglect of the personal dimensions of freedom which are no less important. This is somewhat surprising since freedom is one of the preoccupations of the great schools of Christian spirituality.

The importance of freedom is especially evident in the writings of the Spanish Carmelite St John of the Cross — a point not overlooked by his commentators. Marilyn May Mallory, for example, does not hesitate to summarize the saint's doctrine in terms of freedom;[14] and Jacques Maritain says of him that he "leads liberty through all the nights of renunciation" and calls the path that leads to the heights of Carmel "the sole road of liberty."[15] Even the theologians of liberation have begun to pay attention to St John of the Cross.[16]

The fact is that in the works of St John of the Cross, and in particular in the *Ascent of Mount Carmel* and the *Dark Night of the Soul*, freedom terms, images and analogies occur with such regularity and prominence that there can be no doubt that in some sense freedom and unfreedom are major concerns of the saint. But if we raise the question as to whether or not the mystical doctrine of St John of the Cross is relevant to our theological examination of our contemporary crisis of freedom, we face several difficulties of a distinctly academic nature. The first of these is the fact that man today perceives himself in a very different fashion from the way a sixteenth-century Spaniard thought of himself. This means that we cannot content ourselves with comparing or applying sixteenth-century phenomena and models to present-day man but must seek to understand the saint's doctrine of liberation in terms of our present-day understanding of man. Although he writes about liberty, St John of the Cross was not especially interested in man's self-realization in a secular sense. We cannot assume that he is addressing our problem just because he employs a familiar vocabulary. Much of the data of interest to us must be extrapolated from his writings at the risk of misrepresenting his thought. This task is complicated by certain idiosyncracies of John the author and by some deficiencies in his formal theological education. But we must exercise caution, too. It is entirely possible that his basic intuition on a subject may be correct notwithstanding objections on our part to his theological or psychological exposition. Where we encounter difficulties, a statement of that fact is of more service than a bowdlerized version of the saint — our interpretation may be at fault! We must also avoid the danger of confusing psychological and theological methodologies and of reducing the saint's doctrine to a kind of psychology of mystical experiences.

These difficulties appear formidable enough and suggest that anything one might derive from the saint's mystical doctrine would be useful constructs for theological inquiry but only tenuously related to his actual thought. Our experience has been the contrary. It is our belief that the mystical doctrine of the Spanish saint in his *Ascent* and *Dark Night* provides us with precious insights into growth in freedom, insights that are applicable to Christian life in general and for all times and not merely to the life of those called to mystical union.

FREEDOM, UNION AND SALVATION

Does St John of the Cross speak of the problem of freedom and alienation experienced by modern man? If so, is his doctrine theologically valid for us today? This is our primary question. To answer it we will have to examine both the saint's writings and what theology has to tell us about freedom and alienation.

St John's Literary Exposition

1. Frame of Reference: The Soul's Journey

The main analogy which St John uses to explain his doctrine is that of *flight and rendezvous* by night. The symbol of night is so powerful that the reader often overlooks the element of motion in the analogy. Much of the saint's doctrine regarding liberation makes sense only by reference to the motion of the soul in its journey toward union with its beloved.

2. The Principal Terms Used

In expounding his doctrine St John frequently employs words and comparisons[17] which indicate various kinds of possibilities and impossibilities. While these are sometimes mere figures of speech they may often have analogical meanings that speak of freedom and alienation. This is especially true when John uses such words with a negative particle in a sense that clearly indicates an undue *impediment* to an activity: "Joy is blinding to the heart and does not allow it (*no le deja*) to consider and ponder things . . ."; and, "The third sign . . . is the powerlessness . . . to meditate (*el no poder ya meditar*). . . ."[18]

The basic journey analogy is found in many of these references to impeded activity, though not every motion word is directly applicable to the basic analogy. For example, we find *volver atras* in chapter eight of the First Book of the *Night* and it seems to be an ordinary figure of speech, similar to the English "backslide."

Even though we may not always be sure how a term is to be interpreted, the fact remains that St John of the Cross' diction relies heavily on the analogical use of words referring to motion and to physical freedom. Among the most frequently employed such terms are: *embarazar* (hinder),[19] *impedir* (impede),[20] *asir* and *desasir* (grasp and let go of).[21] Less common are *estorbar* (obstruct),[22] *detenir* (détain),[23] and their cognates. The word *cautiverio* (slavery) and its synonyms[24] are surprisingly rare in contrast with *liberatad*[25] and 'its related forms. The saint often reinforces the sense of the foregoing words by combining them with substantives which turn them into more extended analogies. Examples of these include: *lazo* (snare), *presa* (capture), *daño* (injury-probably the most common), *empacho* (obstacle), and *carcel* (jail).[26] Sometimes words indicating the impediment of motion are used explicitly of psychological activity.[27]

By extension, several terms which have no intrinsic connection with freedom or slavery acquire it through the contexts in which they appear. These are chiefly descriptions of states of the subject and include: *desnudez* (nakedness), *pobreza* (poverty), *soledad*(solitude), *vacío* (void), *propiedad* (propensity for), *sosiego* (calmness) and their cognates.[28]

In several instances, the analogy of physical impediment and personal freedom is presented in extended metaphors. The most celebrated and effective of these are that of the bird held captive by a thread, the remora which prevents the ship from reaching port,[29] and the comparison of the obscuring of reason with the wine of Babylon and the enslavement of Samson by his enemies.[30]

A Problem of Interpretation

It does not necessarily follow from St John's deliberate use of freedom terms and comparisons that he intends to address himself to what we have referred to as the problem of freedom and alienation. They are sometimes only metaphors for growth.[31]

For example, Book Two of the *Dark Night* begins with one of the most explicit freedom images in the saint's writings:

> If God intends to lead the soul on, he does not put it in the dark
> night of the spirit immediately after its going out from the ar-
> ridities and trials of the first purgation and the night of sense.
> Instead, after having emerged from the state of beginners, it
> usually spends many years exercising itself in the state of profi-
> cients. In this new state, as one liberated from a cramped prison
> cell, the soul goes about the things of God with much more
> freedom and satisfaction of spirit. . . . [32]

A cursory examination of this passage might suggest that the
first night (of sense) is the prison from which the soul is
liberated. But the paragraph continues:

> . . . and with more abundant interior delight than it did in the
> beginning before entering the night of sense. Its imagination
> and faculties are no longer *bound* to discursive meditation and
> spiritual solicitude, as was their custom (*no trayendo atada ya la
> imaginación y potencias al discurso y cuidado espiritual, como solía*).[33]

It is clear that the new freedom celebrated here is the "liberation" of the faculties from dependence on discursive meditation,
a skill acquired through hard work. In moving beyond mediation the soul is not moving from an alienating state but toward
a simplification of activity and greater maturity. It would seem,
then, that at least in this case the saint is not talking about
liberation from alienation.

John teaches a similar doctrine in the eighth chapter of the
First Book of the *Night* where he tells us that God wishes to
withdraw beginners (*sacarlos*) from their base manner of loving
and to liberate them (*librarlos*) from meditating. He goes on to
say that God wishes to put them into the [state of] exercise of
the spirit "in which freer from imperfections they may more
abundantly communicate with God — *en que más abundantemente y
más libre de imperfecciones puedan comunicarse con Dios*."[34] Once
again, St John portrays as liberation the growth of the subject
beyond meditation. Yet here he adds that the soul is freer from
imperfections and seems to imply that there is a causal relationship between that fact and the newly increased communication

of God to the soul. What are these imperfections? If by them the saint means merely a less mature stage of development which has been left behind in due order, then the passage treats of growth only. But if he is speaking of a disorder which has prevented or impeded the actualization of the subject, then we may safely guess that we are on the trail of freedom and liberation.

It should be clear from the foregoing examples that it is not enough to examine semantically the sense of individual passages in order to apply the mystical doctrine of St John of the Cross to a theology of freedom. It is necessary to determine from the full context of his teaching whether or not he is speaking on an obstruction which detains the soul in its journey. And we must establish whether or not the goal at the end of that journey is our goal of self-realization and whether or not the obstacles foreseen by the saint are the ones that alienate us on our pilgrimage.

The Theological Basis of Freedom

Let us briefly examine the principal theological issues involved in our quest for freedom. We will take as our starting point some descriptions of freedom taken from the *Theological Investigations* of Karl Rahner whom we will follow as a kind of guide on our quest because of the frequency and thoroughness of treatment with which he has addressed the subject of freedom.

He states that freedom is to be understood as: ". . . the possibility, through and beyond the finite, of taking up a position toward God himself. . . . Freedom is self-achievement of the person, using a finite material, before the infinite God."[35] And he adds: "Freedom, however, does not consist in always being able to do the opposite of what one has done up to now, but it consists in being able to effect oneself once and for all into finality."[36] Or, if we may paraphrase Abraham Maslow's description of freedom, it is the possibility of becoming a *fully* actualized person.[36a]

Rahner's reference to the finite material of freedom is of
critical importance for, "Everything depends on the object of
one's freedom."[37] If man seeks his realization in things, his
future can only be a (theoretically) numerically infinite series of
ultimately sterile choices, for man can experience himself (and
thus realize himself) "by experiencing the other *person* and not
the other *thing*."[38] But no single human person can realize the
full possibilities of his own nature and therefore no human person can begin to find his self-realization fulfilled in such other
human persons as he may love, let alone satisfy his spiritual
hunger for the infinite.[39] It is this hunger for the infinite *person*,
for God himself, which constitutes the very possibility of free
choices and makes of God "the freedom of our freedom by the
grace of his self-communication, without which our free will
could only choose bondage no matter what choice it would
make."[40] Without God man would be caught in a web of determinism.[41] Yet God is never present to man as an object. Man
must seek his self-realization in God through object choices.[42]
In those choices God is present to the spiritual person as "an
unreflected horizon which determines everything else and
within which the whole spiritual life is lived,"[43] and as the
"ground . . . which is the permanent basis for all other
spiritual activities and which . . . is always more 'there' and
less objectively 'there' than everything else."[44]

Human freedom, therefore, is always a "situated" freedom,[45]
dependent on circumstances for its realization and faced with
the possibility that it would be presented with no object of choice
which would allow it to achieve its final actualization.[46] It is
also a task which man cannot evade and which makes a total
demand on man out of the situation in which he uniquely lives;
"He is demanded, he himself is ventured. . . ."[47] Freedom
may be alienated by the refusal of a person to effect his own
self-realization or by circumstances which would render such a
final realization impossible.

Underlying these theological statements is a vision derived
from Christian revelation. It speaks both of man's perfect
self-actualization in God and the obstacles to its achievement.

This vision is essential to an understanding of freedom and of the relevance of St John's mystical doctrine for liberation in Christ.

1. Freedom in the Scriptures

As Nicholas Lash has pointed out, in both the Old Testament and the Synoptic Gospels, the word which we translate as "freedom" is rare. What we would call freedom is a theological reality brought about by God and is expressed by the words for "salvation." To judge by the Synoptic Gospels, freedom was never the direct object of the teaching of Christ.[48] In contrast, in the Gospel according to St John and in the Letters of Paul, salvation in Christ appears theologically elaborated in terms of *eleutheria* — freedom — and its cognates.[49]

A full exposition of this involved theme would take us beyond the scope of this article. But we may note that the problematic of freedom as developed by St Paul, especially in chapter eight of his Letter to the Romans, and the soteriological presentation of freedom in chapter eight of the Fourth Gospel converge in a number of important respects.[50] For both, freedom is an eschatological reality already present in the life of the Christian. For both, it is a liberation from Sin and Death (Paul sees tham as personified!) which cannot come about by man's natural generation or by the institution of the law but only through rebirth in Christ. In Paul's presentation this freedom is linked to baptism and the Spirit, while in John it is more clearly linked to the word spoken by the Son.[51] It is achieved in the Pauline vision through union with the death and resurrection of Christ and in that of John through faithful discipleship. In both of these presentations, freedom is seen as being above all final fulfillment. It is won in the face of the alienation that is sin and in spite of the great alienation — death.

In addition, each of these sacred authors has a special insight which relates directly to our theme. In Romans 7:15–23, Paul speaks of the experience of inner disorder, of alienation from himself which has come to be called concupiscence. John's message of salvific freedom is developed in terms of love: "For while the law came through Moses, this enduring love came through Jesus Christ."[52] The unitive dimension of love is most richly developed in the Last Supper discourse.[53]

We might briefly explore some of the theological implications of these scriptural themes.

2. Sin As Alienating

Sin is often described as a "free transgression of the law of God."[54] While correct, this definition does not do justice to the insight in John's Gospel and in the writings of Paul that alienation and death are an *intrinsic* consequence of sin. The same objection may be raised against the notion of sin as an *"aversio a Deo, conversio ad creaturam."*[55] Sin can be called truly alienating only if it is seen that guilt is not merely an extrinsic qualification of a sinner by the divine Judge but the sinner himself in his own self-realization:[56] he makes himself good or evil. As Monden says, sin *"becomes the man himself in a relation of refusal* to God's love," and the punishment "meted out" to sin is the "enduring invitation of love itself as the torment of him who rejects it."[57] Or, as Rahner has put it, guilt is "theological and metaphysical suicide but one which does not thereby allow the subject to escape from itself into nothingness" so that "freedom fails also to attain itself. . . ."[58]

Not every act of sin or state of guilt is final. So long as man is in time the radical possibility remains open for him to change his mind[59] and, through grace,[60] to repent. This possibility raises the question of Sin and sins and of the distinction between object choices and what has come to be called the fundamental option.

3. Object Choices and the Fundamental Option

A human choice is self-determining before God and leads to man's self-realization "not only in virtue of a juridical or moral interpretation of this act but on the ground of its metaphysical structure,"[61] but *ultimately* so only insofar as it proceeds from the innermost center of his being, from his real spiritual core, "from that core . . . from which man's whole metaphysical essence arises and is compacted. . . ."[62] But that center of his being is in no way directly accessible to him and a here-and-now choice may actually be at odds with the fundamental orientation he has been making for himself in his history of choices. This unknown, deeper, chosen orientation has been called the "fundamental option." Louis Monden has described it as:

> The choice in human activity becomes really a free choice only from the fact that it comes from a much deeper root than ordinary actions. That deeper source, too, is some kind of choice, not with respect to specific subjects but with respect to the totality of existence, its meaning and its direction . . . the fundamental option is made between a "yes" and a "no" in which man, as a spirit, unconditionally commits or refuses himself . . . In order to realize itself this basic option must enter into dialog with a complete psychophysical situation and development, assume all acquired determinisms within its free directedness and thus bestow on them, out of that freedom, a new shape for the future. The continual object-choice which this entails will be a free choice only to the — very often restricted — extent in which it shares the freedom of the basic option.[63]

The only act possible for man in which the full freedom of the fundamental option is brought into play in an object choice is the act of dying because it is the only choice possible to man in which he as a spirit unconditionally commits or refuses himself to God. Death leaves nothing over as the basis of further choice. In dying man welcomes or rejects his final fulfillment and chooses either total liberation or complete self-alienation.[64] Insofar as it is the latter, it has been identified as the scriptural sin against the Holy Spirit. As Schoonenberg observes, an impenitent death cannot be forgiven because it cannot be repented for.[65]

4. Sins and the "Sin of the World"

Besides the individual sinful object choices which a man might make and the sin of an unrepentent death, theology often speaks of a "sin of the world." This notion, which is based

on the use of *hamartia* by Paul and John,[66] refers to a moral
solidarity "which consists not merely in the punishment [of
sins] but also in this, that the children imitate their father's
sin,"[67] in other words, a sinful situation. Piet Schoonenberg explains this situation, which is an essential element in the
development of human freedom, as follows:

> *We are not interested in the situation but in the fact that the person is
> situated*, in what scholastic philosophy might call "situatio
> passive sumpta." What matters ultimately as a component of
> the sin of the world is not a connecting link between personal
> sins . . . but the fact that man himself is affected.[68]

Louis Monden has graphically portrayed the implications of
this sin of the world for human freedom. He writes:

> Even before the child can consciously experience his freedom,
> he is profoundly influenced, often marked for life, by a world
> and community, and by all the greed, the cupidity, the pride,
> the divisions, quarrels and jealousies, the inherited handicaps
> and the moral corruption which exist in that world and in that
> community. By far the greatest proportion of the suffering, the
> isolation and the despair which a man ever has to undergo
> . . . comes from the evil and the insufficiencies which have
> been brought to bear on him through his education, his en-
> vironment and all his contemporaries . . . who carried within
> their own being the shadows of former generations and the
> burden of a long human inheritance.[69]

Freedom must labor against these interiorized determinisms as
it seeks to bring itself to full final actualization. Yet while the
sin of the world is an alienating influence, alienation is realized
only in objective and freely chosen guilt for, as Rahner says:
"Sin take place in sins."[70]

In both the sin of the world and in sin as a freely rejected
self-realization there is an element of psychological un-
wholeness. As Schoonenberg says, "Sin always contains a certain amount of immaturity . . . But precisely as moral evil it is

willed immaturity, a refusal to grow, a shutting oneself off from what the Spirit is about to ask."[71]

The operative basis for the distinction between object choices and a fundamental option as well as the vehicle for the damage wrought by the sin of the world is a theological reality central to the understanding of St John of the Cross' doctrine regarding freedom. It is what is called concupiscence.

5. Concupiscence

Concupiscence is often represented as fallen man's inclination to evil or as that tendency toward sin within himself which St Paul lamented.[72] It is through concupiscence that sin rules in unregnerate man. But there is a positive aspect to concupiscence as well which relates directly to freedom.

Because man is a spiritual person situated through his corporality in time and space, he can only choose for himself what is given to him as person to choose. He needs to perceive a good in order to choose it. Concupiscence is that "act of the appetite in regard to a determinate good or determinate value, in so far as this act takes shape spontaneously in the consciousness on the basis of man's natural dynamism, and as such forms the necessary presupposition of man's personal decision."[73] This definition could be applied to any person in a finite nature. But in man since sin entered into his history (and thus in the present order of salvation), man's spontaneous desire not only precedes a free decision as its necessary condition but it also *resists* that decision.[74] As Rahner puts it:

> In the course of its self-determination, the person undergoes the resistance of the nature given prior to freedom, and never wholly succeeds in making all that man is into the reality and the expression of all that he comprehends himself to be in the core of his person. There is much in man which always remains in concrete fact somehow impersonal; impenetrable and unilluminated for his existential decision; merely endured and not freely acted out. It is this dualism between person and nature, in so far as it arises from the dualism of matter and spirit and not

from man's finitude . . . Concupiscence consists essentially in
the fact that man in this regime does not overcome even by his
free decision the dualism between what he is as nature prior to
his existential decision and what he becomes as a person by this
decision, not even in the measure in which it would absolutely
speaking be conceivable for a finite spirit to overcome it. Man
never becomes wholly absorbed in good or in evil.[75]

The fact that theological concupiscence is seen as rooted in
the opposition of a person to his nature and not *merely* in the opposition of spirit and body is significant for the theme of
mystical liberation. If concupiscence were rooted in the fact of
corporality only, there would be no need for the radical
purification of the spirit on which St John of the Cross insists.
Indeed, the proof that the person/nature dualism is the source
of theological concupiscence is the fact that man's "nature"
resists the free decision of the "person" even when the object of
choice is a spiritual reality.

We may think for example of a persistent temptation against
faith, or to despair. In such cases we are clearly faced with the
acts of the appetite which bear the typical marks of *concupiscentia*
in the theological sense, namely the spontaneity of the act in its
persistence in opposition to a free decision. And yet the act in
question is plainly one which belongs specifically to the spiritual
appetite.[76]

This fact will have important consequences.

6. Suffering and Death

The theological alienation we call guilt leads to personal,
social, and even cosmic suffering. Because of human solidarity
in a sinful situation, apart from and even prior to his free decision, the innocent person is made by sin to suffer as well. Suffering is, therfore, a symptom or "constitutive sign" of guilt,
though not necessarily of personal guilt.[77]

This statement requires some refinement. Suffering in its
most personal form, in the sense used uniquely of persons, is

the *"renisus voluntatis ad id quod est vel non est"* — an opposition of the will to the being or non-being of something.[78] It may be the state of relative self-realization (or lack of it) effected through object choices which constitute a person in opposition to his situation or it may be the final failed self-realization of the devils or of the damned. The ultimate ground for the possibility of this moral suffering is the same transcendent Person who constitutes the ground of his freedom:

> A purely finite person as such, however, cannot suffer either, since as such it does not yet need to have an *eternal* destiny which pre-exists its free decision, so that at most there may be suffering only in an analagous sense in its case, as a *result* of its guilty decision . . . Suffering, as an independent phenomenon different from guilt, is therefore possible only where, on account of a nature capable of suffering, the person can experience an external fate running counter to the meaning-structure of its nature, either because this opposition concerns the pure nature, or because fate contradicts this nature in so far as it has already been existentially formed in a quite different way by a personal decision.[79]

But what we call suffering may also be the mere sensation of pain taken prior to a human act — that pain which the Scholastics call one of the four passions in the appetitive part of the soul.[80] As an act of the appetites it pertains to concupiscence. In a person with an integral nature, such sensitive pain — whatever its origin or intensity — would be wholly and without resistance assumed into the free act of the subject. It would never become a moral disorder. The fear experienced by Christ in his agony is a true sign of concupiscence in an integral nature.[81] In a fallen nature, such pain would create resistance to the free decision.

Normally both aspects of pain are present in human suffering in this life, and their connection with guilt should be more than evident in the long lists and descriptions given us by St John of the Cross of the damages wrought in the soul by moral disorder.[82] Conversely, the absence of moral suffering in the presence of pain might be regarded as a constitutive sign of an at least partially achieved final freedom. We find just such a reference to pain in St Teresa's "Spiritual Relation" of October, 1581, one of the great descriptions of a soul in union:

> In some respects my soul is not really subject to the miseries of the world as it used to be: it suffers more but it feels as if the sufferings were wounding only its garments; it does not itself lose peace.[83]

Suffering is more than a consequence of individual moral acts and bears a relationship to death which is analogical to that of object choices and the fundamental option. As Rahner says, "Dying takes place throughout life itself, and death when it comes is only the ultimate and definitive completion of the process."[84]

Man is oriented toward death by metaphysical as well as biological necessity. Freedom demands an act of self-transcending fulfillment. "It is this, ultimately speaking, that makes man mortal, and mortality in the biological sense is only the manifestation and realization in the concrete of this mortality, which has its origin and basis in the freedom with which man is endowed as spiritual."[85] "Death is the breaking in of finality upon mere transience — that finality which is the concretisation of freedom come to its maturity."[86]

But the manner in which finality breaks in on transience and the manner, therefore, of "passing on" must differ according to the effects of concupiscence in an integral or a fallen nature. Integrity takes up the fundamental option in each choice;[87] and for a person blessed with integrity dying cannot be his fundamental act of total surrender to God. Rather, it must be his final transformation by complete self-donation and fruition in love. John of the Cross sees dying in just such terms for those who have reached the state of union.[88] In fallen man, the act of transience takes on the character of a full actualization of a fundamental choice. But as a person may make such a self-disposition only reflexively and through an appropriate object of choice, dying man can dispose of himself totally before God only in virtue of the fact that in dying he experiences his own violent dissolution. Thus death is necessarily the "culmination of concupiscence,"[89] and of a concupiscence which resists his free decision. Man *suffers* his death, and this suffering makes of death a constitutive "sign of the guilt in Adam of the whole race, a manifestation of the sinfulness of all.'[90]

Psychological Parallels

Because of the limits of the method of the empirical sciences and the transcendental nature of freedom, the latter cannot be directly the object of psychological investigation. Nevertheless, references to freedom or states we would describe as free abound in contemporary psychological literature. Erich Fromm relates it directly to the emergence of the mature person in the process known as individuation.[91] We may easily recognize in the disturbances of a neurotic personality a state of alienation which is usually indicative of a failure in self-realization.[92] The disturbed person is unfree because he did not fully "become a person."[93] The parallels to theological freedom and alienation worked by sin should be obvious.

The parallels between the insights of theology and the findings of psychology deserve greater attention than we are able to give them. Several details, however, are particularly useful for our understanding of St John of the Cross. Personality integration involves a twofold activity in which a person both differentiates himself from the world so that his identity and autonomy are never called into question,[94] and forms relationships with other people and the world of things.

Being in oneself and in the world are necessary because the human personality is embodied and man experiences himself and the world in the locus of his body. As R.D. Laing says, "In ordinary circumstances, to the extent that one feels one's body to be alive, real and substantial, one feels alive, real, and substantial." And he adds, "To the extent that he is thoroughly 'in' his body, a person is likely to have a sense of personal continuity in time."[95] A mature person feels one with his body. He is alive or "in touch with" his own feelings. Being able to trust one's feelings is a characteristic of a more fully achieved person.[96] Dissociation and alienation occur to the extent that a person instrumentalizes his body and experiences it as something other than himself and apart from his personality.[97] Finally, disorders in the higher levels of the personality are reflected in body states, and many body states in turn are indications of personality disorders.

The process of individuation and integration takes place by means of the purposeful, though not always conscious, gratification of needs and drives. The psychophysical organism seeks its own good in accord with what the psychoanalytic school, for example, calls the pleasure principle. If the instinctive needs and drives are denied or repressed, they manifest themselves in pathological states and behavior.

Inner conflicts tend to be embodied in exterior actions and in symbolic expressions. The resolution of these conflicts and the liberation for further growth which results usually require a confrontation of the conflicts and leads to increased self-awareness.[98]

Journey Beyond Alienation

It should be evident that if we can find that St John's categories and doctrine regarding union can be seen as coinciding with the categories and dynamics we have examined in our theological reflection on the nature of freedom and alienation, we may safely assert that the mystical doctrine of the saint is directly relevant to the theology of freedom. In fact, as we shall now see, the goal which John sets for his journey is a personal self-realization in God. The conditions which prevent the soul from reaching its goal are the same conditions which normally alienate the human person from his personal final end. Finally, the means by which the soul journeys to God are the same means as are used by any Christian to reach his theological self-fulfillment, although the mode of realization is exceptional.

1. Union as A State of Freedom

The word "union" refers to a relationship rather than a state of the subject. Nevertheless, the texts in St John's writings which refer to union as the highest state and delight — we would perhaps speak of fulfillment — possible in this life[99] allow us to say that a person who reaches union does so as a free person.

In an important text in his *Living Flame of Love*, the saint explicitly compares and contrasts the state of union, under the image of attaining to one's deepest center, to the beatific vision:

> Although a person attains to as lofty a state of perfection in this mortal life as that which we are discussing, he neither does nor can reach the perfect state of glory, although perhaps in a passing way God might grant him some similar favor . . . Since this center is the furthest attainable in the present life — although not as perfectly attainable as in the next — it refers to it as the deepest center.
>
> Even though the soul can perhaps possess in this life a habit of charity as perfect as in the next, yet the operation and fruition of charity in this life will not be so perfect; although the operation and fruition of love increase to such a degree in this state that it greatly resembles the beatific state. Such is the similarity that the soul dares to affirm only what it would dare affirm about the next life, that is: in the deepest center of my soul.[100]

In speaking of the difference in the habit and operation of charity, John is saying that the person reaches in union a state of perfection not essentially different from what is to come even though the perfect realization of the love relationship must follow death.

The emphasis on love is important, for as Karl Rahner has noted, "Considered as the capacity of the 'heart,' [freedom] is the capacity of love."[101] In the perfection of love *as a habit*, the *capacity of love* reaches its perfection.

In chapter five of the Second Book of the *Ascent*, St John speaks of the participant transformation of the soul in God which is an effect of union.[102] We may see in this a foretaste of perfect final freedom.[103] He continues his exposition by speaking of the capacity of the soul *and its fulfillment*:

> Although a person may have truly reached union, this union will be proportioned to his lesser or greater capacity, for not all souls attain an identical degree of union. This depends on what the Lord wishes to grant each one. Here we have a resemblance to the saints' vision of God in heaven: some see more, others less, but all see him and are happy owing to the satisfaction of their capacity.
>
> In this life we may encounter individuals who are in the state of perfection and enjoying equal peace and tranquility, and the capacity of each will be satisfied, yet one may be many degrees higher than the other. A person who does not reach purity in the measure of his capacity never achieves true peace and satisfaction, for he will not have attained in his faculties the nakedness and emptiness required for simple union.[104]

The coincidence of freedom in union and final freedom as far as it may be attained to in this life is confimed by the fact that according to St John of the Cross, the purification which prepares the soul for union is necessary also for the beatific vision; for, "Until a man is purged of his attachments he will not be equipped to possess God, neither here below through the pure transformation of love, nor in heaven through the beatific vision."[105]

The references to a "nakedness and emptiness" and to the purification from attachments brings us to our second issue, the obstacles to union and the roots of theological alienation.

2. Alienation from Union and from Freedom

According to the doctrine of St John of the Cross, the attainment of the capacity for union is impeded or prevented by either of two causes. The first of these is moral disorder in the form of disordered affections for creatures. The second of these is the use of human modes of psycho-spiritual activity which cannot of themselves attain to God.

As we shall see, the natural psycho-spiritual operations of

the person are actually perfected by the nights. They cannot in themselves be considered alienating. The danger of their use consists in the fact that they must have a creature — the concept — for the object of their activity. To insist on their use when God is calling the soul to union is to substitute a creaturely notion[106] for God himself who wishes to communicate himself in a direct way through the new mode of activity informed by the theological virtues. Their inappropriate use, therefore, is nothing more than a case of disordered affection for a creature; this second cause of alienation is but an instance of the first.

St John's teaching regarding attachments to creatures is one of the more difficult elements of his doctrine. The difficulty arises from the fact that at times he condemns *inordinate* affection for creatures and at other times he seems to censure attachments pure and simple.[107] His notion of inordinate affection compounds the verbal difficulty with theological ones.

According to the saint, an inordinate attachment or affection is a voluntary act or habit — that is, an attitude acquired through free choices — of the subject by which he esteems a creature over and above or together with God. Esteem for a creature is judged inordinate if it is not willed *purely* for the love of God, that is,

> . . . for the honor and glory of God, and the greatest honor we can give him is to serve him according to evangelical perfection; anything unincluded in such service is without value to man.[108]

Creatures are to be loved in God and for God, as part of the one habit and act of love for God and not in and for or by themselves.

The justification for this teaching is found in the important fourth chapter of the First Book of the Ascent. There John enunciates two classic axioms which are unexceptionable in themselves: two contraries cannot exist together in the same subject; and love effects a likeness between the lover and the object loved.[109] The difficulty lies in his application of these principles.

If we may reduce to its conceptual substratum the series of applications of these principles made by John in this and the succeeding chapters, we are faced with the following syllogism:

A creature is nothing in comparison with God. Love for a creature makes a person like a creature. Therefore, a person who loves a creature is nothing.

But since God is infinite being, it follows that: "In no way, then, is such a man capable of union with the infinite being of God. There is no likeness between what is not and what is."[110]

There are three difficulties with this line of argument. The first is that John consistently ignores the analogical character of his major premise and commits a classic example of logical equivocation. His conclusion should read: "Therefore a person who loves a creature is nothing in comparison with God." But that is only his natural state. And to say that man is nothing in comparison with God is not to say that man is nothing at all. The argument, therefore, is beside the point.

A second difficulty with this teaching is that it ignores the fact that God in his transcendent being is never the object of natural human choices and that, apart from the special case of "substantial touches," even the supernatural acts of love for God made by a person in virtue of the theological virtues always involve object choices of creatures as a necessary condition of loving God. For example, faith does not dispense with Christ's creaturely humanity in order to attain to God but rather presupposes it.[111] Human acts of theological love are made on the basis of practical judgements which involve propositions of faith, themselves creatures, even though the judgement itself is illumined by the Holy Spirit and the act of theological love has God also as an object.[112] Implicit in this difficulty is the third: it fails to recognize that God is reflexively present in every free choice as the ground which makes that choice possible.

The truth of the matter is that even in St John's own system, a pure and perfect love for creatures in God is possible only in acts of union. His objection to affections for creatures would seem, then, to put the cart before the horse. It is no wonder that St Teresa poked fun at him in her famous "Vejamen":

> It would be bad business for us if we could not seek God until we were dead to the world . . . God deliver me from people who want to turn everything into perfect contemplation, come what may.[113]

If we read the *Ascent* carefully we may find reasons to justify the saint's stern caution regarding appetites and attachments, notwithstanding our difficulty with his theoretical position. He states; "Any inordinate act of the appetite causes both . . . privative and positive damage."[114]

If we examine briefly the privative damage, we see that it is based on the fact that "Since love of God and attachment to creatures are contraries, they cannot coexist in the same will."[115] In other words, it is not the act of the appetite which is alienating but the act of the person who desires or wills. Human choosing brings about the privative damage because it is a moral disorder.

The positive damage consists in the fact that the appetites "weary, torment, darken, defile and weaken" the person.[116] They oppose his free God-centered choosing.

We may conclude from this that an inordinate attachment would be better described as a voluntary act or habit by which a person chooses a creature in preference to God. John seeks to root out the indiscriminate or irrational use of the appetites because they lead to moral disorder. His target is concupiscence in the strict theological sense, as is obvious in the following:

> I am speaking of the voluntary appetites, because the natural ones are little or no hindrance at all to the attainment of union, provided they do not receive one's consent and pass beyond the first movement in which the rational will plays no role . . . A man can easily experience them in his sensitive nature and yet be free of them in the rational part of his being.[117]

And:

> If anyone is to reach perfect union with God through his will
> and love, he must be freed from every appetite however slight.
> That is, he must not give the consent of his will knowingly to an
> imperfection, and he must have the power and freedom to be
> able, upon advertance, to refuse his consent.[118]

3. Concupiscence and the Night of Sense.

In his exposition of the positive harm the appetites effect in
the soul, it is clear that the saint is concerned with overcoming
concupiscence. He even goes so far as to say that "The appetite
causes this in the soul: it enkindles concupiscence and over-
whelms the intellect so that it cannot see its light."[119] In this and
other passages John appears to use the term to mean concu-
psicible appetites.

It should be noted that St John of the Cross has a theological
understanding of concupiscence that is more traditional than
Rahner's and which attributes the interior resistance the soul
experiences to the fact of corporality and original sin: "The soul,
through original sin, is a captive in the mortal body, subject to
passions and natural appetites. . . ."[120] But the extraordinary
emphasis John places on the need for a radical purification of
the spirit makes it more than clear that concupiscence in the
strict sense applies to man as a whole, body and spirit.

If we keep in mind St John's special emphasis on the need to
reform the appetites so that they do not interfere with choosing
God, we may begin to understand a curious feature of the rules
the saint gives for entering actively into the night of sense.[121]
They refer to attitudes more than to acts, for St John wishes to
reach the depths from which human choices proceed. His first
rule speaks of having an habitual *desire* of imitating
Christ — *traiga un ordinario apetito de imitar a Cristo*; and the second
rule is directed toward preventing the desire for satisfaction in
anything that is not purely for the honor and glory of God —
basta que no quiere gustar de ello.[122] These rules are further expounded in the celebrated antithetical injunctions which follow

his basic rules as a set of corollaries.[123] Their intent is the con-
quest of the appetites, for conquering the appetites suffices to
bring the soul into the night.[124] Yet something very different is
taking place here than what one might be led to understand.

According to the saint, the following change is effected by
God in the night:

> . . . the concupiscence and the appetites are brought into sub-
> jection, reformed, and mortified. The passions as a result, lose
> their strength and become sterile from not receiving any satis-
> faction.
>   . . . For when the appetites and concupiscences are quenched,
> the soul dwells in spiritual peace and tranquility. Where neither
> the appetites nor concupiscence reign, there is no disturbance
> but only God's peace and consolation.[125]

These lines and the theory of return to original justice which
John had already begun to develop while writing the *Dark Night
of the Soul*[126] suggest something like the patristic theory of
apatheia. This idea certainly seems incompatible with the affective activity portrayed by the saint in his later works, and it
does not seem to fit in with certain elements of the doctrine of
the *Ascent* and *Dark Night*. In the nights the activity of the appetites are perfected and ordered, rather than quenched. This
takes place by drawing them into the choice-making activity so
that they may be directed by reason toward God. St John describes this by employing what amounts to a technical phrase of
some significance: *"Las cuales passiones, poniendolas en obra de razón
en orden a Dios. . . ."*[127] When the appetites are placed in
reasonable order, their strength is made to *increase* in the service
of God. Insofar as they have been ordered, their tragic and
alienating dimension is overcome. A person is thus more free to
choose God with all his being.

4. The Perfection of Choice-Making in the Nights

Throughout the *Ascent* and *Dark Night* the progress of the
human person toward union is presented, for the most part, in

terms of the removal of alienating appetites and choices, that
is, imperfections. This perspective may create the impression
of a pure passivity:

> All these sensory means and exercises of the faculties
> must . . . be left behind and in silence so that God himself
> may effect the divine union in the soul. . . . If a person does not
> turn his eyes from his natural capacity, he will not attain to so
> lofty a communication; rather he will hinder it.[128]

Such an impression would be incorrect. At every stage of its
journey human choices are necessary. The foremost clearly reflexive choice asked of the individual is one of renunciation and
detachment. But such a course of action makes sense only in
virtue of a divine invitation.[129] The real state of affairs is that
the individual is constantly choosing God. This fact is especially
evident in the active aspect of the night of spirit which consists
in a loving attentiveness to God. The inattentiveness to the
natural and supernatural apprehensions of the spiritual faculties are the outward expression of a deeper choice making.

It is important to keep in mind that by the metaphysical
structure of a human act, every free choice tends to shape man
himself in his relationship to God. This means that in the night
of spirit even more than that of sense, man — with the help of
grace — takes himself in hand as a whole and freely cooperates
in his purification and preparation for union. John emphasizes
the role of the spirit since, after all, "all good and evil habits
reside in the spirit."[130] But the fact that he also teaches that the
senses, which were only curbed in the night of sense, are purified here shows that man is in fact, one *suppositum*. Therefore,
without doing violence to the saint's doctrine, we may assert
that in the apparent inactivity of the night of spirit, man freely
cooperates in reshaping himself as a whole. He transforms
himself into the image of Christ by reciprocating the love given
him in Christ.

5. Choices and the Theological Virtues

Man's liberation through choosing would never get beyond a

moral self-improvement program by the force of his own spiritual power. The attainment to God as one's final end in this
world is an eschatalogical state, a reality both "here now" and
"yet to be" which places man's existential center "beyond the
realm of the tangible and the empirical."[131] The positive appearance of that eschatalogical reality is impossible in any
choice pertaining to this world because of the structure of object
choices. Yet Rahner allows an exception to this rule and admits
of one moral act which makes man's eschatalogical hope visible
in this world. That act is renuncation. It is possible by reason
of its connection with the mystery of the death of Christ,[132] and
allowable only by the "special and express permission" of God
"for going beyond the world."[133]

> For, precisely in its negative characteristics, renunciation is a
> profession of action in the tangible order, a profession of man's
> shifting the centre of his existence out of the world, since renun-
> ciation of the highest positive values of this world is either
> meaningless and perverse within this world or must be regarded
> as the believing gesture of that love which reaches out beyond
> the world and its goods (even those of a personal nature).[134]

Rahner is speaking of the renunciation imposed by the evangelical counsels, but his assertion is applicable to the renunciation
effected in the rights. There one shifts one's center out of this
world in a manner not only allowed by God but in a certain sense
caused by him. And this renunciation leads to a participation
in the dying and death of Christ.

The talk of man "shifting the centre of his existence" should
alert us to the fact that the principal object of choice in this
renunciation is not the experience of a void but an unfelt
something which transcends every good. The *intent* is plenitude
and fulfillment in the beloved.

But this raises a problem. By the structure of human acts
man cannot choose that which is not given to him. An eschatalogical good, like any transcendent good, cannot be perceived
or apprehended by the person and therefore cannot be the di-

rect, formal object of a human choice. Notwithstanding his openness as a spiritual person to the infinite, man cannot efficaciously intend or achieve his eschatalogical fulfillment or any of the values, like final freedom, inherent in it. Man needs the help of the theological virtues which theologize or divinize his spiritual activities and make God attainable as a formal object of human choices.

In classic theology, the theological virtues are operative habits which have God as their formal object. The dynamic aspect of an operative habit is perhaps better expressed by the contemporary description of them as transcendental intentional tendencies of attitudes (with the full force of that word) toward God.[135] But a theological virtue is only a principle of action; God is not attained to except in a theological *act*, that is in every morally honest choice which is informed by the theological virtues, whether or not he is thought of in a reflexive manner.[136] Yet so long as the object of one's eschatological longings does not appear, each of these choices will be object choices. Conversely, any object of choice which does not direct the person toward God must stand in the way of attaining to God. Therefore the theological virtues by their intrinsic directedness toward God lead the human person to renounce everything that would diffuse or obstruct his love for God.

Since this eschatalogical perfection must be the work of the theological virtues, the attainment of union must come about by their means, as St John clearly teaches, and — in complete harmony with what we have seen regarding renunciation and the virtues — the phenomenologically characteristic act of these virtues is renunciation:

> These virtues, as we said, void the faculties: Faith causes darkness and a void of understanding in the intellect, hope begets an emptiness of possessions in the memory, and charity produces the nakedness and emptiness of affection and joy in all that is not God.[137]

As Federico Ruiz-Salvador says of the working of the theological virtues in the doctrine of the saint:

> . . . the theological virtues are global tendencies toward God which, when present, require the will to strip itself of everything which is opposed to the virtue (insofar as it can actively do so) *by means of the corresponding theological virtue.*[138]

Contrary to appearance and even to isolated statements by the saint, renunciation follows the infusion of the virtues as an exigence of the virtues' further development.[139]

Man in grace is never entirely without God while not fully in possession of him. Realized eschatology is a dimension of everyday Christian life. Yet the kind to possesion and fulfillment that is union are so final as to require a morally definitive degree of renunciation ordinarily possible only in dying. By his active dying, man lets go of himself and entrusts himself to God with his whole being in a perfect final actualization of his fundamental option. He does this by the power of the theological virtues. Similarly, the mystical nights lead to union and to an anticipated realization of final freedom. In the nights, through the manner in which they inform the faculties, the theological virtues perfect man's self-renunciation and choice for God. They do this in the infused activity we call contemplation.

6. Contemplation and Liberation

The Second Book of the *Dark Night* is dominated by a single theme which explains how the Lord frees the soul from the alienating impediments to union and brings union about: "The Lord works all of this in the soul by means of a pure and dark contemplation."[140] Contemplation itself is nothing more than an inflow of God into the soul; it is the dark night.[141] It is characterized by a secret, loving knowledge of God which renders the person forgetful of all that is not God.[142] Contemplation produces in each of the faculties the effect ascribed to the theological virtues, but on a more intense level. God does not merely move the soul to renounce goods for his sake but by his presence deprives the soul of the acts natural to the faculties, or seems to.[143] Teófilo de la Virgen del Carmen explains this purifying effect of contemplation:

> The understanding and the will . . . are purified through a

radical restriction of the operations natural to them. Psychologically the soul suffers because of the impossibility of directing itself to God by means of [the natural] acts of these faculties; "He cannot beseech God nor raise his mind or will [*afecto*] to Him" (N, 2, 8, 1). In reality, its true purification consists in preventing the dispersion of its strength by occupying itself in natural things — in the sanjuanistic sense. This, in fact, is the scope of the divine action: to impede the natural operation of the [soul's] powers, conserving, intensifying and channeling their energies in the direction of the supernatural, toward God (See N, 2, 11, 3–5; 16, 4).[144]

This is true, but it leaves an important aspect of activity in the nights unstated. If the powers of the soul and their energies are directed toward God, then it is not quite true to say that the soul is doing nothing. In moments of contemplation all activity *seems* to cease. This is because love "does not reside with tenderness in the sense, but in the soul,"[145] at a suprasensible level. As a consequence, unless there also happens to be a sensible overflow, there can be no sensory object nor even spiritual object (concept, phantasm, etc.) in an act of contemplation by which the subject can perceive himself reflexively as being in act. He *feels* inactive; rather he feels nothing at all. His spiritual activity can be judged only by its effects. As Dom John Chapman notes, "An interruption from outside causes a distinct sense of detaching the will from some unfelt act."[146]

Sensible overflow from contemplation need not be joyful or be concerned directly with God. Often it is an illumination of creaturely imperfection which causes intense moral suffering. In this, we may see traces of suffering as a constitutive sign of guilt.[147]

As both Teófilo and Ruiz-Salvador have demonstrated,[148] contemplation is not faith or any of the theological virtues nor an act of those virtues. Rather it is a presence of God for which the theological virtues are man's active disposition.

Liberation for the contemplative and non-contemplative alike is a redemptive gift of grace which he cannot arbitrarily

seize for himself but for which a person must wait in patience
and hope. By the exercise of the theological virtues, the Christian — whatever the manner of God's self-communication to
him — cooperates with God to free his own freedom at the hour
that is given to him. Because union is a state of self-realization
in God and because the means for attaining to it are common to
every Christian life, St John's doctrine is relevant to any
theology of freedom.

INTENTIONALITY AND THE PSYCHOLOGY OF LIBERATION

St John's ascetical doctrine, as we have seen, raises some
difficulties. To attempt to direct one's appetites *purely* to the service of God by denying them in all that is not God would be to
undermine choice-making, put an end to maturation and leave
the soul in apathy. John's doctrine seems to assume that general maturation precedes God's mystical intervention. In reality, a person does not first mature with respect to his natural
mode of existence and then begin a radical God-directed activity. This reality is reflected in the progressive character of the
nights. The saint's practical doctrine often transcends the limits
of its theoretical justification. The psychological details make of
his writings an exceptionally rich resource. They allow us to
relate his doctrine to insights of the behavioral sciences. Using
this tool, we will try to clarify our understanding of freedom by
means of a hypothetical modern interpretation.

Fruition or Intention

Readers of the saint's teaching are familiar with the term
fruition. St. Thomas calls it the perfection of an appetitive
power.[149] Since a person's chief appetitive power is his will,
fruition is properly speaking the possession by — or its fulfillment in — the will of its final, transcendent Good. Final fruition
and final freedom coincide. Thomas, however, admits of the

possibility of a perfect fruition in the actual possession of an end and an imperfect fruition in the intentional possession of an end.[150] Intention is the name of the act of the will which moves all the powers of the soul toward their end.[151] In words that have a striking echo in John's phrase *"ponerlos en obra de razón,"* Thomas states: "Intention is the movement of the will toward something preordained by reason."[152] Then, in the discussion which follows, he adds two points which are of interest to us; the intentionality of an act need not be directed toward a final end, and it is possible to intend several ends in one act. As a result, in human choices man may perfectly well do what is popularly called "killing two birds with one stone."

When John of the Cross writes of the necessity to *"poner en obras de razón en orden a Dios,"* he is speaking of intentionality.[153] Love directs all human choices toward God by its intentionality.

The intentionality of love is given an especially beautiful expression in chapter thirteen of the Third Book of the *Ascent*:

> As a result he tells her to set him as a mark upon her heart [Sg 8:6], there where all the arrows of love (the actions and motives of love) that come from the quiver strike. He does this so that all the arrows might strike him who is there as their target, and thus all are directed to him.[154]

In contrast to cognitive intentions which are mediated by concepts, the conative intentions of the will tend toward their object as it is in itself. And as the function of intentionality is the integration of the acting person with the object of his intention, intentionality is most perfectly realized in the act of personal love. As Arrigo Colombo says:

> In truth, love is nothing else than personal assimilation and identity (see *Summa Theologica*, I, q. 20, a. 1 ad 3), and therefore the highest degree of integration realized through the tending of the will which enters into its object by means of an intentional form, through the tending, that is, of two wills which mutually

take on one another and realize unity where there is fundamental distinction.[155]

In words that call to mind the working of the theological virtues, Jacques Maritain uses the fact of intentionality to explain the activity of the soul in union:

> Thus, the espoused soul loves and gives itself love itself; it is by infinite love that the soul operates according to the *intentional being of love* the while it operates according to the *entitative being of its own finite acts*.[156]

That intentionality is to be understood as a mutual directedness of God and the soul is clearly expressed in St John's poem "The Living Flame of Love." In his commentary on that poem, the saint explains the important phrase "deepest center of the soul — *centro más profundo del alma*" in terms which recall Rahner's phrase about shifting one's center from the world. When the soul attains to the center of its intentions it will have fruition:

> The soul's center is God. When it has reached God with all the capacity of its being and the strength of its operation and inclination, it will have attained to its final end and deepest center in God, it will know, love, and enjoy God with all its might.[157]

Because the concept of intentionality is used in some schools of modern philosophy and psychology, it provides an important clue for our contemporary discovery of the meaning of the saint's doctrine.

Eros, Caring and Intentionality

The concept of intentionality is used by Rollo May in his modern classic *Love and Will*, together with the other theologically significant notion of "eros,"[158] to elucidate the crisis of loving and willing which is the subject of his book. May argues that the suppression of eros is a fundamental factor in this crisis because it results in a failure of intentionality.

1. Eros

Rollo May describes eros for us without actually defining it. In contrast with the biological drive of sex, eros "is the experiencing of the personal intentions and meaning of the act." It is both the "power that *attracts* us" and the "drive toward union with what we belong to — union with our own possibilities, union with significant other persons in our world in relation to whom we discover our own self-fulfillment."[159] Eros is to be distinguished from classic Freudian libido[160] in that libido is an undifferentiated drive toward gratification while eros is love in its tendency toward unity. But eros of itself does not effect that unity, for it is irrational.

Eros is a "daimon." And we would say with Rollo May that:

> *The daimonic is any natural function which has the power to take over the whole person.* Sex and eros, anger and rage, and the craving for power are examples. The daimonic can be either creative or destructive and is normally both. When this power goes awry and one element usurps control over the total personality, we have "daimon possession," the traditional name through history for psychosis. . . .
>
> . . . All life is a flux between these two aspects of the daimonic. We can repress the daimonic, but we cannot avoid the toll of apathy and the tendency toward later explosion which such repression brings in its wake.[161]

The destructive side of a daimon derives from its irrationality. Its creative aspect follows from its integration into the personality. To use St John of the Cross' phrase, a daimon must be *puesto en obras de razón.*

2. Caring

According to May, the creative aspect of eros is developed through caring. He writes:

> Eros, the daimon, begins *physiologically*, seizing us and whirling

us up into its vortex. It requires the necessary addition of care, which becomes the psychological side of Eros.[162]

In our opinion, care is not merely what gives eros its intention. Care *is* intentionality because it directs the powers of the person toward the object of its love.[163]

May argues that there is a need today for a "mythos of care" because man has "lost his world."[164] A similar insight may be found in the *Spiritual Canticle* of St John of the Cross:

> How do you endure
> O life, not living where you live?

> To understand these lines it should be known that the soul lives where she loves more than in the body she animates; for she does not live in the body, but rather gives life to the body, and lives through love in the object of her love.[165]

Caring is perfected in the intentional being of love.

Philosopher Milton Mayeroff takes up the theme of being "in place" in his extended essay *On Caring*. He writes, "We are 'in place' in the world through having our lives ordered by inclusive caring."[166] A strongly outward-directed intentionality is recognizable in his explanation of caring as a relationship in which the person who cares engages his own possibilities in loving the other as "my appropriate other":

> My appropriate others, speaking now simply of those separate from me, are not ready-made and waiting for me. They must have developed in relation to me to the point where, in conjunction with other carings, *they have become a center around which my life can be significantly ordered.*[167]

The development of those significant others may not occur or may be realized only imperfectly. The failure to encounter significant others, as the work of Eric Berne and R.D. Laing

show, may handicap of even prevent a person's normal self-
actualization.[168]

3. Egocentricity and the Failure of Intentionality

A person who lacks the ability to relate to others or who
refuses to do so is said to be egocentric. Paradoxically, such a
person often has a poorly developed ego identify or sense of
self. The schizoid personality, for example, because it lacks a
secure "self," is unable to relate. It fragments intself into
secondary "inner selves" and attempts to relate these to one
another in an interior socialization. As Laing puts it:

> In this, the self attempts to become 'a relationship which relates
> itself to itself' to the exclusion of everything and anything . . .
> The substitution of the interaction with the other results in
> the individual coming to live in a frightening world in which
> dread is unmitigated by love. The individual is frightened of the
> world, afraid that any impingement will be total, will be im-
> plosive, penetrative, fragmenting, and engulfing. He is afraid
> of letting anything of himself 'go,' of coming out of himself, of
> losing himself in any experience, etc., because he will be
> depleted, exhausted, emptied, robbed, sucked dry.[169]

He is incapable of erotic intentionality. He loses his world and
has no place to which to journey — for lack of a center for caring.

He also fails to achieve the inner integration of his personality which eros brings about when a person cares for another. It
brings order out of inner confusion because it requires renunciation and the unification of one's energies.

4. Caring and Renunciation

Caring itself is expressed in the renunciation enjoined on the
soul in its journey. As Mayeroff says: "When a man who has
been unable to care or had no one or nothing to care for comes
to care for some other, many matters previously felt to be important fade in significance, and those related to caring take on
new importance."[170] He then adds:

Such inclusive ordering requires giving up certain things and activities, and may thus be said to include an element of sub-mission. But this submission, like the voluntary submission of the craftsman to his materials, is basically liberating and affirm-ing.[171]

In a theological sense, intentionality, or caring, places all the powers of the personality—what St John calls the *fortaleza del alma*[172]—in reasonable order with respect to that value or those values which form a center or centers for a person's life. When God is that center, caring directs all the person's choosing toward God and helps to liberate him from everything not or-dered toward God. Caring accomplishes all of this because it is an aspect of unitive love, of eros.

5. Eros and the "Fuerza del Amor"

St John of the Cross cites Pseudo-Dionysius more than any other non-scriptural author, and eros is a central concept in the Syrian monk's *Divine Names*. Nevertheless, St John of the Cross never mentions eros. Marilyn May Mallory attributes this fact to St John's lack of knowledge of the original Greek texts.[173] But she identifies an equivalent concept in the writings of the Spanish mystic:

In the terminology of John of the Cross no real equivalent for eros or eroticism can be found simply because Spanish has no satisfactory work for translating this Greek word, eros. Latin . . . too has no real equivalent for 'eros.' Translators of Pseudo-Dionysius into Latin usually translate 'eros' with 'amor' and use the terms 'dilectio' or 'amor beneficus' or 'caritas' to translate 'agape.' John of the Cross' equivalent for purely sensual pleasure in love is luxury ('lujuria'). His equivalent for agape is charity ('caridad'). But apart from the term 'amor,' he seems at first glance to have no other way to translate eros. Thus, in quoting the text from Pseudo-Dionysius which says that it is eros which leads to ecstasy, John of the Cross says to Doña Ana de Peñalosa that it is love ('amor') which leads to ecstasy.[174]

But she goes on to note:

> The aspect of dynamism or motor, which so characterized eros in Pseudo-Dionysius, is also present in the special terms which John of the Cross devised, namely 'force of love.' Therefore this term seems in fact to be a more accurate translation of 'eros' than 'amor'.[175]

Her hypothesis, which she claims to substantiate on the basis of the high correlation between libidinal energy and progress in contemplation in the test results of contemplatives,[176] seems to us reasonable in its identification of the saint's term *fuerza del amor* with eros or unitive love.

It should be noted that term *fuerza del amor* does not occur in either the *Ascent* or *Night*, although the concepts behind it are clearly present. The term *fuerza*, which can mean simply a force or energy, occurs with increasing frequency in the latter part of the *Night*, and in chapter thirteen of the second book we read:

> It should be explained here why, even though the soul feels as miserable and unworthy of God as it does in these purgative darknesses, it possesses an energy bold enough to go out to be joined with God — *tenga tan osada y atrevida fuerza para ir a juntarse con Dios.*
> The reason is that since love now imparts a force — *le va dando fuerzas* — by which the soul loves authentically, and since the nature of love is to seek to be united, joined, equaled, and assimilated to the loved object in order to be perfected in the good of love, the soul hungers and thirsts for this union or perfection of love still unattained. And the strength love has now bestowed, and by which the will has become impassioned — *y las fuerzas que ya el amor ha puesto en la voluntad y le ha hecho apasionada* — makes this inflamed will daring.[177]

Rollo May notes that an effect of eros is that love grows with its own passion. In speaking of the enkindling of love in the soul John expresses a similar idea, "The passions even help it experience impassioned love."[178]

The concept of eros, then, is not inappropriately used to explain the doctrine of the *Ascent* and *Night*. Through the intentionality of psychologically erotic or unitive love, the soul is led to "preserve its strength for God, and come to love him with all its might."[179]

6. The Pleasure Principle

Gratification of needs is necessary for the achievement of any healthy psychological growth. This fact is explained in various ways by different personality theories. Psychoanalytic theory invokes what it calls the pleasure principle.[180]. Without entering into a discussion of the merit of the orthodox Freudian use of this term, we may note that pleasure is an important element in the spiritual dynamic of the soul:

> A love of pleasure, and attachment to it usually fires the will toward the enjoyment of things that give pleasure. A more intense enkindling of another, better love (love of one's heavenly Bridegroom) is necessary for the vanquishing of the appetites and the denial of this pleasure. By finding his satisfaction and strength in this love, a man will have the courage and constancy to deny readily all other appetites. The love of one's Spouse is not the only requisite for conquering the strength of the sensitive appetites; and enkindling with longing of love is also necessary. For the sensory appetites are moved and attracted toward sensory objects with such cravings that if the spiritual part of the soul is not fired with other more urgent longings for spiritual things, the soul will neither be able to overcome the yoke of nature nor enter the night of sense, nor will it have the courage to live in the darkness of all things by denying its appetites for them.[181]

Thus, when God moves someone according to his own mode,[182] he does so by means of a kind of pleasure principle. But this involves not merely the undifferentiated drive toward gratification represented by libido but the eros necessary to effect its sublimation into personal meaning. We may, in fact, see in libido and eros a relationship analogous to that of the sensitive and spiritual parts of the soul.

Personal Integration

The process of integration which leads to personal maturation is characterized by certain activities and states which may
help us to understand the teaching of St John.

1. "Naming the Daimon" in the Nights

Rollo May explains the sublimating activity by which a
daimon is integrated creatively into the personality as "naming
the daimon." In "naming" it, a person "forms *personal meaning*
out of what was previously a merely threatening chaos."[183]
When the daimon is named, it is confronted as a part of oneself
and taken up into a deeper and wider consciousness. This
enlarged consciousness bestows freedom. May understands
freedom as "the other side of consciousness of self,"[184] and
asserts: "That consciousness of self and freedom go together is
shown in the fact that the less self-awareness a person has, the
more he is unfree."[185]

2. Memory, Feelings and Unselfconscious Awareness

The self-awareness described by May must be distinguished
from the morbid preoccupation with self that is characteristic of
pathological states. Carl Rogers clearly illustrates these different kinds of self awareness in his description of therapy as a
growth process in seven stages.[186] In the first stage there is little
self-awareness so that feelings and personal meanings are not
recognized. The person is described as "structure-bound,"
"That is he reacts 'to the situation of now by finding it to be like
a past experience and then reacting to the past, feeling *it*.'"[187]
As one progresses in therapy notable changes occur. For example, in the third stage the person gains awareness of himself,
but as an *object*. This alienation is overcome as feelings are
recognized and then owned so that experience becomes more
immediate. By the sixth stage, the experience of self as an object begins to be superseded: "The self *is*, subjectively, in the
existential moment. It is not something one perceives."[188]
Finally, in the seventh stage, feelings are experienced directly
and trusted as a referent for the reality of one's situation. "Experiencing has lost almost completely its structure-bound as-

pects and becomes process experiencing—that is, the situation is experienced and interpreted in its newness, not as the past."[189] And most important of all: "The self becomes increasingly simply the subjective and reflexive awareness of experiencing. The self is much less frequently a perceived object, and much more frequently something confidently felt in process."[190]

To use Laing's term, as the individual gains ontological security, he begins to live with the world and experience it in the immediate present as it is and not merely as he wishes to construe it. He does not make his ego defense needs the referent for reality. In this sense, as E.W. Trueman Dicken has noted, "The essence of humility . . . is unselfconsciousness."[191]

The insistence of the saint on the need to purify the memory through the virtue of hope makes sense psychologically.[192] As long as a person is structure-bound with respect to any other person, he cannot encounter the other in his reality and cannot effectively make him the center of his intentionality. Unless the memory is purified, the person can never love God as he is but only as he is conceived.

Rollo May describes this new awareness, which he calls the "creative consciousness of self," in terms reminiscent of St Thomas' definition of contemplation as a "simple intution of truth—*simplex intuitus veritatis.*"[193]

> This fourth level of consciousness cuts below the split between objectivity and subjectivity. Temporarily we can transcend the usual limits of conscious personality. Through what is called insight, or intuition, or the other only vaguely understood processes which are involved in creativity, we may get glimpses of objective truth as it exists in reality, or sense some new ethical possibility in, let us say, an experience of unselfish love.[194]

3. Love, Death, and Loss of Ego.

As the daimon eros leads a person to this self-transcending state of awareness, it also creates a vulnerability of mortal intensity. In May's words:

For death is always in the shadow of the delight of love. In faint
adumbration there is present the dread, haunting question,
Will this new relationship destroy us? *When we love, we give up the
center of ourselves.* We are thrown from our previous state of existence into a void; and though we hope to attain a new world, a
new existence, we can never be sure. Nothing looks the same,
and may well never look the same again. The world is annihilated; how can we know whether it will ever be built up
again? We give, and give *up* our own center; how shall we know
that we will get it back? We wake up to find the whole world
shaking: where or when will it come to rest?

The most excruciating joy is accompanied by the consciousness of the imminence of death—and with the same intensity. And it seems that one is not possible without the other.[195]

Giving up one's center here refers not merely to the ecstatic experience of transcendence in sexual intercourse but to the intrinsic, intentional movement of unitive love in making the
other the deepest center of one's loving. May continues:

The experience of annihilation is an inward one and, as the
myth rightly puts it, is essentially what eros does to us. It is not
simply what the other person does to us. To love completely
carries with it the threat of annihilation of everything.[196]

It is no wonder that love and death are so closely associated in
art and literature.

Love is most "tragic" when it is returned, not when it is re-
quited. "It is when love *is* realized that eros may literally 'break
the limb's strength,' as with Anthony and Cleopatra. . . . "[197]
When a person begets a child, even if he is the bravest of men,
he becomes vulnerable to dread of death. We might say that
this is because one lives in the beloved, the extent of one's surrender of his center is that complete.

Psychophysical Depression

The suffering endured by the soul in the nights is so similar
to depression that St John himself takes pains to distinguish the

passive night of sense from melancholy.[198] Melancholy is a
classic term for a kind of depression state. A brief review of
psychiatric literature on the subject of depression reveals that
there is no hard and fast set of symptoms for this syndrome,[199]
but several factors seem to be general to cases of depression.
First of all, there is the loss of an object of love. This object may
be a person, a thing, or even an abstract value such as liberty
or self-esteem. Secondly, the person usually places unreal expectations on the object of his love. He is often dependent on it
and suffers from a conflict of mixed feelings of love and hatred.
Finally, the depression-prone person tends to have a height-
ened, overcritical concern with himself.

Some degree of depression is normal following the loss of a
loved one. Depression due to mourning is usually temporary
and self-remitting. The pathological depressive, however, depends on the object of love for his self-esteem. When he loses
the object of his love, his sense of self-value and identity is called
into question.

Symptoms of depression may vary from patient to patient
and are often classed according to the type of disorder.

Depression may be serious to the point of fatality. In the
"anaclitic" depression of infants it often leads to death. In
adults, it may lead to a lack of will to live and even to suicide.
There were reports of depression-induced deaths among American soldiers in prison camps during the Korean war. Marilyn
Mallory makes an interesting observation regarding depression
and contemplation:

> . . . . In the Questionnaire on Spirituality, this description
> of spiritual torment correlated highly with neuroticism. Neuro-
> tic subjects who were in no way advanced mystics had neverthe-
> less experienced this inner lack of integration. On the other
> hand, very advanced mystics, who were unusually stable, had
> also gone through such experiences during the dark night. The
> implication is that the 'dark night' of passive purification is a
> depressed state which occurs in the mystic as a transitional
> period in a growth process, but which is chronic in the
> neurotic.[200]

Keeping in mind that we must observe caution about general-izing on the basis of a single experimental study, we suggest that the dark night is in fact experienced as a depression state. In the dark nights the person is deprived of any affective ap-prehension of the object of his love and, because of the radical change in his intentionality, is unable to find fulfillment in any creature outside of God. He experiences, likewise, a height-ened and critical awareness of his subjective state and most especially of the moral disorders that separate him from God. His experience of himself is one of depression, the depth of which is a function of the intensity of the "darkness" of the night and the moral misery of the soul. John even tells us that its in-tensity could be capable of inducing death.[201] Yet unlike a pathological depression, in the nights the person does not rest in apathetic passivity but actively loves God and neighbor. The psychological depression in the nights is real and is the obverse side of the theologically transformed acts of a person still ex-periencing the resistance of sin and concupiscence.

Christ as the Center of Intentionality

In her psychological testing of Carmelites, Marilyn Mallory discovered no correlation between the practice of sanjuanistic ascesis and progress in contemplation.[202] It was a love for Christ which seemed to correlate with progress in contempla-tion. These findings would seem to further confirm the view that renunciation is an exigence of the virtues and of inten-tionality and not a cause of them. In the *Ascent* and *Dark Night* references to Jesus Christ are relatively few, though not without significance for the question of psychological inten-tionality. We may conveniently class these texts into three groups. The first group includes references to the person of Christ, to his teaching and to the love of the saints (especially Mary Magdalen) for him. These texts would relate to medita-tion and cognitive intentionality.[203] The second group, not always clearly distinguishable from the first, would make of Christ what the scholastics might call an exemplary cause.[204] They are of little direct concern in themselves to conative intentionality. They are typified by the first rule for entering actively into the nights. The third series of texts is typified by the second rule: "Do this out of love for Christ."[205] In addition, the mystical journey is often represented under the image of the *esposa* searching for her *amado*, a clearly erotic image which in the saint's writings is always indicative of unitive love. However, the spouse is clearly identified as Christ in only three passages.[206] Nevertheless, these texts are so clear that it is plain that Christ is the center of the soul's loving intention. In its caring for Christ, who is God's revelation of himself, the soul directs all its energies toward God.

Spititual growth, then, is not a process of repressive renunciation but of the perfection and integration of the human personality. It leads to a union of the entire person with the object of its caring. We believe that this interpretation does justice to the doctrine of St John of the Cross.

MYSTICAL DEATH AND LIBERATION

The Christian attains to his full and final freedom of being when he enters with Christ into glory, yet he participates already in that eschatological reality if he has died with Christ.[207] Liberation is impossible without dying. But death is the ultimate alienation. Is the Christian asked to live in alienation from the world?

Karl Rahner censures those mystical asceses which pretend a mystical death.[208] Being "dead to the world" cannot mean a mere moral disengagement from it. But the German theologian also suggests a "daring" hypothesis that mystics do indeed die and he proposes this theory in order to explain the subjective knowledge of the mystic who has been "confirmed in grace":

> It must . . . be asked whether 'death,' as the decisive caesura in the history of salvation . . . must always necessarily coincide with the moment of time when biological life ceases. . . . If one may question the identification, our principle can be referred to

the impossibility of knowledge of future salvation which precedes death as the caesura in the history of *salvation*. In this sense, the mystic in question may be regarded as dead so to speak as regards the history of salvation, and he may be conceded such absolute knowledge without detriment to the truth in question.[209]

We believe that St John of the Cross' teaching provides grounds for the theological acceptance of this hypothesis and that the freedom attained by the human person in union is unintelligible without an anticipated active dying and passive suffering of death.

The Death of Christ and the Death of the Christian

As we saw in our first section, death is a universal metaphysical necessity which has become, because of sin, a violent passion and the culmination of concupiscence. Man endures his death. He also makes of it the material of his self-donation to God. Man's active dying, in fact, is the only moral act possible to him which engages the full freedom of his fundamental option in a final option which totally self-determines him with respect to his end.

1. The Redemptive Death of Christ

Death is a moral act; it is not the only moral act. For a person in a human nature blessed with integrity it would not even be the only act of total self-disposition — any moral act would do.[210] Jesus was such a person. Yet Scripture singles out his death as *the* act by which we were redeemed. As Karl Rahner observes:

> . . . It must be recognized that the Bible, when it asserts that we were freed and redeemed precisely through the blood which Christ shed for us and through his body which was given for us and when it insists that the redeeming act was a bloody sacrifice in the ritual sense, which, of its essence, presupposes the death of the victim and, finally, when it stresses that the transformation and expiation of the material universe is brought about

through Christ's death, it obviously considers death as redemptive precisely under the characteristics which are proper to death alone and not to any other moral act. The efficacy of Christ's death, consequently, cannot be attributed to it in its general quality as a moral act but in its precise character as death. . . . [211]

Christ's redemptive participation in death is seen as a consequence of the Incarnation:

> Inasmuch as Christ became man from out of the fallen race of Adam, he assumed the "flesh of sin." He assumed human existence in a situation in which that existence could reach its consummation only by passing through death in all its darkness. Therefore, he took death upon himself inasmuch as it is an expression of the fallen state of creation in both angels and in man. Even though Christ was not in the state of belief, he nevertheless experienced in himself the darkness which is the specific character of human death and the unmastering of the personal consummation in the emptiness of the bodily end. He not only offered satisfaction for sin, but he enacted and suffered death as death is the expression, the manifestation and the revelation of sin in the world. He did all this in absolute liberty, as the act and the revelation of that divine grace which rendered divine the life of his humanity and which, by reason of his own divine person, belonged to him of natural necessity.[212]

In speaking of death, including the death of Christ, Rahner emphasizes its darkness which constitutes the condition of death becoming an unconditional surrender in obedience:

> It is precisely in its darkness that the death of Christ becomes the expression and the incarnation of his loving obedience, the free offering of his entire created existence to God. What had been, therefore, the manifestation of sin, thus becomes, without its darkness being lifted, the contradiction of sin, the manifestation of a "yes" to the will of the Father.[213]

It is obvious that in the life of Christ death is the culmination of his fidelity to doing the will of his Father. This lifelong obedience finds its perfection in the final option of death. We might rightly call obedience the "axiological presence"[214] of a person's active dying. As Rahner remarks, Christ's "obedience is our redemption, because it is death, and also . . . his death effects our redemption, because it is obedience."[215]

The Descent into Hell is an element of death which deserves our attention. Rahner observes that in the New Testament it is not presented as "a soteriological act on behalf of the saved who had lived before Christ," but rather as an essential element of human death "implying the absence of the eschatological glorification of the body."[216] At the same time, it effects an "open, real-ontological relationship to the world in its oneness."[217] This last aspect stands in marked contrast to the pretended death to the world which is mere volitional solipsism. Death draws a person into the fullness of relation, not a sterile self-sufficiency.

2. The Death of the Christian.

The Christian's subjective redemption comes about as he shares with Christ a death which is a total and unconditional "yes" to the Father. He does this by virtue of the grace of Christ given him in the sacraments which join him to Jesus in his saving mysteries. This is especially evident in the sacrament of baptism:

> Baptism is the beginning of Christian death, because it is the initiation of the life of grace, by virtue of which alone death becomes Christian. We may even say that the life of grace *is* the Christian death, while outside that state, man's death is the whole meaning of his life. . . . Through baptism we are crucified with Christ and the crucifixion of our Christian life is consummated in the act we call our death. Baptism, the beginning of Chritian life is also the first step in Christian dying.[218]

Christ's death and his grace do not substitute for the person's active dying but transform that act. In its phenomenological aspects, that is, viewed empirically, it remains dark, ambiguous, and the ultimate alienation. The theological virtues make it an act of surrender to God.

This Faith, Hope and Charity are not, however, mere feelings accompanying the brutal reality of death, lasting only until death really occurs, persisting powerlessly beside the hard reality which is death. They are, rather, because transformed by grace, the true reality which transforms death but which, in order that faith should be preserved, transforms it in such a way that death is still encountered as the wages of sin. The trinity of Faith, Hope and Charity makes death itself the highest act of believing, hoping, loving . . . In so far as these fundamental acts become constituents of death as an act of man, death itself is changed; the dreadful falling into the hands of the living God, which death must appear as a manifestation of sin, becomes in reality: "Into thy hands I commend my spirit."[219]

And because the death of Christ is "axiologically" present in the life of a Christian, these same theological virtues are able to make a choice for God of every good act of self-determination the Christian makes.

3. Martyrdom and the Contemplative Life.

Karl Rahner observes that the nature of a Christian's death is given external witness in the death of the martyr. That death is a free act of liberty, "a death which is caused by external violence and which could have been avoided by the exercise of freedom."[220] It "discloses the essence of Christian death, the death through free faith, which character would otherwise be hidden under the veil of ambiguity which obscures all human events."[221] It does this by its special relationship to the Church which is the sacrament of God's holiness and grace.

Since the patristic period there has existed in the Church a tradition which has identified the monastic life, and more specifically the contemplative life, with martyrdom. That the contemplative had died with Christ was forcefully and—from our viewpoint, perhaps—somewhat bizarrely signified in the funereal elements of the late medieval rite of enclosure of anchorites.[222] There was undoubtedly a romantic element in this tradition, but that does not diminish the theological importance of its basic insight. Contemplative life, at least in its ideal realization, can be called a white martyrdom in that it expresses the mystery of death-with-Christ through a free and complete act of self-donation in which the person, in the Church, by a free and inconditional act of self-surrender gives himself to the Father in loving obedience. The white martyr places all his hope in God as he suffers from alienating powerlessness in a death-like darkness. He might have avoided this suffering by refusing to go out from himself, yet the contemplative freely chooses to respond to the invitation of love in spite of the "death" that love will demand of him. Through his "death," the power of sin is overcome and the contemplative begins to live fully by the power of the Spirit of the Risen Lord.

Strangely, while the paranormal perceptual states of the mystics have been of continual interest to psychology, there has been no significant work on the psychology of apophatism. Equally odd is the dearth, until the last decade, of studies of the psychology of dying. It should be no surprise, therefore, that a serious comparative study of death and apophatic mysticism has yet to be undertaken.[223] The lack of empirical data is especially to be regretted, but the considerations on the psychology of intentionality in our second section and the teaching of St John of the Cross regarding the sufferings of the night of spirit seem to fully support a theory of mystical dying in the dark nights. The contemplative is indeed a white martyr.

Death in the Doctrine of St John of the Cross

The theological reality of dying with Christ is reflected in the doctrine of St John of the Cross.

1. Sanjuanistic References to Death

St John of the Cross refers to death and dying in a variety of ways which we may conveniently list under six headings. These categories are not rigid divisions.

(1) The saint cites scriptural passages which speak of death in terms not directly applicable to soteriology. They include references to the death of a person or persons and quotations from psalms that are expressive of human anguish.[224]

(2) He often calls the state of the soul in sin "death" and, by extension, uses death as an analogy for the natural operations of fallen man, e.g.: "Gall refers to their lack of God, which is death to the soul," and "Let it be known that what the soul calls death is all that goes to make up the old man: the entire engagement of the faculties . . . in the things of the world, and the indulgence of the appetites in the pleasures of creatures."[225]

(3) The saint often speaks of the redemptive death of Christ or makes reference to the Cross, often only indirectly and in the context of a spiritual or an ascetical principle.[226]

(4) St John sometimes mentions a desire for death which is not due to existential anguish but rather to the vehemence of love. This type of "dying" is found mostly in the *Canticle* and *Living Flame* and is considered an imperfection.[227]

(5) In the *Ascent* and *Dark Night*, another kind of death predominates: dying to natural modes of operations and with them to concupiscence and the effects of sin and to everything that prevents union.[228]

(6) Finally, St John speaks of death caused by the vehemence of love when the soul in union comes to the end of its earthly existence.[229]

Of these uses, the fifth has the most direct bearing on our study. Dying to natural operations and through them to the world is a martyrdom in which the mystic anticipates his final option in dying. The proof that this is so can be found in the mystic's death by love.

2. Death and the Operations of the Soul

To understand the liberation-by-death significance of the nights, we must turn briefly to the *Living Flame*. There John writes; "For death is nothing else than the privation of life . . ."; and "Every living being lives by its operations. . . ."[230] We may derive from these statements that from the viewpoint of St John of the Cross spiritual or mystical death *is the privation in a human person of the activity of the faculties and of the appetites.*

Death is a *privation.* This implies an intervention of an outside force and a kind of violation of the integrity of the human person. Even mystical death — like the martyr's — is a passion that alienates. This notion prescinds somewhat from the question of physical demise. The operation of animation of the body by the soul continues, but from the viewpoint of moral activity, the choice which constitutes the final self-determination of a person and which is the essential element of dying as a moral act, may somewhat anticipate the separation of body and soul. As in the gradual deterioration of the human body, the faculties and appetites may be progressively deprived of their operations. Even from the sanjaunistic point of view, spiritual death is axiologically present in life, and individual choices will involve death to the world as a condition for life in Christ.

The paradoxical moral import of every moral act for life or death is found in the teaching of St Paul whom St John of the Cross quotes in defense of his doctrine.[231]

It may be objected that since death is a deprivation and choices are voluntary, no act of mortification can be considered a moral death or moral act of dying. This is true, but it misses the point. In the night the human person turns all the *fuerza del alma* toward God. Renunciation follows as a consequence of each act of centering on God and becomes the condition for further development of the soul's intentionality. So long as the renunciation goes against the inclination of the appetites, it is suffered as an undesired, though sometimes foreseen, consequence of the basic choice. Voluntary mortification may, then, be suffered in the second instance as an intrusion from without.

Though the active aspect of dying is implicit in the teaching of the saint, we find nothing like a developed theory of death as a redemptive act in the writings of the mystic.[232]

3. Dying with Christ

The extreme ascesis proposed in the thirteenth chapter of the First Book of the *Ascent* is proposed in imitation of Christ. But St John does not develop his doctrine explicitly in terms of dying and of the Cross of Christ until chapter seven of the Second Book of the *Ascent*.

The saint teaches that the journey itself demands of the human person "a dispossession and annihilation in the spiritual part of his nature," and justifies his doctrine by appealing to the teaching of Jesus: "If anyone wishes to follow my way, let him deny himself, take up his cross and follow me. For he who would save his soul shall lose it, but he who loses it for me shall gain it" (Mk 8:34–35). From this he develops his doctrine regarding total self-abnegation and then adds:

> O, who can explain the extent of the denial Our Lord wishes of us! This negation must be similar to a complete temporal, natural, and spiritual death, that is, in reference to esteem of the will which is the source of all denial. (. . .)
>
> His Majesty taught this to those two disciples who came to ask him for places at his right and left. Without responding to their request for glory, he offered them the chalice he was about to drink as something safer and more precious on this earth than enjoyment (Mk 20:22).
>
> This chalice symbolizes death to one's natural self through denudation and annihilation. As a result of this death a man is able to walk along the narrow path in the sensitive part of his soul, as we said, and in its spiritual part (in his understanding, joy, and feeling). Accordingly, one can attain to dispossession in both parts of the soul. Not only this, but even in his spirit a person will be unhindered in his journey on the narrow road, for on this road there is room only for self-denial (as Our Savior asserts) and the Cross. The Cross is a supporting staff and greatly lightens and eases the journey.[233]

There follow additional reflections on dispossession, nakedness, self-abnegation and annihilation. He then adds:

> Because I have said that Christ is the way and that this way is a death to our natural selves in the sensory and spiritual parts of the soul, I would like to demonstrate how this death is patterned on Christ's. For he is our model and light.
>
> First, during his life he died spiritually to the sensitive part, and at his death he died naturally. He proclaimed during his life that he had no place whereon to lay his head (Mt 8:20). And at his death he had less.

Second, at the moment of his death he was certainly annihilated in his soul, without any consolation or relief, since the
Father left him that way in innermost aridity in the lower part.
He was thereby compelled to cry out: *My God, My God, why have
you forsaken me?* (Mt 27:46) This was the most extreme abandonment, sensitively, that he suffered in his life . . . That is, he
brought about the reconciliation and union of the human race
with God through grace. The Lord achieved this, as I say, at
the moment in which he was most annihilated in all things: in
his reputation before men, since in beholding him die they
mocked him instead of esteeming him; in his human nature, by
dying; and in spiritual help and consolation from his Father, for
he was forsaken by his Father at that time so as to pay the debt
fully and bring man to union. David says of him: *Ad nihilum
redactus sum et nescivi* (Ps 72:22) . . . When the spiritual person is
brought to nothing, the highest degree of humility, the spiritual
union between his soul and God will be effected. The journey,
then, does not consist in recreations, experiences and spiritual
feelings, but in the living, sensory and spiritual, exterior and interior death of the Cross.[234]

Two other important, though (mercifully!) much briefer
references to the mystical journey as a death occur in the Second Book of the *Dark Night*. In chapter thirteen the saint
teaches that God cleanses the soul in its sensory and spiritual
parts "by darkening the interior faculties and emptying them of
all these objects, and by restraining and drying up the sensory
and spiritual affections" of the soul. As a result, *"God makes the
soul die to all that he is not."*[235] And in chapter sixteen he says:

> . . . these faculties must also be darkened regarding the divine
> so that weaned, purged, and annihilated in their natural way
> they might lose that lowly and human mode of receiving and
> working. Thus all these faculties and appetites of the soul are
> tempered and prepared for the sublime reception, experience
> and savor of the divine and supernatural, which is unreceivable
> until the old man dies.[236]

In these passages, a number of important theological
elements of death are applied to the journey in the night.

The means by which union in grace is effected—and thus freedom also—is the redemptive death of Christ. This death is not viewed so much as a physical passion as much as a moral act. Christ is seen as having lost everything by which the natural man lives and as abandoning himself to the Father in the essential obscurity of existential darkness this loss involves. As we have seen, the dark and unconditional abandonment of the totality of one's being is the essential element of dying as a human act.

The only door to life is Christ who is entered by conformity to him in obedience and death. Thus the same kind of self-abandonment is required of the soul on its journey.

From the viewpoint of the saint, the principal element of dying is the "denudation and annihilation in the sensory and spiritual parts of the soul," that is the deprivation of the natural operations. The active element is not so clearly developed.

Because the purification which leads to this death is the work of contemplation and the theological virtues, the anticipated death is a theologically-informed act.

Oddly, the sacramental implications of the death of Christ as the starting point of the Christian life are not developed. We find only a single, somewhat indirect, reference to baptism in the writings of the saint.[237] On the other hand, death is seen as morally present throughout the life of Jesus, but while the saint says that he died to the sensitive in his life he cannot be referring simply to disordered appetites, as Christ was perfectly free in this respect. Rather, he died to a human mode of activity which was in itself completely just.

This has important consequences for the disciple of the Master in whose life death must also be spiritually present. The overcoming of concupiscence is only part of the work done on one's journey. He is asked not only to put his appetites in reasonable order but also to die to their natural mode of operations. And the reason for this is found in the beginning of the paragraph from chapter sixteen of the Second Book of the *Night* which we have quoted above:

And even if God were to give these natural faculties the activity and delight of supernatural, divine things, they would be unable to receive it except in their own way, very basely and naturally. As the philosopher says, whatever is received is received according to the mode of the receiver.[238]

Mortal flesh cannot bear the weight of God's glory!

4. Annihilation and the Mystical Death

In these passages we have frequently encountered the word "annihilation — *aniquilación*" or one of its cognates. In typical indifference to technical precision, St John uses this term often and in several different senses without bothering to define it or to distinguish among its various meanings. In only two cases does he use it in the strict metaphysical sense of reduction of being to nothing.[239] More often it has a clearly accomodated sense, e.g.: "As for God, who will stop him from accomplishing his desires in the soul that is resigned, annihilated, and despoiled?"[240] At times, however, he uses it to describe an oppressive or violent interference with the activity of the faculties, to the point that they are unable to do anything. Because they are deprived of their activity, they—and the person—are morally dead.

John generally predicates annihilation of a power of the soul or of the entire soul as an operative subject. The operative sense is made clear by his use of the phrase *acerca de*—with respect or regard to—or by the context.

Without knowing where it is going, the soul sees itself annihilated with respect to all things.[241]

The annihilation of the memory in regard to all forms is an absolute requirement for union with God.[242]

This was great happiness . . . because through the annihilation and calming of my faculties, passions, appetites, and affections . . . I went out from my human way of acting.[243]

The experience of annihilation may be the effect of active renunciation or passive contemplation:

. . . He wishes us to do likewise by annihilating the strength and satisfaction of the faculties in regard to sensory and visible objects.[244]

We clearly explained this sickness and languor in respect to all things when we mentioned the annihilation of which the soul becomes aware when it begins to climb the ladder of contemplation. It becomes unable then to find satisfaction, support, consolation, or a resting place in anything.[245]

St John emphasized the oppressive character of the feelings of the soul in the sixth to ninth chapters of the Second Book of the *Night*. There, in addition to "annihilation," he sometimes uses the word "undoing — *deshacimiento*" which is so close in meaning to annihilation that Kavanaugh and Rodriguez even translate it as such. Taken reduplicatively with annihilation, it seems to point up the sensible suffering which, because of the nature of human acts, is the sensible pre-condition for the moral act of dying. Unless the person experiences his undoing, he cannot surrender himself totally and unconditionally into the hands of God:

For the sensory part is purified by aridity, the faculties by the void of their apprehensions, and the spirit by thick darkness.

God does all this by means of dark contemplation. And the soul not only suffers the void and suspension of these natural supports and apprehensions . . . but is also purged by this contemplation. . . . in order to burn away the rust of the affections the soul must, as it were, be annihilated and undone — *se aniquile y deshaga* — in the measure that these passions and imperfections are connatural to it.

Because the soul is purified in this forge like gold in the crucible . . . it feels terrible annihilation [lit., undoing — *deshacimiento*] in its very substance and extreme poverty as though it were approaching its end.[246]

In modern terms, the feelings of annihilation are the feelings of depression states. By interfering with natural operations, contemplation sabotages the natural psychological dynamic of the person and reduces him to a state of frustration in which he is neither able to direct his natural energies toward anything or find fulfillment in any creature. Ordinarily, the operative inactivity this provokes would be fatal in its consequences, as in the case of infants who die from a lack of fondling. As the saint says, "And if he did not ordain that these feelings, when quickened in the soul, be soon put to sleep again, a person would die in a few days." [247] The "depressed" person lives by virtue of the unfelt theological activities which characterize him in this state. Since he is unable to love in any other manner, he rapidly perfects himself in God who is the transcendent object of his hope.

5. Substantial Darkness and Substantial Touches

The extent of the annihilation may best be understood if we reflect on a word which St John frequently employs while speaking of this "annihilating" purification: *substance* and its cognates.

Normally the word "substance" is not employed in its strict metaphysical sense of reduction of being to nothing. Rather it expresses what is more important or "essential" in the popular acceptation of that word. [248] But there are exceptions to this popular usage. Consider the "substantial darkness" that annihilates the spirit:

> That the intellect reach union with the divine light and become divine in the state of perfection, this dark contemplation must first purge and annihilate it of its natural light and bring it into obscurity. It is fitting that the darkness last as long as is necessary for the expulsion and annihilation of the intellect's habitual way of understanding which was a long time in use, and that the divine light and illumination take its place. Since that strength of understanding was natural to the intellect, the darkness it here suffers is profound, frightful, and extremely painful. *This darkness seems to be substantial darkness, since it is felt in the deep substance of the spirit.* [249]

Substantial clearly indicates a degree of intensity or other quality of the experienced darkness. Taken by itself it suggests a kind of tangible or palpable darkness, but more seems to be intended, as is shown by being related to the "substance of the spirit."

"Substance of the spirit" is a synonym for "substance of the soul" which is a favorite technical expression of the saint. In its general sense it is equivalent to the "center" or "ground-*fondo*" of the soul, that is, "that which is most intimate or interior to the being."[250] It should be obvious that a soul cannot experience anything in its metaphysical substance but only through its sensitive powers. Therefore, some kind of accomodated sense must be intended here. Henri Sanson explains the saint's use of the phrase in three ways. It may mean (1) the deeper level of a person's being as opposed to his powers and their natural operations; or (2) the soul insofar as it is poor and naked, that is despoiled of accidents or apprehensions; or (3) the soul itself insofar as its "profound caverns" or transcendental capacities are rooted in God.[251] This latter sense is reflected in Teófilo de la Virgen del Carmen's definition: "In truth, by the term 'substance of the soul' St John sometimes explicitly indicates the spiritual potencies insofar as they are passively placed in act and from the very roots."[252]

In examining the activities of the parts of the personality it is easy to forget the person behind them. The roots of a faculty cannot be anything other than the subsisting person, the one who acts and experiences. Human faculties in ordinary life are moved passively. In the language of scholastic epistemology, this happens to the possible intellect as well as to the will in fruition. But it is the person who knows and enjoys. Therefore it seems that St John's reference to the substance of the soul is an expression of a person's holistic experience of fulfillment.

This holistic interpretation is confirmed by the meaning of the related term, "substantial touch." Though the fully-developed notion occurs but twice in the *Night*,[253] and not at all in the *Ascent*, references to "touches-*toques*" abound in these works and are often characterized as "substantial." When the word "touch" occurs alone it ususally means any passive activation of a sensible or spiritual power by God. Some of these touches are merely sensible delights. But the saint also speaks about other special touches which he calls "touches of union."[254] These are fugitive, indistinctly felt (in the saint's sense of supra-conceptually) acts of contemplation. The saint may say that these touches are experienced in the substance of the soul and so may be referred to as substantial touches. In chapter twenty-four of the Second Book of the *Night* we read:

> The soul obtains habitually and perfectly (insofar as the condition of this life allow) the rest and quietude of the spiritual house by means of the acts of substantial touches of divine union which, in concealment and hiding from the disturbances of the devil and of the senses and passions, are received from the divinity. With these touches the soul is purified, quieted, strengthened, and made stable that it may be able to receive permanently this divine union, which is the divine espousal between the soul and the Son of God.[255]

These touches are experienced in concealment because their subject is not a single faculty but the spiritual person himself. But since the person is an integrated whole, God's presence will be intuited or felt after the fact of his being there and, if at all, in the intellect and will. This is why the touches seem to be activations of the spiritual potencies, "from their roots and according to their dynamic totality."[256] But to speak of dynamic totality from their roots is to say the whole person experiences the touch of union.

The question must be asked, however, how these touches are to be distinguished from full fruition if the person as a whole is moved by them. The answer to this can be seen in the function which John assigns them of purifying and preparing the soul for union. They are experienced passively, and in the way the person is drawn toward God, but he must add his own active response to the love of God which is poured into his heart. Only by his own free choice can he be effected into his final fulfillment.

Unlike the terrifying experience of darkness that contemplation more often brings, these substantial touches are cataphatic or illuminative experiences of the inflow of the same love of God. The fact that they purify demonstrates that it is not the suffering which the soul feels that purges it but rather the love which provokes suffering until the soul is able to receive and reciprocate it in a divine manner.

God gives himself to the soul as his significant other when through the nights the human person has so developed in relationship to God so that their mutually intentional love may be realized. In experiencing the touches of the "substance of God in the substance of the soul,"[257] the human person tastes the love he hopes for. God not only empowers him to love divinely but by doing so throws him into a crisis of mortal intensity. As May says, "It is when love *is* realized that eros may literally 'break the limb's strength.'"[258] The soul is made totally vulnerable by a love which asks it to give everything.

Through the substantial touches which enable the person to dispose of himself as a whole into God's hands, and through the unitive power of theological love, the person surrenders himself in "substantial" darkness or annihilation and, hoping against hope, is brought to his final fulfillment. As the saint puts it: "When he is brought to nothing, the highest degree of humility, the spiritual union between his soul and God will be effected."[259] The soul chooses God as its supreme Good. Its fundamental option for God is made its only option, in a certain sense of the person's life. He no longer lives in his object choices. As the bride of the saint's *Canticle* proclaims, "Nor have I any other work, now that my every act is love — *ni ya tengo otro oficio, que ya sólo en amar es mi exercicio.*"[260]

John of the Cross would develop the implications of what we have called a moral anticipation of dying in his later works. In the *Living Flame of Love* he writes:

> It should be known that the death of persons who have reached this state is far different in its cause and mode than the death of others, even though it is similar in natural circumstances. If the death of other people is caused by sickness or old age, the death of these persons is not so induced, in spite of

their being sick or old; the soul is not wrested from them unless by some impetus of love, far more sublime than previous ones, of greater power, and more valiant, since it tears through this veil and carries off the jewel, which is the soul.

The death of such persons is very gentle and sweet, sweeter and more gentle than was their spiritual life on earth. For they die with the most sublime impulses and delightful encounters of love. . . . [261]

In commenting on this passage, Federico Ruiz-Salvador says;

We protest: such a manner of dying is not to be taken seriously. Where is the feeling of human anguish caused by one's natural dissolution which Christ felt on the Cross?

The system of St John of the Cross does not do away with death and its horrors. It simply displaces them from the place where they belong according to the life of natural man to the place which belongs to them in a life of faith. St John of the Cross calls for the achievement of death consciously and in broad daylight during a man's life. The dark night is a true death.[262]

And it is a rebirth to true freedom.

SUMMARY

The mystical journey in the dark night is a liberation because it is an effective means of attaining, insofar as it is possible in this life, to the perfection of one's being in a union of love in Christ between the human person and God. By overcoming the obstacles to union, which also are the obstacles to beatitude, we attain to our final freedom. At once attracted and impelled by God's love, the human person begins actively to enter into the night of sense through Christ-centered choices which put an end to the dispersion of his psychological and spiritual energies and direct his intentionality or caring more perfectly toward his end. His efforts would be unable to achieve anything more than moral self-improvement were it not for the fact that they are sustained by the theological virtues. These virtues, as transcendental intentional tendencies and operative habits, allow a person to know and love God and to begin to choose him in himself and not simply as a good intuited in creatures and striven for by natural transcendence. Charity, especially in its unitive or erotic aspect, directs the person's energies toward God in an increasingly inclusive caring. As the person begins to choose in a theological manner, he becomes more and more God-centered and by his choices he begins to liberate himself of his voluntary imperfections. By means of the theological virtues, God infuses dark contemplation. In contemplation, human choices undergo change and the person begins to choose God in an ordinarily unfelt manner. The attraction of God's love and the person's response effect a renunciation which detaches the person from creatures and re-orders his concern for them as part of his all-inclusive caring for God. As contemplation penetrates ever more deeply into the "substance" of his personality, the person gains dominion over his appetites and overcomes the effects of concupiscence. His love for God then grows with its own passion, and the person comes to love God with all the strength of his soul.

The interference with his normal psychological activities which the theological virtues effect in contemplation begin to detach him forcibly from memories and from his defensive modes of using his perceptions and feelings: he gives up his structure-bound attitude and becomes present to reality. At the same time he develops an acute consciousness of his own defects, finiteness, and misery in the sight of God who, since he is no longer sensibly felt, seems lost to the soul. The psychological interference provokes a depression of sometimes mortal intensity. But contrary to what the person perceives, in this "depression" he is actively engaged in increasingly inclusive choices directed toward God. When "substantial touches" of contemplation draw him into a deeply personal experience of God and when the apophatic darkness of contemplation leads the person to the "substantial" experience of moral annihilation, the person surrenders himself completely to God in an act of unitive love; he lets go of himself and by analogy to death entrusts himself to God. In so doing he achieves a full spiritual participation in the death of Christ.

Moral imperfections and the sin of the world no longer have any hold over him, as all he lives for and loves is God. He loves God by the supernatural operations of the theological virtues which have transformed his acts, and not by force of natural human transcendence. He has effected himself into final freedom by accepting from God the gift of his self-bestowal in union.

NOTES

1. Karl Rahner, *Grace in Freedom*, trans. and adapted by Hilda Graef (New York: Herder and Herder, 1969), p. 221.

2. Karl Rahner, "Theology of Freedom," in *Theological Investigations*, VI, trans. Karl-H. and Boniface Kruger (Baltimore: Helicon Press, 1969), pp. 190–191. See also his remarks on the method of transcendental investigation in "Theology and Anthropology," *Theological Investigations*, IX, trans. Graham Harrison (New York: Herder and Herder, 1972), pp. 29–33.

3. It is remarkable that almost all the current theologies of freedom are based on an Hegelian or Marxist dialectic. Typical of this approach is Paul Tillich's description of freedom as the structural element of reality in polarity with destiny "which makes existence possible because it transcends the essential necessity of being without destroying it." *Systematic Theology*, I (Chicago: University of Chicago Press, 1951), p. 182. See also James H. Cone, "Freedom, History, and Hope," in *Liberation, Revolution and Freedom*, ed. Thomas M. McFadden (New York, Seabury Press, 1975), p. 57.

4. The behaviorist school of psychology, for example, which follows an empiricist metaphysics, reduces freedom and all other mental states which seem to explain behavior to feelings caused by conditioned responses to environmental contingencies. In this way the human person is explained away as well. See B.F. Skinner, *Beyond Freedom and Dignity* (Harmondsworth: Penguin Books, 1973).

5. Carl R. Rogers, *On Becoming a Person: A Therapist's View of Psycotherapy* (Boston: Houghton Mifflin Company, 1961), p. 192.

6. Rollo May, *Love and Will* (London: Souvenir Press, 1970), p. 184.

7. E. W. Trueman Dicken, *The Crucible of Love* (New York: Sheed and Ward, 1963), pp. 73–74.

8. Eric Josephson and Mary Josephson, *Man Alone: Alienation in Modern Society* (New York: Dell Publishing Company, 1962), pp. 13–26. See also

Thomas Merton, *Contemplation in a World of Action*, Image Books (Garden City: Doubleday, 1971), p. 90.

9. Any such description of freedom must remain incomplete. As a transcendental value it may be experienced positively in different ages. The same may be said of alienation.

10. Rahner, *Grace in Freedom*, pp. 211-213. Italics added.

11. 1 Jn 3:2.

12. Jn 8:31-32.

13. It would be sufficient to consider the importance which freedom as a recurring theme has in the writings of Karl Rahner.

14. Marilyn May Mallory, *Christian Mysticism: Transcending Techniques: A Theological Reflection on the Empirical Testing of the Teaching of St John of the Cross* (Amsterdam: Van Gorcum Assen, 1977), p. 11.

15. Jacques Maritain, *Distinguish to Unite or the Degrees of Knowledge*, trans. under the supervision of Gearld B. Phelan (New York: Charles Scribner's Sons, 1959), p. 356.

16. Segundo Galilea, "San Juan de la Cruz y la espiritualidad liberadora," in *Medellín*, (June, 1975), 216-222. This article, unfortuantely, is more significant for its title than for its contents.

17. We group under figures of comparison all the analogies, allegories and symbols used by the saint. For a discussion of the differences in their usage, see Federico Ruiz-Salvador, *Introducción a San Juan de la Cruz: el Hombre, los Escritos, el Sistema* (Madrid: B.A.C., 1968), pp. 111-122, and his "Il linguaggio di S. Giovanni della Croce" in *La Comunione con Dio secondo San Giovanni della Croce* (Roma: Edizioni del Teresianum, 1968), pp. 41-48.

18. A, 3, 18, 5; N, 1, 9, 8. Except where otherwise noted, the quotations are from the *Complete Works of St. John of the Cross*, trans. Kieran Kavanaugh, O.C.D. and Otilio Rodriguez, O.C.D. (Washington: ICS Publications, 1973). Spanish language citations are taken from the *Vida y Obras de San Juan de la Cruz, Doctor de La Iglesia Universal*, 9th edition, (Madrid: B.A.C., 1975). All citations from the *Canticle* and *Living Flame* are from the second ("B") redaction.

19. A, Prologue, 7; 1, 3, 4; 1, 11, 2; 1, 11, 16; 2, 7, 3; 2, 7, 4; 2, 11, 11; 2, 15, 4; 2, 16, 4; 2, 16, 5; 2, 16, 6; 2, 17, 1; 2, 17, 7; 2, 18, 2; 2, 23, 1; 2, 23, 4; 2, 24, 8; 2, 28, 1; 2, 29, 12; 3, 2, 2; 3, 2, 14; 3, 5, 3; 3, 7, 1; 3, 12, 1; 3, 17, 2; 3, 39, 1; N, 1, 10, 4; 1, 12, 4.

20. A, Prologue, 4; 1, 5, 2; 1, 5, 8; 1, 11, 3; 1, 11, 4; 1, 12, 5; 1, 13, 11; 2, 5, 3; 2, 8, 1; 2, 8, 5; 2, 9, 4; 2, 11, 3; 2, 13, 1; 2, 15, 4; 2, 16, 5; 2, 16, 10; 2, 17, 7; 2, 22, 1; 2, 23, 4; 2, 24, 5; 2, 24, 8; 2, 29, 7; 2, 32, 4; 3, 3, 1; 3, 5, 1; 3, 5, 2; 3, 7, 1; 3, 8, 1; 3, 11, 1; 3, 11, 2; 3, 13, 3; 3, 13, 4; 3, 24, 3; 3, 21, 2; 3, 35, 3; 3, 37, 1; 3, 37, 2; 3, 38, 2; 3, 39, 2; 3, 45, 5.

N, 1, Explanation, 2; 2, 6, 3; 2, 8, 1; 2, 14, 1; 2, 15, 1; 2, 16, 2; 2, 16, 3.

21. A, Prologue, 3; 1, 2, 2; 1, 5, 5; 1, 6, 1; 1, 7, 2; 1, 11, 4; 1, 11, 5; 1, 11, 8; 2, 4, 4; 2, 4, 5; 2, 12, 6; 2, 12, 8; 2, 16, 6; 2, 16, 14; 2, 17, 6; 3, 20, 1; 3, 20, 2; 3, 20, 3; 3, 20, 4; 3, 22, 5; 3, 28, 5; 3, 28, 7; 3, 35, 5; 3, 35, 8; 3, 37, 1;

3, 38, 1; 3, 38, 5; 3, 40, 1.
    N, 1, 3, 1; 1, 3, 2; 2, 9, 1.
22. A, Prologue, 3–7; 1, 1, 4; 2, 4, 4; 2, 16, 10; 2, 26, 18; 2, 29, 5; 3, 2, 2; 3, 2, 14; 3, 3, 1; 3, 14, 7.
    N, 1, 9, 7; 1, 10, 2; 1, 10, 5; 1, 10, 6; 2, 14, 1.
23. A, 2, 1, 1; 2, 4, 3; 2, 11, 7; 3, 24, 6; 3, 39, 2.
24. A, 1, 4, 5; 1, 4, 6; 1, 15, 1; 3, 20, 3; 3, 22, 5; 3, 25, 4. N, 2, 4, 3.
25. A, 1, 3, 4; 1, 4, 6; 1, 7, 1; 1, 11, 3; 1, 11, 4; 1, 11, 6; 1, 11, 7; 1, 12, 6; 1, 15, 1; 1, 15, 2; 2, 4, 6; 2, 12, 9; 2, 16, 11; 2, 17, 7; 2, 19, 11; 2, 19, 12; 2, 21, 11; 3, 2, 14; 3, 3, 2; 3, 3, 3; 3, 4, 1; 3, 4, 2; 3, 5, 3; 3, 6, 2; 3, 6, 3; 3, 10, 2; 3, 12, 1; 3, 16, 6; 3, 18, 1; 3, 18, 6; 3, 20, 2; 3, 20, 3; 3, 22, 2; 3, 23, 1; 3, 23, 5; 3, 23, 6; 3, 24, 6; 3, 25, 6; 3, 29, 1; 3, 29, 5; 3, 32, 1; 3, 37, 2; 3, 39, 3.
    N, 1, 4, 3; 1, 8, 3; 1, 8, 4; 1, 10, 4; 1, 11, 4; 1, 12, 4; 1, 13, 2; 1, 13, 3; 1, 13, 11; 1, 13, 14; 2, 1, 2; 2, 7, 4; 2, 9, 1; 2, 9, 2; 2, 14, 1; 2, 14, 3; 2, 15, 1; 2, 16, 2; 2, 16, 7; 2, 22, 1; 2, 23, 2; 2, 23, 3; 2, 23, 12.
26. A, 3, 20, 3; 3, 15, 13; 1, 12, passim. N. 1, 9, 9; 2, 1, 1.
27. For example: A, 3, 12, 1; 2, 24, 8; 1, 11, 3; 3, 19, 4.
28. See A, 2, 15, 4; 2, 17, 7; N, 2, 14, 1; 2, 14, 3; S, 2, 23, 4.
29. A, 1, 11, 4.
30. A, 3, 22, 5.
31. Growth can be called a liberation in the strict sense only where it is wrested from an alienating situation. Thus a chick hatching from an egg is not strictly liberated. Analagous experience of "liberation" occur in psychological and spiritual growth.
32. N, 2, 1, 1.
33. *Loc. cit.* Italics added.
34. N, 1, 8, 3. Translation ours.
35. Karl Rahner, "The Dignity and Freedom of Man," in *Theological Investigations*, II, trans. Karl-H. Kruger (Baltimore: Helicon Press, 1963), pp. 246–247.
36. *Ibid.*, p. 248.
36a. EDITOR'S NOTE: See J. Ruth Aldrich's article *infra*.
37. Karl Rahner, "Freedom in the Church," in *Theological Investigations*, II, trans. Karl-H. Kruger (Baltimore: Helicon Press, 1963), p. 92.
38. Karl Rahner, "Experience of Self and Experience of God," in *Theological Investigations*, XIII, trans. David Bourke (New York: Seabury Press, 1975), p. 127.
39. See Jacques Maritain, "L'Idée Thomiste de la Liberté," *Revue Thomiste*, 40 (1939) 3, 440–459; and Jean Mouroux, *The Meaning of Man*, trans. A.H.G. Downes, Image Books (Garden City: Doubleday, 1961), pp. 119–126.
40. Rahner, "Freedom in the Church," p. 94.
41. Skinner's behaviorist model would make good sense without man's spiritual openness for God. On the other hand, St John of the Cross' picture of the moral freedom of a person separated from God is scarcely more optimistic. See A, 1, 6–12. Without God man is truly alienated. See Rahner, "Theology of Freedom," pp. 190–191.

42. Karl Rahner, "Guilt and its Remission: The Borderland Between Theology and Psychotherapy," in *Theological Investigations*, II, trans. Karl-H. Kruger (Baltimore: Helicon Press, 1963), pp. 269–270.

43. Karl Rahner, "Dogmatic Reflections on the Knowledge and Self-Consciousness of Christ," in *Theological Investigations*, V, trans. Karl-H. Kruger (Baltimore: Helicon Press, 1966), p. 209.

44. *Loc. cit.*

45. Rahner, "Freedom in the Church," pp. 94–95.

46. Karl Rahner, "Does Traditional Theology Represent Guilt as Innocuous as a Factor in Human Life?" in *Theological Investigations*, XIII, trans. David Bourke. (New York: Seabury Press, 1975), p. 137.

47. Rahner, "Theology of Freedom," p. 188.

48. Nicholas Lash, "The Church and Christ's Freedom," in *Jesus Christ and Human Freedom*, eds. Edward Schillebeeckx and Bas van Iersel (New York: Herder and Herder, 1974), pp. 100–108.

49. For a fuller discussion of freedom in the New Testament see Heinrich Schlier, ελευθερος, in *Theological Dictionary of the New Testament*, II, ed. Gerhard Kittel, trans. and ed. Geoffrey W. Bromley (Grand Rapids: Erdmans, 1964), pp. 496–502.

50. See *The Jerome Biblical Commentary*, eds. Raymond Brown, Joseph A. Fitzmyer and Roland E. Murphy, 2 vols. in one, (London, Dublin and Melbourne: Geoffrey Chapman, 1968), II, 53:54; and the comments of Raymond E. Brown, *The Gospel According to John (i-xii)*, Vol. 29 "Anchor Bible," intro. trans. and notes by Raymond E. Brown (Garden City: Doubleday, 1966), pp. 352–368 (esp. 361–362).

51. It would be possible to develop the Johannine theme in terms even closer to Paul by examining John's understanding of the role of the Holy Spirit and baptism (Jn 3), the Holy Spirit and truth (Jn 16:13), divine sonship and sin (1 Jn 3), the annointing of truth (1 Jn 2:20–27), and the eschatalogical hope of God's children (1 Jn 3:2).

52. Jn 1:17.

53. The eucharistic context and the convergence of major themes from throughout the Fourth Gospel make chapters fourteen to seventeen especially significant for a theological understanding of the perfection of love in union with Christ.

54. Henri Rondet, *The Theology of Sin*, trans. Royce W. Hughes (Notre Dame: Fides, 1960) pp. 82–83. Rondet insists forcefully on the objective character of sin as a transgression of divine law.

55. As we will see, this notion is particularly inadequate if interpreted as meaning love for a creature precludes love for God as does St John of the Cross. See A, 1, 12, 3.

56. Karl Rahner, "Guilt — Responsibility — Punishment Within the View of Catholic Theology," in *Theological Investigations*. VI, trans. Karl-H. Kruger and Boniface Kruger (Baltimore: Helicon Press, 1969), pp. 201–202.

57. Louis Monden, *Sin, Liberty and Law*, trans. Joseph Donceel (New York: Sheed and Ward, 1965), pp. 8, 9.

58. Rahner, "Guilt—Responsibility—Punishment," p. 210.

59. The possibility of repentence is a result of the theological notion of concupiscence, which we will discuss later. It is perhaps most clearly seen in the case of Adam after his loss of integrity as opposed to his state before the fall. See Karl Rahner, "The Theological Concept of Concupiscentia," in *Theological Investigations*, I, trans. and intro. Cornelius Ernst, (Baltimore, Helicon Press, 1961), pp. 372-373.

60. Rahner, "Guilt and its Remission," pp. 278-279.

61. Rahner, "Concupiscentia," p. 361.

62. *Ibid.*, p. 362.

63. Monden, *Sin*, p. 31.

64. See Monden, *Sin*, p. 35; Karl Rahner, *On the Theology of Death*, Coll. "Quaestiones Disputatae," 2, trans. Charles H. Henkey (New York: Herder and Herder, 1961), pp. 30-39.

65. Piet Schoonenberg, *Man and Sin: A Theological View*, trans. Joseph Donceel (Notre Dame: University of Notre Dame Press, 1965), p. 14.

66. *Ibid.*, pp. 98-123 and especially 100-101.

67. *Ibid.*, p. 104.

68. *Ibid.*, p. 105.

69. Monden, *Sin*, p. 71.

70. Rahner, "Guilt—Responsibility—Punishment," p. 211.

71. Schoonenberg, *Man*, p. 42.

72. Piet Schoonenberg calls concupiscence in a pejorative sense "the tendency toward sin within man or mankind as it stands under sin; that is, in the flesh or in the world." *Op. cit.*, p. 82.

73. Rahner, "Concupiscentia," p. 359.

74. *Ibid.*, p. 360.

75. *Ibid.*, p. 364.

76. *Ibid.*, pp. 353-354. Rahner notes that in Paul's writings, the opposition between *sarx* and *pneuma* is not based on a body/spirit dualism. Rather it is an expression of the state of unredeemed man as contrasted to "the divine spirit graciously bestowed from above which must cleanse and sanctify man's higher part too, so that it should not be—*sarx*." *Ibid.*, p. 355, note 2.

77. Rahner, "Guilt and its Remission," pp. 274-275.

78. *Summa Theologica*, Ia, q. 64, a. 3, c.

79. Karl Rahner, "The Passion and Asceticism: Thoughts on the Philosophico-theological Basis of Christian Asceticism," in *Theological Investigations*, III, trans. Karl-H. Kruger and Boniface Kruger (Baltimore: Helicon Press, 1967), pp. 70-71.

80. See *Summa Theologica*, Ia-IIae, q. 35, "De dolore, seu tristitia secundum se."

81. Rahner, "Concupiscentia," p. 368.

82. Compare the positive harm worked by the appetites (A, 1, 6-12) and the intense sufferings of the spirit in the night (N, 2, 5-9).

83. St. Teresa, "Spiritual Relation" from Palencia, 1581, in the *Complete*

Works of St. Teresa, trans. and ed. E. Allison Peers, 3 vols. (London and New York: Sheed and Ward, 1944–1946), I, p. 334. (= Spiritual Testimony No. 65, 1, I.C.S. ed., p. 363.)

84. Karl Rahner, "On Christian Dying," in *Theological Investigations*, VII, trans. David Bourke (New York: Herder and Herder, 1971), p. 290.

85. *Ibid.*, 287. See also his remarks regarding concupiscence and death and the dogmatic questions related to this in "Concupiscentia," pp. 379–380.

86. Rahner, "On Christian Dying," p. 289.

87. Rahner, "Concupiscentia," pp. 371–374.

88. F, 1, 30.

89. Karl Rahner, *On the Theology of Death*, p. 22.

90. Rahner, "On Christian Dying," p. 288.

91. Erich Fromm, *Escape from Freedom* (New York: Avon Books, 1969). pp. 39–55.

92. See Abraham H. Maslow, *The Farthest Reaches of Human Nature* (New York: Viking Press, 1971), pp. 25–40.

93. Rogers, *On Becoming a Person*, pp. 191–192.

94. R.D. Laing refers to this as "ontological security." See his book, *The Divided Self* (Baltimore: Penguin Books, 1965), pp. 40–41.

95. *Ibid.*, pp. 66–67.

96. Rogers, *On Becoming a Person*, pp. 111–113.

97. For a holistic approach emphasizing the somatic component of the experience of alienation see Alexander Lowen, *The Betrayal of the Body* (New York: Collier Books, 1967), pp. 1–18.

98. Rollo May, *Love and Will* (London: Souvenir Press, 1970), pp. 172–177.

99. See: A, 2, 4, 4; N, 2, 5, 2; C, 1, 6; C, 1, 11; C, 20–21, 11; C, 22, 3; C, 38, 3.

100. F, 1, 14. See the comments of Ruiz-Salvador, *Introducción*, pp. 668–670.

101. Rahner, "Theology of Freedom," p. 187.

102. A, 2, 5, 7.

103. Georges Morel sees in participant transformation the perfection of man's being — an idea which implies freedom of being. See his book *Le sens de l'existence selon Saint Jean de la Croix*, II, (Paris: Aubier, 1960), p. 245.

104. A, 2, 5, 10–11.

105. A, 1, 4, 3.

106. Even the propositions of faith are creaturely concepts and to be preoccupied with them while God is infusing a theological activity is to close the door to God. See John's remarks regarding each of the faculties in A, 2, 8, 2–4; A, 3, 2, 2–4.

107. A, 1, 6, 1 qualifies appetites as *inordinate*, but the illustration that follows seems to ignore this qualification. See the discussion of concupiscence, *infra*.

108. A, 3, 17, 2.

109. A, 1, 4, 2–3.

110. A, 1, 4, 4. Here "nothingness" is seen as an obstacle to union while in A, 2, 7, 11 it is a condition for union: "When the soul is brought to

nothing . . . the union between God and his soul will be effected."
111. See A, 2, 22, 5 and A, 2, 22, 7.
112. See Karl Rahner, "Reflections on the Unity of the Love of Neighbor and the Love of God," in *Theological Investigations*, VI, trans. Karl-H. and Boniface Kruger (Baltimore: Helicon Press, 1969), pp 244-248.
113. St. Teresa, Peers ed., III, p. 267. (May we recognize in A, 2, 7, 5, which verbally echoes St Teresa's words, a reply by John?)

Marilyn Mallory attributes St John's somewhat inadequate theological position here to an understanding of desire derived from Augustine and mediated by a number of popular medieval writings, most notably Book Two of Peter Lombard's *Book of Sentences*. See her *Christian Mysticism*, pp. 128-129.
114. A, 1, 6, 1.
115. *Loc. cit.,*
116. *Loc. cit.*
117. A, 1, 11, 2.
118. A, 1, 11, 3.
119. A, 1, 8, 3. See also, S, 1, 7, 1; S, 3, 19, 3-4; N, 1, 13, 3.
120. A, 1, 15, 1.
121. A, 1, 13. Note especially paragraph 11.
122. A, 1, 13, 3-4.
123. A, 1, 13, 6-11.
124. A, 1, 13, 8.
125. N, 1, 13, 3.
126. N, 2, 23, 14-24, 2. (The chapter division is the later work of an editor.) See Pierluigi di S. Christina, "Il ritorno alla guistizia originale," in *Sanjuanistica* (Rome; Collegium Internationale, 1943), pp. 227-255.
127. A, 3, 16, 2. See also N, 1, 4, 7-8.
128. A, 3, 2, 2.
129. Rahner, "The Passion and Asceticism," p. 83.
130. N, 2, 3, 1.
131. Karl Rahner, "Reflections on the Theology of Renunciation," in *Theological Investigations*, III, trans. Karl-H. Kruger and Boniface Kruger (Baltimore: Helicon Press, 1967), p. 53.
132. *Ibid.*, p. 54.
133. *Loc. cit.*
134. *Loc. cit.* Note, Rahner is speaking of the *existential* appearance of the eschatological presence of God's salvation; this mystery also appears sacramentally.
135. Karl Rahner, "The 'Commandment' of Love in Relation to the Other Commandments," in *Theological Investigations*, V, trans. Karl-H. Kruger (Baltimore: Helicon Press, 1966), p. 447. See also his article, "On the Theology of Hope," in *Theological Investigations*, X, trans. David Bourke (New York: Herder and Herder, 1973), pp. 445, 451.
136. Because the love of God is not a value alongside others but is identical with the "*a priori* horizon of the will and with that of freedom in general." See Rahner, "The 'Commandment' of Love," p. 446.

137. A, 2, 6, 2.

138. Federico Ruiz-Salvador, *Vida teologal durante la purificación interior en los escritos de San Juan de la Cruz*, unpublished doctoral thesis, Teresianum, Rome, 1959, p 77. Translation ours. [Extract published in *Revista de espiritualidad*, 18 (1959), pp. 34–379.]

139. John of the Cross is celebrated for his application of hope to the memory which he grants the dignity of a full faculty. Karl Rahner's approach is somewhat different and in terms which echo the idea of "efficient" and "sufficient" grace, proposes hope as the virtue which manifests the specific and concrete saving will of God in individual cases. As unrelated as this perspective may seem to that of St John of the Cross, it assigns to hope a similar function: it makes a person immediately present to saving reality in his there-and-then unique circumstances. This would necessarily involve purification of the memory since without it a person cannot be freed from structure-bound behavior. See Rahner, "On the Theology of Hope," in *Theological Investigations*, X, trans. David Bourke (New York: Herder and Herder, 1973), p. 254.

140. N, 2, 3, 3. See esp. N, 2, 5.

141. See N, 2, 5, 1.

142. See A, 3, 2, 8–9.

143. See N, 2, 9, 2–4. For the implications of the doctrine presented here, see our third section, *infra*.

144. Teófilo de la Virgen del Carmen, "Estructura de la contemplación infusa sanjuanista," in *Revista de espiritualidad*, 23 (1964), 364. Translation ours.

145. A, 2, 24, 9.

146. Dom John Chapman, "What *is* Mysticism?", reprinted in his *Spiritual Letters* (London and Sydney: Sheed and Ward, 1959), p. 318.

147. N, 2, 10, 2. Urbano Barrientos in his *Purificación y purgatorio: Doctrina de San Juan de la Cruz sobre el purgatorio, a la luz de su sistema místico* (Madrid: Editorial de Espiritualidad, 1960) pp 98–100, states that the pain of contemplation is willed by God for the sake of purification. It seems to us that he fails to distinguish between the cause of purification and its concomitant effects in the senses. His argument turns on his understanding of the pleasurable interstices of the night as being typical of contemplation, an assumption which raises questions regarding the teaching of the saint in N, 2, 3, 2, and F, 1, 1, 19 that God positively wills pleasure as a relief to the soul and to strengthen it. It seems to us that the alteration of feelings can be explained by the make-up of the human personality and the progressive penetration of purification to the deepest center.

148. Ruiz-Salvador, *Vida teologal*, p. 87; and Teófilo, *Estructura*, p. 418.

149. *Summa Theologica*, Ia-IIae, q. 11.

150. *Ibid.*, a. 4, c.

151. *Summa Theologica*, Ia-IIae, q. 12, a. 1, c.

152. *Ibid.*, a. 3, ad 2.

153. See A, 3, 16, 2 and N, 1, 4, 7–8.

154. A, 3, 13, 5.

155. Arrigo Colombo, "Intenzionalità," in *Enciclopedia filosofica*, 2nd ed. rev.

(Firenze: Sansone, 1967), vol. II, p. 990. Translation ours.

156. Maritain, *Degrees*, p. 373.

157. F, 1, 12.

158. Though May's work is of special interest to us, he unfortunately seems to have had no direct knowledge of medieval Christian thought. Several of his statements are derived, not very accurately, from Paul Tillich. Fortunately, his basic insight regarding eros is corroborated by the independent work of Marilyn May Mallory and together they contribute to the possibility of restating in contemporary terms the ascetical doctrine of St John of the Cross.

159. May, *Love and Will*, pp. 73–74.

160. *Ibid.*, pp. 81–88.

161. *Ibid.*, p. 123.

162. *Ibid.*, p. 289. Note the psychological parallel to the theological notion of concupiscence.

163. It seems that the introduction of care here is due to May's philosophical presuppositions which are derived from Hegelian idealism as mediated by Tillich. He sees intentionality as part of the structure of reality and introduces care as its subjective counter-structure in the person.

164. May, *Love and Will*, p. 295. Interestingly, May quotes here from T. S. Eliot's "East Coker" a passage influenced by the Psalms and, according to William Johnston, by the *Book of Privy Counsel* from the author of the *Cloud of Unknowing*, a writer noted for his affinity to St John of the Cross. In his poem, Eliot repeats his message a few lines later with an explicit gloss of the verses of St John of the Cross on his drawing of Mount Carmel. See William Johnston, *The Mysticism of the Cloud of Unknowing* (New York, Rome, Tournai, Paris: Desclée, 1967), p. 175, note 12.

165. C, 8, 3.

166. Milton Mayeroff, *On Caring* (New York, Hagerstown, San Francisco, London: Harper and Row, 1971), p. 54.

167. *Ibid.*, p. 59.

168. Eric Berne's theory of transactional analysis is too well known to need comment. It stresses the social etiology of psychological trauma. See his *Transactional Analysis in Psychotherapy* (New York: Grove Press, 1961), pp. 52–59. R. D. Laing's work has stressed the familial etiology of schizophrenia. See his *The Politics of the Family* (New York: Random House, 1969) and *Knots* (New York: Vintage Books, 1970).

169. Laing, *The Divided Self*, p. 83.

170. Mayeroff, *On Caring*, p. 51.

171. *Ibid.*, pp. 52–53.

172. See N, 2, 11, 3–5.

173. Mallory compares the Greek of the Syrian monk with three modern translations. Unfortunately, she does not use a version known to St John. The translations all exhibit a dualistic conceptual bias in handling Greek terms with no exact Latin or modern-day equivalents. In point of fact, there was a long-standing medieval tradition of interpretation of Pseudo-Dionysius

in Augustinian-influenced terms. Furthermore, as Mallory notes, the Syrian monk had little to say about sin and this lacuna was filled in with Augustinian speculation. To these influences she attributes St John's ascetic pessimism.

174. Mallory, *Christian Mysticism*, p. 125.

175. *Ibid.*, pp. 169–170.

176. We question her apparent identification of emotions and affections (in the English sense of the word) with the conative tendency of the soul toward God. The theological activity of the soul is not developed. Furthermore, she seems to identify libido pure and simple with eros, which is an oversimplification. Rollo May's treatment seems to us more adequate. Yet the intentional aspect of love can be developed from her data and is even suggested by the importance she attaches to the notion of *centro más profundo del alma*. See *Christian Mysticism*, p. 170.

177. N, 2, 13, 9.

178. May, *Love and Will*, pp. 278–279; N, 2, 13, 3.

179. A, 3, 16, 2.

180. Sigmund Freud, *A General Introduction to Psychoanalysis*, trans. Joan Riviere (New York: Permabooks, 1953), p. 365.

181. A, 1, 14, 2.

182. See A, 2, 17.

183. May, *Love and Will*, p. 167.

184. Rollo May, *Man's Search for Himself* (New York: New American Library, 1967), p. 138.

185. *Ibid.*, p. 164.

186. Rogers, *On Becoming and Person*, pp. 125–158.

187. *Ibid.*, p. 133.

188. *Ibid.*, p. 147.

189. *Ibid.*, p. 152.

190. *Ibid.*, p. 153.

191. Trueman Dicken, *The Crucible of Love*, p. 46.

192. A, 3, 2–15.

193. *Summa Theologica*, IIa-IIae, q. 180, 1, 3.

194. May, *Man's Search*, p. 120.

195. May, *Love and Will*, p. 191. Italics added.

196. *Loc. cit.*

197. *Loc. cit.*

198. See A, 2, 13, 6.

199. See Alexander Lowen, *Depression and the Body* (Baltimore: Penguin Books, 1973), pp. 17–39: E.A. Gutheil, "Le depressioni reattive," and Walter Bonime, "Psicodynamica della depressione nevrotica" in *Manuale di psichiatria*, ed. Silvano Ariete (Turin: Boringhieri, 1969), I, pp. 362–372, 371–390; Frank J. Ayd, Jr. *Recognizing the Depressed Patient* (New York and London: Grune & Stratton, Inc., 1961), p. 1–22; Leonard Cammer, *Up from Depression* (New York: Pocket Books, 1971), pp. 66–73 and passim.

200. Mallory, *Christian Mysticism*, p. 201.

201. N, 2, 6, 6.

202. This finding suprises us. If a literal application of the ascetical rules proposed by the saint is destructive, any serious attempt to implement them should correlate *negatively* with progress in contemplation. Mallory's findings would suggest ascesis is irrelevant. The fact is that she sometimes overstates his ascetical doctrine, and the propositions in the ascetical section of her test (*Christian Mysticism*, p. 239) often need qualification. One may dispute her claim to have tested actual sanjuanistic ascetical practice. On the other hand, the correlation between progress in prayer and libidinal energy is significant.

203. A, 2, 7, passim.; A, 2, 11, 12; A, 2, 16, 3; A, 2, 16, 15; A, 2, 19, 7-9; A, 2, 19, 12; A, 2, 20, 3; A, 2, 22, 3-8; A, 2, 22, 11; A, 2, 22, 15; A, 2, 26, 10; A, 2, 27, 5; A, 3, 23, 2; A, 3, 25, 4; A, 3, 28, 4-6; A, 3, 29, 2-3; A, 3, 30, 4-5; A, 3, 31, 2; A, 3, 31, 5; A, 3, 31, 7-10; A, 3, 36, 3; A, 3, 38, 2-3; A, 3, 39, 2; A, 3, 40, 1; A, 3, 44, 2; A, 3, 44, 4; A, 3, 45, 3; N, Prologue; N, 1, 4, 7; N, 2, 14, 1; N, 2, 19, 4; N, 2, 20, 6; N, 2, 23, 3; N, 2, 23, 7. In addition there are numerous ambiguous references which may refer to God or to Christ.

204. A, 1, 5, 8; A, 1, 13, 3; A, 2, 7 passim.; A, 3, 23, 2; A, 3, 35, 5; A, 3, 39, 2.

205. A, 1, 13, 4; N, 2, 13, 6-7; and N, 2, 21, 3 which refers to Christ as the soul's spouse. In addition, there are numerous references to the soul's intentionality for God without specifying whether or not he is referring to the Incarnate Word.

206. A, 1, 14, 2-3; A, 3, 27, 4 (by an accommodated reference to Scripture); and N, 2, 21, 3.

207. See Rom 8:12-17; Phil 3:10-11.

208. Rahner, "The Passion and Asceticism," p. 67.

209. Karl Rahner, "The Hermeneutics of Eschatological Assertions," in *Theological Investigations*, IV, trans. Kevin Smyth (Baltimore: Helicon Press, 1966), p. 339, note 14. It seems to us that two separate questions are involved in this hypothesis. The first is the fact of "confirmation in grace," which would have to be a kind of final freedom. The second is the question as to whether a subject of this gift would have knowledge of the fact of it. Subjective certitude of salvation is not a necessary part of the extraordinary grace.

210. See Rahner, "Concupiscentia," pp. 372-373.

211. Rahner, *On the Theology of Death*, pp. 68-69.

212. *Loc. cit.*

213. *Ibid.*, p. 70. See also p. 49.

214. *Ibid.*, p. 51.

215. *Ibid.,* p. 71.

216. *Ibid.*, p. 72.

217. *Loc. cit.* See also p. 27-33.

218. *Ibid.*, p. 83.

219. *Ibid.*, pp. 79-80.

220. *Ibid.*, p. 105.

221. *Ibid.*, p. 109.

222. See Edward E. Malone, *The Monk and the Martyr* (Washington: Catholic University, 1950).

223. Lynda Maxwell's "Mystical Consciousness and Dying" in *Contemplative Review*, 10 (1977) Summer, pp. 7-13.; Fall, pp. 1-9; Winter, pp. 9-17, compares the experiences of near-death as recorded by Raymond A. Moody in *Life After Life* with the paranormal perceptual states of mystics. The parallels are striking, but of no direct interest to us as they illustrate the mystic illumination of the dying and not the dying of living contemplatives. In any case, phenomenological comparisons, which are colored by the imagination, must be handled with caution. More significant for our study is the description by Elisabeth Kübler-Ross of the last stages of dying. These are depression and acceptance. Death itself is seen as a last stage of growth. See *On Death and Dying* (New York: McMillan, 1969), pp. 84-137.

224. A, 2, 19, 4; A, 2, 21, 6; A, 2, 6, 1-2.

225. C, 2, 7; F, 1, 33.

226. A, 2, 7 passim; N, 1, 7, 4; C, 3, 5.

227. C, 11, 8. See also the *coplas* which begin: *Vivo sin vivir en mi*, I.C.S.ed., pp. 720-21.

228. A, 2, 7, passim.

229. C, 40, 1.

230. F, 2, 34 and 34.

231. Rom 8:13 and Eph 4:22-24 in F, 2, 32-33.

232. As, for example, in the writings of St Paul of the Cross. See Basileo de San Pablo, *La espiritualidad de la pasión en el magisterio de San Pablo de la Cruz* (Madrid: El Pasionario, 1969). His comparison of the doctrine of the two mystics, however, is decidedly unobjective. See pp. 207-212.

233. A, 2, 7, 6-7.

234. A, 2, 7, 9-11.

235. N, 2, 13, 11. Italics added.

236. N, 2, 16, 4.

237. C, 23, 6.

238. N, 2, 16, 4.

239. See A, 2, 5, 3; C, 11, 3.

240. A, 2, 4, 2.

241. N, 1, 11, 1. Translation ours.

242. A, 3, 4, 2.

243. N, 2, 4, 2.

244. A, 3, 37, 2. See also N, 2, 8, 2 and N, 2, 21, 11.

245. N, 2, 19, 1.

246. N, 2, 6, 4-5.

247. N, 2, 6, 6.

248. Victoriano Capánago tends to interpret this word in a more strictly metaphysical sense than do the saint's other commentators. See his *San Juan de la Cruz: valor psicológico de su doctrina* (Madrid: [no publisher indicated], 1950), p. 289.

249. N, 2, 9, 3.

250. Eulogio de la Virgen del Carmen, "La antropologia sanjuanistica," in *El Monte Carmelo*, 69 (1961), 64. Translation ours. For "fondo," see also B.

García-Rodriguez, "El fondo del alma," in *Revista española de teologia*, 8 (1948), 457–477.

251. Henri Sanson, *L'esprit humain selon Saint Jean de la Croix* (Paris: P.U.F., 1952), pp. 71–73.

252. Teófilo, "Estructura," p. 382. Translation ours.

253. N, 2, 23, 11 and N, 2, 24, 3.

254. See A, 2, 32, 4 and A, 3, 2, 5–6.

255. N, 2, 24, 3. For the way in which substantial touches prepare the soul for union, see Laureano Zabalza, *El desposoria espiritual segun San Juan de la Cruz* (Burgos: [no publisher indicated], 1964), pp. 54–63.

256. Teófilo, "Estructura," p. 385. Translation ours.

257. N, 2, 23, 12.

258. May, *Love and Will*, p. 201.

259. A, 2, 7, 11.

260. C, 28.

261. F, 1, 30.

262. Ruiz-Salvador, *Introducción*, p. 671. Translation ours.

TERESA, A
SELF-ACTUALIZED WOMAN

J. Ruth Aldrich, Ph.D.

Doctor Aldrich teaches college English to U.S. Army troops in Turkey. She submitted her doctoral thesis on St Teresa to the faculty of Philosophy and Letters of Salamanca University in Spain.

INTRODUCTION

The significance of including Teresa among the class of self-actualized people cannot be appreciated without recalling the attitude of most twentieth-century psychologists toward mystics and mysticism in general and toward Teresa of Avila specifically. Abraham Maslow expressed the scientific consensus succinctly: ". . . like most scientists, I had sniffed at them (mystic experiences) in disbelief and considered it all nonsense, maybe hallucinations, maybe hysteria—almost surely pathological."[1] Speaking specifically of Teresa, the French neurologist Charcot has written: "She was undeniably hysterical."[2] Many psychologists of the twentieth century accepted and supported that judgment.[3]

Certainly Teresa found defenders in great numbers. Still, until Abraham Maslow began to study mentally healthy people in the 1940's in an attempt to discover what he called "the higher ceilings of human nature," Teresa's defenders had no systematic framework upon which to base their arguments. Maslow, in his description of the self-actualized person, has provided such a framework, a formula with which to organize a logical, scientific defense.

In the development of his description of the self-actualized

81

person, the healthiest of people mentally, Maslow used many historical subjects, but he seems not to have even known about Teresa. As a matter of fact, none of the historical figures used by Maslow at first were religious (in the sense of "professional" religious); and the psychologist stated concretely that he wanted to avoid all association with, or even the suggestion of association with, organized religion. Toward the end of his career, however, as he studied more intensely the mystical experience and its presence in the self-actualizers, avoidance of "religious" language and symbolism became quite impossible.[4]

I should mention here that Maslow is also well known for his development of the idea of what he called a "hierarchy of needs." Essentially, the idea is that self-actualization marks the final step in human personality development. Before a person begins to strive toward this final step, other basic needs, both physiological and psychological, must have been met.[5] My own study shows that Teresa achieved self-actualization, but further work demonstrating her development toward that level is still to be done.[5a]

THE SELF-ACTUALIZED PERSONALITY: A BRIEF DESCRIPTION

> There are in the world people who are good, strong, triumphant: they are saints, wise men, recognized leaders, winners instead of losers, constructive rather than destructive people.[6]

With these words, Maslow begins his description of the self-actualized person. The personality characteristics used to describe such people might be divided into several classifying groups, beginning with the "purely personal" qualities such as spontaneity, aggressiveness, the need for solitude, serenity in times of crisis and a "philosophical" sense of humor. These qualities, of course, have their influence in the other groupings. A second set of characteristics refers primarily to the quality of the interpersonal relationships of the self-actualizers. Included here is the sense of mission and the democratic attitudes of these persons. Other characteristics of the personality refer directly to the self-actualizer's relationship with established authority and societal norms, i.e., attitudes toward and interaction with The Establishment. Here I include such qualities as the resistance to enculturalization, an acute keenness of discernment and perception of reality, and the determination to fulfill one's mission in life.

It is on this final group of personality qualities that I should like to focus attention in this abbreviated description of Teresa of Jesus — saint, educator and Doctor of the Church — as one of those extraordinary personalities that deserve to be called "self-actualized."

TERESA'S REALISM

Teresa lived comfortably in two worlds. All of the saint's modern biographers have marvelled at her ability to combine "celestial experience and efficacious earthly activitiy."[7] Maslow, had he known about Teresa, would not have been at all surprised by such ability, since the quality is found in most self-actualized people. One of Teresa's worlds is the one the saint called "the interior world," that world which is the source of celestial experiences called "mystical." The other world was the physical one into which Teresa was born, sixteenth-century Spain — a world, like the present one, hostile to the self-actualized person, male or female, but an especially difficult world in which to survive as a woman, self-actualized or not. The self-actualizer possesses qualities that facilitate survival — psychological, spiritual and physical — within the confines of existing power and political structures. Self-actualized people are rarely "drop-outs." "They do, however, enjoy exceptionally keen insight into the reality of any situation and the ability to detect the spurious and the deceptive and the dishonest."[8]

About one reality of her time, Teresa wrote little — and the few words that she wrote on the subject have rarely, if ever, been quoted by scholars. Many have cited the famous words from her *Life*, ". . . just being a woman is enough to have my wings fall off. . . ." as proof she was aware of her position in the ambient of sixteenth-century Spain.[9] But few have cited the clarity with which she saw a much harder reality of the epoch: the physical danger of being female.

Teresa's own mother had borne nine children in eleven years, a statistic that causes wonderment among moderns but not fear for the mother's life. Perhaps at the time of her mother's death, the child Teresa was not old enough to understand the reasons, but by the time she wrote the extraordinary document called *Foundations* she would have seen enough to know that her mother's experience was not atypical. Her acute perception of reality is clear to us when she suspects that some of the nuns fail to be grateful for ". . . the great favor that God has shown them in choosing them for his service and thus saving them from subjection to a man, which may end their lives . . ."[10] The convent may have been the "living tomb" that Salvador de Madariaga has called it,[11] but the women there were spared inclusion among the appalling mortality rate statistics that have haunted women until the twentieth century.

Three reasons lead us not to classify Teresa among militant feminists (the Spanish have an old saying that is apt here: "One swallow does not a summer make"). Teresa was too busy *living* feminist ideals to write about them, and to have done so would probably have resulted in her being silenced by the authorities. More importantly, her mission in life was far greater than the mere socio-economic improvement of women's lives—Teresa sought to enhance opportunities for the development of *human* potential, male and female. And finally, had she restricted herself to the narrow confines of feminism, her work would most assuredly have been stopped at its inception.

In her work, Teresa's ability to clearly discern reality and her concern that her sisters be free of the suspicion engendered by the religious in Spain who would take advantage of that society's susceptibility to the "miraculous" led her to write often to those less perceptive than herself. She advises against deceptions of all sorts—whether the source was the devil, spiritual advisors or one's own desire to experience the "divine gifts." Writing in *The Interior Castle*, Teresa notes that the intellect can help the soul to realize that

> the whole world is filled with falsehood, and so too that the joys the devil gives it are filled with trials, cares, and contradictions.[12]

The "joys the devil gives" lead the soul to a false sense of peace, about which Teresa writes throughout chapter two of the *Meditations on the Song of Songs*, to cite one of the lengthier warnings. The chapter begins "God deliver you from the peace of many kinds that worldly people have," and continues with Teresa's advice to her "daughters" that contentment which comes easily is to be mistrusted as false, since "there must be war in this life."[13]

At another point in *The Interior Castle*, she says "For certainly I see secrets within ourselves that cause me to marvel. And how many more there must be!"[14] Certainly she speaks there of spiritual secrets and her keenness in discerning reality is especially in evidence. The case which she describes in this fourth dwelling place would not be extraordinary in any atmosphere of intense spiritual searching in which "a great amount of penance, prayer and keeping vigil" work upon women so that when

> they feel some consolation interiorly and a languishing and weakness exteriorly, they think they are experiencing a spiritual sleep (which is a prayer a little more intense than the prayer of quiet) and they let themselves become absorbed. The more they allow this, the more absorbed they become because their nature is further weakened, and they fancy that they are being carried away in rapture.[15]

With the frankness characteristic of her own personality and of every self-actualizer, the saint analyzes a specific case as the paragraph continues:

I call it being carried away in foolishness because it amounts to nothing more than wasting time and wearing down one's health. . . . One person happened to remain eight hours in this state. By sleeping and eating and avoiding so much penance, this person got rid of the stupor, for there was someone who understood her. She had misled both her confessor and other persons, as well as herself — for she hadn't intended to deceive.[16]

Teresa tells another such story in the sixth chapter of *The Foundations*. Two sincere women, one a sister, the other a lay sister in the convent, had convinced themselves that they had to have daily Communion. The two began to be "enraptured" with such frequency that the prioress had written to Teresa about their situation. The founding mother refused to pass judgment by correspondence and went in person. She found two intensely devout women who were eating so little and so infrequently that they simply fainted. One of Teresa's earliest biographers, Francisco de Ribera, tells many other such stories, commenting on the foundress' special "gift" in detecting the true from the false.[17]

TERESA AND AUTHORITY

Of particular interest to Maslow would have been Teresa's relationship with the hierarchy of the Church, especially with the Inquisition officials and with her immediate superiors. Teresa didn't stutter on that subject, either: "Discretion is required in everything."[18] And in *The Interior Castle* she counsels about letting those who have visions or similar experiences becoming publicly known: ". . . a great deal of discretion is necessary in this matter and I highly recommend it to the prioresses."[19] The fact is that Teresa was so successfully discreet that she was often called "hypocrite" and "disobedient" by those who did not approve of her activities as reformer and founder of convents. Teresa's own very open account of her dealings with Church superiors on the founding of her first monastery in Avila offers a splendid example of the attitude with which she approached the Establishment. In chapter thirty-six of the *Life*, she tells us about being "called on the carpet," as it were, and asked to appear before the Provincial to explain her reasons for establishing a new house of prayer:

> After having received a serious reprimand . . . I didn't want to excuse myself; I had been determined about what I did. Rather, I begged to be pardoned and punished and that he not be vexed with me. I saw clearly that in some matters they condemned me without any fault on my part . . . But in other matters I knew plainly they were speaking the truth . . . None of what they said caused me any disturbance or grief, although I let on that it did so as not to give the impression I didn't take to heart what they said to me . . . I gave the explanation in such a way that neither the Provincial nor those who were present found anything to reprimand me for.[20]

The circumstances dictated her behavior at that moment. Human nature being what it is, had Teresa insisted upon the rightness of her position, or appealed to the Provincial's sense of logic, or dwelt upon the negative reasons for leaving La Encarnación, the Carmelite reform would have probably been stifled before it was really started. Teresa had advised the ladies-in-waiting of Doña Luisa de la Cerda that they must "live in their own century" and the saint practiced what she preached — on this occasion, anyway. Women were expected to be humble in the presence of authoritarian figures, contrite when confronted by reprimand; and Teresa, like all self-actualizers, knew how to live within the confines of the Establishment and make it work for her.

On other occasions, confronted with a different set of circumstances, Teresa does not humble herself in the presence of authority. Such contradiction in behavior is consistent with that expected of the self-actualized personality. ("Consistency is the hobgoblin of little minds," Emerson says, and both Maslow and Saint Teresa would have understood perfectly.) In the *Interior Castle*, Teresa speaks of "a lengthy controversy . . . among some spiritual persons" about one of the techniques of prayer, clearly choosing sides in the argument and stating her own position: "For my part, I must confess my lack of humility, but those in favor of stopping the mind (during prayer) have never given me a reason for submitting to what they say."[21]

One of the reasons for such inconsistency of behavior is to be found in another quality often characteristic of the self-actualized person — the refusal to be inhibited by tradition or conventional behavior when confronted with something that the self-actualizer has decided is necessary or important.[22] Teresa's famous phrase "determined determination" expresses perfectly the attitude of the self-actualized: nothing must be allowed to stand in the way of the accomplishment of one's chosen mission in life.[23] Once again the reader of Teresa's autobiography can see that in spite of her genuine humility and submission to the Church, she was not afraid to contradict her superiors if it meant that their opinions would halt or hinder the success of the Reform. In chapter thirty-five of the *Life*, she tells of the difficulties of deciding whether to allow income in the convents or to interpret strictly the Carmelite vow of poverty. She consults numerous authorities. Friar Peter of Alcantara argued in favor of complete poverty. Fr Ibáñez, the more "official" authority because of his higher position in the hierarchy, argued against poverty, giving many practical and theological reasons for accepting money. Teresa made her decision and wrote to Ibáñez,

> that I didn't want to benefit from theology if it wasn't conducive to my following my vocation, my vow of poverty and the counsels of Christ with total perfection, and that in this case he would do me no favor with his learning.[24]

This rebuke is mild, however, when one considers Teresa's confrontation with the Establishment in Toledo in 1569. Teresa had fulfilled all of the necessary bureaucratic requirements for founding a new monastery of the Reform in that city. For two months, she waited patiently for the final signature of permission from the governor of the archdiocese,

Don Gómez Tello de Girón, who at that time was the highest authority in both civil and religious matters. Finally, she asked for and was granted a personal interview with him. If she had worried about punishment by the Inquisition authorities, she forgot the worries. As she herself recounts the incident in chapter fifteen of the *Foundations*, her anger at the unnecessary delay and her fear that the foundaton would be denied led her into an angry tirade in which she even made not-so-veiled allegations about the sumptuous and sexually profligate life of the Church hierarchs in that decadent era. If she thought that women should be humble and contrite in the presence of authority, she forgot her principles, speaking to the governor/archbishop with such "rigor" that the license she requested was signed before she left the room that day.

Such attitudes and behavior by the self-actualized person seem merely one more aspect of that kind of reaction classified by Maslow as "resistance to enculturation." Enculturation, or socialization, is the process by which we are taught socially acceptable behavior, the process by which we learn what is right and what is wrong according to our society's values. After childhood, after parents have ceased to be our principal teachers, public opinion and peer pressure take over as "enculturizers." We are taught, for example, that we should eat with a knife and fork rather than with our fingers. On another level, we are taught that "nice" girls avoid certain kinds of behavior and that "men" don't cry when they are injured, frustrated or angry.

When Maslow uses the expression, "resistance to enculturation," he does not mean to suggest that the self-actualized personality rejects all of society's rules just for the sake of doing so. The self-actualized person is not the rebellious teen-ager who rejects his parents' mores because they are his parents', or neckties because The Establishment's representatives wear them. On the contrary, the self-actualized are usually quite conventional in their dress and in adherence to other social customs.[25] Thus, any deviation of theirs from the conventional is not "blind" rebellion but rather a thoughtful, premeditated rejection based upon their higher ("meta") needs.

Teresa's attitude toward women and toward herself as a woman in her society is one case in point, and there are others.

SOME REACTIONS OF TERESA TOWARD SOCIETAL ATTITUDES IN SPAIN

Society's attitudes toward women in Teresa's Spain were dictated by the pauline injunctions to "Let the woman learn in silence with all subjection . . ." and not to allow her ". . . to teach, nor to usurp authority over the man, but to be in silence" (1 Tm 2:10–11, King James Version).[26]

Teresa knew this, of course, knew very well that the single woman in her epoch had few socially-acceptable recourses: she lived either in a convent or in the home of relations. Teresa entered a convent. She became a reformer, a founder of other convents. Contrary to the social norms and expectations of her society, she insisted that a first duty of prioresses was to teach the illiterates who applied for admission to Carmelite monasteries to read.[27]

However, she worried about the pauline injunction and its applicability to her own life and needs. Not until July of 1571 does she record having heard that inner voice so important to all of the self-actualized people, religious or not. In Spiritual Testimony 15, written at Avila, she mentions her knowledge of "what St. Paul said about women." Then she tells us that the voice of the Lord gave her the answer for those who attempted to "socialize" her by reminding her of it: "Tell them they shouldn't follow just one part of Scripture but that they should look at other parts, and ask them if they can by chance tie my hands."[28]

The history of the second foundation, that of Medina del Campo, provides another example of Teresa's turning her back on public opinion, tradition and even the advice of her friends. When the people of that city heard of plans to establish another convent there, they reacted strongly to what they thought would be further strain on the city's finances. As Teresa tells it " . . . there was much complaint: some said that I was crazy; others expected the plan to fail." In fact, the complaints were so vociferous that some of Teresa's friends advised that she abandon the new foundation. The saint's own reaction is to be expected from the self-actualized person:

> . . . I paid little attention to that (the advice), because what they thought doubtful seemed perfectly obvious to me — I could not persuade myself that the plan could be anything but successful.[29]

Such resistance to enculturization is to be found in every self-actualizer.

The determination to complete one's mission also supersedes, at times, even one's own stated principles. The self-actualizers do not always remain true to themselves, that is to say, if by doing so they endanger their mission in life. Teresa saw her mission, at least in part, as one of reform — reform that would be accomplished through the founding of new monasteries. In chapter nine of the *Foundations*, she tells of the founding of the convent at Malagón, the third, in which she was forced to abandon one of her own most beloved principles, that of poverty. The situation at Malagón was such that, without giving in to the advice of those who counselled having a fixed, secure income for the convent, the local license would not have been granted. Confronted with the necessity of choosing between her own principles and the completion of her mission, Teresa chose the latter and gave in to the desires of the authorities. Nothing will keep the self-actualizers from doing what must be done. As Teresa explains the strength of her desire to serve God:

> It seems to me then, that no trial, neither death nor martyrdom nor anything could be offered to me that I wouldn't easily undergo.[30]

CONCLUSION

Maslow was convinced that the study of these extraordinary persons that he called "self-actualized" could result in healthier non-actualizers. That is to say that the attempt to imitate the qualities of the self-actualized personality could result in greater maturity and positive personality development in the average person.[31] The need for heroes, for role models is well-known and it is my belief that Teresa of Avila, sixteenth-century woman, offers an example from which every person might learn and grow.

To prove that such an attitude is characteristic of the self-actualized was not a problem for Maslow; he noted it in a large majority of his subjects. Nor is it a problem to prove that Teresa of Avila should be included among those "most mentally healthy" people that the psychologist could find. The examples offered here deal with only a few of the salient qualities of such people, and other examples abound. On page after page of the *Life*, or the *Foundations*, or of the *Spiritual Testimonies*, the reader who knows Maslow's work says "here is the epitome of the self-actualized person."

So? the reader may ask. And of what import is that to me? Maslow answers the question, in part, in the second edition of *Toward a Psychology of Being*:

> The study of such self-fulfilling people can teach us much about our own mistakes, our shortcomings, the proper directions in which to grow. Every age but ours has had its model, its ideal. All of these have been given up by our culture; the saint, the hero, the gentleman, the knight, the mystic. About all we have left is the well-adjusted man without problems, a very pale and doubtful substitute.[32]

NOTES

1. Colin Wilson, *New Pathways in Psychology: Maslow and the Post-Freudian Tradition* (New York: Mentor New American Library, 1972), p. 3. This study is central for anyone wishing an in-depth look at Maslow and the development of his theories. Wilson had access to much unpublished material, including

hours of taped interviews with the psychologist.

2. Cited by Graciano Martinez, "Santa Teresa ante los neurologos," *España y America*, 23 (1925), 10.

3. A brief but comprehensive survey of these psychologists (along with Teresa's defenders) and their work is presented by Angel L. Cilveti, *Introducción a la mística española* (Madrid: Catedra, 1974).

4. Wilson, *Ibid.* Maslow expounds on the subject at much greater length in an essay called "Religions, Values and Peak Experiences," recently reissued by Penguin (in 1976). Of special interest to students of religion and psychology is Maslow's introduction to the volume, in which he brings the study up to date.

5. Duane Schultz, *Growth Psychology: Models of the Healthy Personality* (New York: Von Nostrand-Reinhold, 1977). This summary of the development of humanistic or "Third Force" psychology contains a succinct description of Maslow's major theories, including definitions of "self-actualization" and "hierarchy of needs."

5a. EDITOR'S NOTE: We present here a partial outline of the author's doctoral dissertation, as it was made available by her. The dissertation was drafted in Spanish and presented to Salamanca University:

"Santa Teresa de Jesus: Unas Consideraciones Nuevas a traves de la Psicologia Actual," Tesis doctoral aceptada en la Facultad de Filiosofia y Letras de la Universidad de Salamanca, Spain, 1977.

Chapter 2 — Self-Actualization, Mysticism and Creativity

> The Personality of the Mystic
> General Definition of Self-Actualization
> Maslow and Mysticism
> Creativity and Teresa

Chapter 3 — "Personal" Qualities

> Spontaneity
> The Need for Solitude
> Security in Times of Crisis
> Recognition of the Importance of Self-Development
> Philosophical Sense of Humor
> Aggressiveness
> Defects

Chapter 4 — Qualities of the Interpersonal Relationships of Self-Actualizers

> Profundity
> Sense of Mission
> Hostile Relationships
> Attitudes of Self-Actualizers toward the Non-Actualizer

Democratic Attitudes
Attitude of the Non-Actualizer toward the Self-Actualizer

Chapter 5 — Relationships with the Establishment

Perception of Reality
Personal Autonomy and Resistance to Enculturation
Determination to Realize Goals
The Sense of the Ethical

6. Abraham Maslow, *Toward a Psychology of Being* (New York: Von No-strand, 2nd ed., 1968), p. 11.

7. William Thomas Walsh, *Saint Teresa of Avila, A Biography* (Milwaukee: Bruce, 1945), p. 380.

8. Maslow, *Being*, p. 211.

9. L, 10, 8.

10. F, 31, 46. Author's translation.

11. See Salvador de Madariaga, *Mujeres espanolas* (Madrid: Espasa-Calpe, 1972), p. 11. Coll. "Austral," 1500.

12. C, 2, 1, 4.

13. *Meditations on the Song of Songs*, 2, 2.

14. C, 4, 2, 5.

15. C, 4, 3, 11.

16. *Ibid.*

17. *Vida de Santa Teresa de Jesus, Fundadora de las Descalzas y Descalzos Carmelitas*, rev. por Inocente Palacios de la Asuncion (Madrid: F. Lizcano, 1863 ed.), pp. 466-69.

18. L, 13, 1. The same statement also appears in L, 22, 18.

19. See C, 5, 8, 9. This avoidance (so often recommended by Teresa) of histrionics is identified by Maslow as another quality characteristic of the self-actualizer.

20. L, 36, 12–13.

21. C, 4, 3, 4.

22. Maslow, *Being*, p. 217.

23. It must be added that the self-actualized person's mission usually involves some altruistic activity, something beyond the mere earning of more money or gaining of more power.

24. L, 35, 4.

25. Maslow, *Being*, p. 232.

26. The same idea is expressed in 1 Co 14:34–35.

27. *Constitutions*, 1, 9 and 1, 12.

28. Spiritual Testimony No. 15 (Avila, Saint Joseph's, July 1571).

29. F, 3, 3. Author's translation.

30. Spiritual Testimony No. 1, 4 (Avila, 1560).

31. Maslow, *Being*, p. 111.

32. *Ibid.*, p. 5.

TOWARD A CONTEMPORARY MODEL OF SPIRITUAL DIRECTION: A COMPARATIVE STUDY OF ST JOHN OF THE CROSS AND CARL ROGERS

Kevin Culligan, O.C.D.

Father Culligan has been teaching with the Loyola University (of Baltimore) Pastoral Counseling Program for the past few years. He obtained his doctorate in the psychology of religion from Boston University. During the sixties he served as Chairman of the I.C.S.

In a position paper written in 1976 for the United States Bishops' Committee on Priestly Life and Ministry, Fr Louis Cameli states: "The relationships between psychology and spirituality — convergence, difference, complementarity, etc. — are yet to be explored in a satisfactory systematic fashion."[1] Cameli's point applies especially to spiritual direction. Writers for years have noted modern psychology's value for spiritual direction,[2] although little has been done to demonstrate systematically its precise place in this ministry.[3] The lack of such interdisciplinary research accounts in part for our current situation in the United States where we are involved in an extensive revival of spiritual direction, yet, as Cameli observes, "working with an incomplete theoretical and systematic framework which would describe the exact function of a spiritual director today."[4]

In response to the need expressed by Cameli, this article presents the results of my own attempt to develop a method for exploring systematically the relationships between traditional theories of spiritual direction and the findings of modern therapeutic psychology. Using St John of the Cross and Carl Rogers as representatives of spiritual direction and therapeutic psychology respectively, I have searched for relationships between these two writers and formulated my findings into hypotheses about spiritual direction that can be evaluated by further psychological and theological research. In presenting these hypotheses, I hope to foster the development of a reliable model or "theoretical and systematic framework" for guiding current practice and research in spiritual direction.[5]

St John of the Cross and Carl Rogers have proven especially rewarding subjects for this interdisciplinary inquiry. An acknowledged master of Christian spirituality, St John was also an experienced spiritual director whose prose writings, the fruit of nearly twenty-five years in this ministry,[6] chart the entire road to union with God with profound insights into human behavior that presage the psychological discoveries of our day.[7] Though written expressly for sixteenth-century Spanish religious and laity, John's treatises continue today to guide thousands throughout the world in their search for divine union.

As formulator of the influential client-centered approach to modern psychotherapy, Carl Rogers also writes out of his years of experience as a psychotherapist. Supporting his theories with extensive empirical research, Rogers attempts to explain a wide range of human behavior (e.g., individual, interpersonal, group, family, etc.) on psychological grounds alone, although many have seen implications in his work for theology, pastoral counseling, and spiritual direction.[8] Comparing two writers so experienced in their subject matter, comprehensive in scope, influential in their field and rich in implication for the work of the other has yielded an abundant harvest of insight into the relationships between spiritual direction and therapeutic psychology.

My research method involved analyzing texts which record St John's experience as a spiritual director and Roger's as a psychotherapist. With St John, I analyzed his *The Ascent of Mount Carmel* and *The Dark Night*, two treatises which together form one coherent literary work[9] explaining "how to reach divine union quickly" [10] and describing the road that leads to this union. Although spiritual direction is not the stated subject matter of the *Ascent-Dark Night*, this work nevertheless reveals both John's understanding of the spiritual director's role in guiding a person along the road to union with God and his own practice of spiritual direction as he attempted in these pages to lead his readers to divine union. I carefully analyzed each book of the *Ascent-Dark Night* to determine both their explicit and implicit teachings on spiritual direction; I then formulated the results of this analysis into a synthesis, a summary statement expressing St John's theory of spiritual direction as found in this one work.

Next, I examined two major articles by Rogers — "A Theory of Therapy, Personality, and Interpersonal Relationships, as Developed in the Client-Centered Framework"[11] and "Client-Centered Psychotherapy" [12] — which succinctly state his psychological theories. I analyzed these articles asking the heuristic question: What do the psychological theories of Rogers have in common with St John's theory of spiritual direction in the *Ascent-Dark Night*? I then formulated the results of this analysis into hypotheses about the nature of spiritual direction that can be evaluated in further research. My contention is that testing these hypotheses will provide the necessary constructs and relationships for a reliable theoretical model or systematic framework to guide practice and research in spiritual direction.

In this article, I will present first the summary statement of John's theory of spiritual direction in the *Ascent-Dark Night*, followed by Rogers' contributions to this theory expressed in hypotheses for further research and implications for spiritual direction, and finally an outline of the steps for completing this research and formulating a contemporary model of spiritual direction.

SPIRITUAL DIRECTION
IN *THE ASCENT OF MOUNT CARMEL* AND *THE DARK NIGHT*

In this first section, I will summarize St John's teachings on spiritual direction as found in the *Ascent-Dark Night*[13] stating the main elements of his teaching in eight major propositions, each followed by a brief explanation. Citations from St John's writings supporting these propositions are given in the footnotes. I express and arrange these propositions, not necessarily in the words and sequence used by St John, but according to a terminology and logic suggested by the teachings themselves. These propositions thus represent his theory of spiritual direction expressed as a synthesis emerging from an inductive analysis of the texts of the *Ascent-Dark Night*.[14]

God is a Person's Principal Spiritual Director

In this proposition, God means primarily the Divinity present within the human person. John occasionally expresses God's guidance within the human person in Trinitarian terminology, such as Jesus Christ (*Jesucristo*) teaching persons by his words and example or the Holy Spirit (*el Espíritu Santo*) infusing divine wisdom into the soul; however, he most frequently attributes divine guidance simply to God (*Dios*) substantially present within the person (*dentro del alma sustancialmente*) as Master, Teacher, or Guide.[15]

The Goal to Which God Leads the Human Person is Union with Himself in Perfect Faith, Hope and Love

John considers the ultimate goal of human life to be perfect union with God resulting from a fully developed faith, hope and love. This union makes the person God by participation, heals all sin and imperfection, and transforms the human faculties, enabling them to know and love in a divine manner. Viewed either theologically or psychologically, union with God perfects the entire human personality.[16]

God Guides the Human Person to Divine Union through Human Nature, Especially the Light of Natural Reason: through Divine Revelation, particularly as Expressed in the Person of Jesus Christ, and through Infused Contemplation

John focuses in the *Ascent-Dark Night* upon the last of these three means of divine guidance. Through infused contemplation, God communicates himself directly to the human person in divine wisdom and love, thereby guiding the person in whom he dwells to divine union according to his unique individuality. Contemplation both purifies a person of his inordinate love of creatures and unites him with Uncreated Love. A person disposes himself for God's unique guidance through infused contemplation by withdrawing his sensory appetites from inordinate attachments to creatures and by directing his spiritual faculties to God through faith, hope and love; in response, God communicates his wisdom and love to the person with increasing intensity, eradicating the soul's imperfections and uniting the entire person, sense and spirit, to himself. Because of the inner deprivation and pain caused in the person by the mortification of the sensory appetites, the theological virtues, and God's self-communication, John likens divine guidance through infused contemplation to a journey in darkness.[17]

Persons Committed to Seeking Divine Union are Capable of Following God's Guidance without the Aid of a Human Spiritual Director

Human reason, divine revelation and infused contemplation, in themselves, are sufficient to guide every person to union with God. Relying only on these sources of guidance, a person journeys more securely toward union with God than he does when following the counsel of someone who is insentitive to the unique way God guides each individual person or who is ignorant of the dynamics of infused contemplation. However, in trying to follow God's guidance all alone, a person can also deceive himself, misinterpret his religious experiences and develop harmful attachments that hinder spiritual growth. For these reasons, God ordains that persons ordinarily journey to divine union with the help of other human persons. Thus, a person may discern God's guidance not only privately through prayer, reflection, spiritual reading and growth in faith and love, but also through an interpersonal relationship with a human guide.[18]

Spiritual Direction is a Ministry in the Church to Help Persons Follow God's Guidance to Divine Union

Spiritual direction is a human relationship between a director or spiritual guide and a directee or one seriously seeking union with God through love which has as its subject matter the entire psychological experience of the directee—thoughts, desires, feelings, emotions and actions—insofar as these reveal his relationship to God and God's action in his life. In this human relationship, the spiritual director helps the directee to discern and follow God's guidance, especially as received in infused contemplation. The director also helps the directee to relinquish his inordinate attachments to creatures and to center his entire life upon God in faith, hope and love, thus becoming disposed to receive God's guidance in infused contemplation. Metaphorically speaking, a director guides the directee through the interior darkness caused by self-denial, faith and contemplation to a loving union with God. A spiritual director thus acts as an instrument in God's guidance of a person to union with himself.[19]

The Essential Function of the Spiritual Director is to Guide the Directee along the Road to Union with God

John's understanding of the spiritual director's role may be seen in the titles and activities he assigns to the director. He calls the director a master or teacher (*maestro espiritual*), spiritual father (*padre espiritual*), confessor (*confesor*), and guide (*guía*). The spiritual director teaches his directee the nature of the journey to union with God and how to cooperate through self-denial and prayer with God's guidance; using advice, counsel, instruction, directives and commands, he trains persons in detachment and the practice of faith, hope and love; he evaluates his directees' religious experience and growth in prayer; with understanding and compassion, he supports them during periods when God prepares them for divine union with intense sensory and spiritual purification. The word which best expresses the role of the spiritual director as implied by these titles and activities is *guidance*: whether he is called father, master or confessor, or whether he is teaching, evaluating, training or supporting his directees, the spiritual director is essentially a *guide* who leads persons along the dark and difficult road of mortification, theological virtue and contemplation leading to union with God through love.[20] As a guide, the spiritual director's unique contribution is the interpersonal relationship he forms with the directee, for in this relationship the directee gains instruction, discernment and support for the spiritual journey, benefits not found in other forms of spiritual guidance such as spiritual reading or self-guidance relying on faith and reason alone.

As a role model for this ministry, a spiritual director may look with profit to Jesus Christ. St John maintains that God gave Jesus to mankind as a brother, companion and master. Similarly, a spiritual director is a brother or sister to the directee in their common sharing of human nature, a companion for the spiritual journey to God and a teacher of the spiritual life.

To be a spiritual director, one need not be a priest. Although John speaks of confessors (*confesores*) when discussing spiritual direction, he does not intend thereby to limit this ministry to ordained priests working in sacramental settings: unordained persons with the necessary knowledge, experience, and skill are also capable of guiding others along the road to God.[21]

To Fulfill the Role of an Instrument in God's Guidance of Persons to Divine Union through Infused Contemplation, the Spiritual Director must Possess Knowledge, Experience and Skill in Helping Relationships

1. Knowledge

John's theory of spiritual direction maintains that God guides persons to divine union through infused contemplation: therefore, the human director must, first of all, possess a *theology* that accounts for God's communication of himself to persons, not only indirectly through divine revelation and human reason, but also directly through infused contemplation. The director's theology should also acknowledge God's transcendence and immanence, the divine attributes which require that persons journey to union with God primarily by faith and interior prayer. The director should also be versed in *Sacred Scripture*, understanding both the history of God's guidance of his people (the prototype of all divine guidance) and the various levels of biblical interpretation (which reveal the full meaning — letter and spirit — of the Scriptures).[22]

Secondly, a director must have a *philosophy of human knowledge* that recognizes a person's capacity to receive God's self-communication in infused contemplation. St John employed the Scholastic theory of active and passive intellect to explain, on the one hand, the human person's inability to formulate adequate images or concepts of God, and on the other hand, his innate capacity to receive a general, loving knowledge of God in contemplation. Although a director may not hold a Scholastic epistemology, his theory of knowledge should account for a person's capacity to receive God's direct self-communication. Lacking such a theory, he may fail to understand how to dispose his directee to receive God's guidance in infused contemplation.[23]

Thirdly, the director's knowledge should include *a theology of the spiritual life*. As a systematic ordering of the principles of Christian spirituality, spiritual theology describes: the relationship of God with men and women through distinct stages, each characterized by predictable and recognizable phenomena; the necessity of mortifying inordinate desires and practicing the theological virtues for disposing oneself to be guided by God; and the nature of prayer and contemplation as a dialogue between the human person and God. Familiarity with these principles enables the spiritual director to recognize the major factors in a person's relationship with God and journey to divine union.[24]

Finally, the director should know *psychology*. God guides persons according to the laws of human nature: the more a director understands these laws, the better prepared he is to assist the directee in responding to God's guidance. The following areas of psychology provide especially helpful information to the director for understanding human behavior: sensation, perception, learning, memory, emotion, motivation, human development, personality and abnormality. Knowing the basic psychological principles in each of these areas prepares a director to appreciate the human factors affecting a person's relationship with God.[25]

2. Experience

Spiritual direction is guiding persons along the dark and difficult road to union with God. To guide others effectively, a spiritual director must know this road from his own experience of self-denial, faith and contemplation. In addition to giving the director a firsthand knowledge of the road to divine union, this personal experience prepares him to perceive and judge his directees more accurately and to interact with them more objectively, thus increasing his effectiveness as an instrument of divine guidance. Also, the added experience of guiding others in their journey toward God enables the director to observe the infinite variety of ways God leads souls to himself as well as the infinite variety of human response to his divine guidance. With this experience, the spiritual director is better prepared to walk in faith with each directee, discerning that person's unique road to God as God gradually reveals it to them and helping each one follow faithfully that road to divine union.[26]

3. Skill in Helping Relationships

Because the relationship between the director and directee is the essential characteristic distinguishing spiritual direction from other forms of spiritual guidance, the spiritual director must possess adequate skills for this relationship. These skills presuppose in the director an awareness of: his own humanity as an instrument for guiding others according to reason and faith; the directee's unique individuality and capacity for self-direction; the presence of Jesus in the relationship clarifying and confirming divine truth in the hearts of both the director and directee; the many dynamics in a helping relationship, such as unconscious communication of attitudes, clarification of personal experience through its verbal expression to an attentive listener, resistance, transference and collusion. Skill in the helping relationship of spiritual direction demands that a director be able: to recognize and handle the dynamic factors as they emerge in his work with a directee; to create an interpersonal climate which enables the directee to relate significant experiences — both positive and negative — on the journey to God; and to communicate to directees a sympathetic understanding of their experiences. With these interpersonal skills, the director makes the helping relationship an effective means for the directee to discern God's guidance.[27]

Knowledge, experience, skill in helping relationships: these three qualities distinguish an effective spiritual director. John recognizes that some Christians may be endowed with other extraordinary gifts and graces, including the biblical charisms of healing, prophecy and discernment of spirits (1 Cor 12:8-11); however, he does not consider them essential for the ministry of spiritual direction. With the necessary human knowledge, personal experience of the spiritual life and competence in human relations, one is adequately prepared to serve as God's instrument in his guidance of persons to divine union.[28]

A Spiritual Director's Work with a Directee Differs in Each Stage of the Directee's Journey toward Union with God

Throughout the entire journey, the director uses his knowledge, experience and skills to help the directee surrender

entirely to God's guidance; however, the precise helping activities performed by the director differ with each stage of the
directee's progress in prayer and the spiritual life.

1. Beginners

To prepare beginners to accept God's guidance, the director
first clarifies with the directee the goal of the spiritual journey
(union with God through love) and the means to this goal (self-
denial, theological virtue and infused contemplation). The
director then helps the beginner to center his affectivity entirely
on God by letting go of habitual, inordinate attachments to
creatures and by enkindling a desire for God through
meditative prayer.

Although truly converted to God and sincere in their desire
for him, beginners are nevertheless disordered in their relationship with themselves, with others and with God as a result of
their inordinate attachments and are motivated primarily by
the desire for sensory pleasure in their religious activities.
These factors cause in a beginner a rationalized resistance to
God's guidance, emotional distress and psychological dysfunc-
tion and denial of their true spiritual condition. For these same
reasons, a beginner is likely to be hostile, manipulative,
dishonest, dependent and sexually aroused in his relationship
with the director. The director must recognize these factors
when they emerge in a beginner and help him to order all of his
behavior according to reason and the demands of true interior
devotion. Working with beginners in these ways, the spiritual
director prepares them for the passive night of sense when God
commences to communicate himself directly to their spirit and
to guide them through infused contemplation.[29]

2. Passive Night of Sense

As persons progress in self-denial and meditative prayer,
disposing themselves for divine guidance, God soon responds
by communicating himself directly to their spirit, leading them
from meditation to contemplation, transforming their motivation from self-love to love of God and replacing their sins and
imperfections with virtue. Although God's communication

strengthens a person spiritually, it also produces an intense sensory dryness characterized by three phenomena occurring simultaneously: loss of consolation in both God and creatures, a painful desire to serve God and an inability to practice discursive meditation. The director's role during this critical transition period is: to recognize these signs when they appear in the directee; to determine whether the phenomena are indeed caused by infused contemplation or by some other cause, such as infidelity or physical and emotional disturbance; to convey an understanding of the phenomena to the directee; to support the directee in the personal trials of this period; and to guide him in the transition from meditative prayer to contemplative prayer. In these ways, the director helps the person through the passive night of sense into the second stage of the spiritual journey, the *via illuminativa* or the stage of proficients in which God communicates his knowledge and love directly to the person in infused contemplation.[30]

3. Proficients

After leading a person through the purifying night of sense, God brings him into the second stage of the spiritual journey, the stage of proficients (also called the *via illuminativa*) in which he continues to draw the person closer to divine union through infused contemplation. Almost everyone who begins the spiritual journey in earnest reaches this second stage, although relatively few pass beyond it to perfect union with God in love. Ordinarily lasting some years, this period is one of relative serenity, interior freedom and spiritual delight, interspersed with brief spiritual trials.

The director's main function in this stage is to encourage the directee's growth in faith, hope and love, the three virtues which unite the human person to God. By teaching his directees to let go of voluntary attachments to distinct images, concepts, memories and experiences of God and to direct the affections of the will away from individual objects toward God, the director disposes his directees to receive in contemplation the transforming knowledge and love of the Transcendent God. In his relationship with the directee, the director must also create an interpersonal atmosphere which allows the directee to express freely his spiritual experiences for purposes of clarification and confirmation. Furthermore, the director helps the directee govern his life according to faith and reason which, more than extraordinary religious experiences, are the ordinary lights for discerning God's will in daily activities. And finally, the director encourages his directee to pray with greater interiority, depending less upon external devotional objects and images and more upon the interior recollection of the entire self—sense and spirit—in God present within. By helping persons to grow in faith, to clarify the meaning of their experiences, to live daily according to faith and reason and to grow in interior prayer, the director best helps those in the stage of proficients to be led by God to final transformation in love.[31]

4. Passive Night of Spirit

Before bringing a person to perfect union with himself, God leads him through a final purification called the passive night of spirit. During this period, God communicates himself to the person with increased intensity, thereby freeing him from every inordinate attachment to creatures and drawing the powers of his being to be centered firmly in himself. In this communication, God infuses his own loving wisdom into the person, filling the human faculties of intellect, memory and will with divine knowledge and love. This contemplative inflow of God into the human person both purges and illumines the person, with alternating periods both of extreme anguish (when one feels God's absence) and of extreme delight (when one feels God's presence), until the person is free of every inordinate attachment and ready for perfect union with God in pure love.

Only a relatively few persons undergo this final purification which may last for some time, even years, depending upon the strength of the final attachments that must be uprooted. For these persons, the director performs an important role. Upon recognizing from the intensity of the person's alternating contemplative experiences of inner anguish and delight and the steady increase in his love that the person has left behind the relatively tranquil stage of proficients, the director prepares to

support the directee through this transition period to union
with God. This support includes: encouraging the directee to
continue the practice of interior prayer and the theological virtues which best dispose a person to receive God's communication of loving knowledge; teaching him the nature and the
necessity of this purifying night; and providing a sympathetic
understanding of his purgative and illuminative experiences.
By these means, the director supports the directee through the
final purification before reaching perfect union with God in
love.[32]

5. The State of Perfection

After purifying a person of all inordinate attachments in the
passive night of spirit, God leads him to the highest stage of the
spiritual journey attainable in this life, the state of perfect
union with God through love (or the *via unitiva*). This stage
begins when the alternating periods of consolation and desola-
tion cease and the person enjoys a habitual, peaceful, joyous
awareness of the presence of God. The few persons who attain
this union are now entirely centered upon God in pure faith,
hope and love: they are transformed in God and live completely
according to the wisdom and love they receive from him.

Because his union with God is now perfect, the person is
guided by God in all his activities. Accordingly, he needs little
external guidance from a spiritual director. When the directee
is at this highest stage of the spiritual journey, the director must
simply recognize the directee's union with God, support the
action of God in his life and not interfere with that action by
advice appropriate only to an earlier stage of the spiritual
journey.[33]

From this brief overview of the stages of the spiritual journey
we can see that the spiritual director performs his guidance role
in a variety of ways depending upon God's unique action in the
directee's life and the directee's stage of progress in the lifelong
spiritual journey. In the earlier stages of the journey, when
God's self-communication is less immediate and less intense,
the spiritual director takes a more active part in helping the

person dispose himself to receive God's guidance in infused contemplation; in the later stages of the journey, when God's self-communication more directly guides the person, the director assumes a more supportive role in helping the person to respond to the divine guidance received in contemplation.

The various guidance functions provided by the director may, in turn, be reduced to one overall task that applies to each stage of the spiritual journey. At each stage of their spiritual journey, the spiritual director must help persons to imitate Jesus Christ and to live according to his teachings, especially his example and teachings of detachment in sense and spirit for the sake of living according to the will of the Father. In following Jesus's example of self-emptying, a person best disposes himself to be guided by the same inner Spirit that guided Jesus throughout his life. Jesus, in fact, personifies the entire road (*camino*) to divine union. In conforming one's life to the example and teachings of Jesus, a person gradually empties himself in sense and spirit of inordinate attachments and centers his life entirely upon God, becoming thereby increasingly open to receive the infused loving knowledge of God. In the terminology of St John of the Cross, the active nights of sense and spirit are fulfilled in the person's conscious imitation of Jesus Christ; the corresponding passive nights of sense and spirit are experienced by the person as the gradual reception of the Holy Spirit in infused contemplation. To the degree one conforms one's entire life — sense and spirit — to the self-emptying of Jesus Christ in response to the will of the Father, to that degree is one led interiorly by the Spirit of God; and when one's life is perfectly conformed to Jesus' sensory and spiritual death to self on the Cross, one is then perfectly quided by the Holy Spirit in all his activity. At that point, the work of the human spiritual director is virtually at an end.[34]

Summary

The theory of spiritual direction contained in *The Ascent of Mount Carmel* and *The Dark Night* maintains that God dwelling

within the person is the primary spiritual director who guides
the person to union with himself in love. God provides this
guidance principally through infused contemplation in which
he communicates himself to the person. The human spiritual
director acts as an instrument in this divine guidance by helping the person to surrender completely to God's action in his
life. To be an effective instrument in this divine guidance, the
human director must have sufficient knowledge, experience and
skill in helping relationships. By means of a human relationship in which the director listens, teaches, advises, discerns,
supports and conveys understanding of the directee's experience, the director guides a person along the dark and
difficult road of detachment, faith and prayer, thus disposing
the person to receive from God the unique guidance given in
infused contemplation. This lifelong process is perhaps best
summarized by saying that the human spiritual director guides
a person in the imitation of Jesus Christ which, in turn, best
disposes him to receive and be led by the Spirit of Jesus who is
given in infused contemplation.

CONTRIBUTIONS OF CARL ROGERS

The preceding pages contain eight propositions which syn-
thesize St John of the Cross' theory of spiritual direction as
found in *The Ascent of Mount Carmel* and *The Dark Night*; let us
now turn to the writings of Carl Rogers to determine whether
modern therapeutic psychology can enhance the usefulness of
this theory. By comparing John with Rogers, can we discover
relationships upon which to build an effective theoretical model
for guiding practice and research in today's ministry of spiritual
direction?

At first glance, Carl Rogers, the twentieth-century American humanistic psychologist, appears to have little in common
with John of the Cross, the sixteenth-century Spanish mystic,
poet, and priest. However, in comparing their writings one
discovers amazing similarities. Both are astute observers of

human behavior in others and in themselves. Both rely heavily upon personal experience when speaking of helping relationships. Both attempt to describe systematically the recurring orderliness they discover in their observations and experience. Both posit goals for human life and describe a process leading to these goals. Both attempt to discover and formulate the functional relationships which explain the entire phenomena of personality—its motivating principles, the conditions for its development, its deviation and restoration, its optimal degree of functioning. Despite their many differences, John of the Cross and Carl Rogers possess a scientific bent of mind which enables us to compare their theoretical systems.[35]

But there are important differences. St John is a priest-poet, Rogers a psychotherapist-scientist. John's world view is built upon Christian faith, Roger's upon philosophical humanism. John's approach to the human person is theological, Rogers' is psychological. John studies the human person using the methods and language of Scholastic theology and Christian mysticism, whereas Rogers relies upon the methods and language of modern science. John sees the human person as intrinsically and dynamically related to God in love. Rogers sees the human person primarily as a natural organism in a social environment and attempts to describe the nature and dynamics of human relationships. Although both view the human person as in the process of becoming more fully functioning, John describes this process according to the more structured view of faculty psychology, whereas Rogers employs the less structured view of perceptual psychology. They apply different meanings to the same word, as when John often uses "self" to describe the entire person unrelated to God,[36] while Rogers uses "self" to describe "a conceptual gestalt composed of the perceptions of the 'me' or 'I'."[37] Rogers places primary emphasis upon a person's experiencing as a source of guidance and values,[38] whereas John subordinates personal experience to the teachings of Sacred Scripture and the Church as a guide for leading one to union with God.[39] Rogers' theory of knowledge, based on perception, makes no attempt to account for knowledge received in contemplation (that is, communicated directly by God through love without sensory experience to persons seeking him in faith). Rogers' primary concern is with knowledge (or personal learnings) gained through organismic experience which depends heavily upon sensory perception, whereas John, while acknowledging the importance of sensory knowledge, is primarily interested in knowledge gained by mystical "unknowing" received passively through infused contemplation. In helping relationships, John stresses the authority of the helper in guiding another to union with God, emphasizing such guidance functions as teaching, advising and correcting; Rogers, on the other hand, emphasizes the authority implicit in the experiences of the one helped, requiring of the helper that he or she create certain conditions in their relationship which enable the one helped to discover the directive meanings of his experience.

In summary, John and Rogers differ in their world view, their scientific frame of reference, their methodology, their terminology, their theories of personality, the importance they attach to personal experience, their theories of knowledge and their approach to helping relationships. Underlying these differences is John's view of the human person based upon pastoral ministry, Scholastic theology and mystical experience and Rogers' view based upon clinical and empirical observation of significant interpersonal relationships, especially psychotherapy.

Despite the differences, the psychological theories of Carl Rogers appear relevant to St John of the Cross' theory of spiritual direction in key areas which may serve as a foundation for constructing a theoretical model to guide practice and research in contemporary spiritual direction. Rogers has noted the applicability of his theory of psychotherapy for other modes of human relationships such as family life, education, business and intercultural relations;[40] it appears also to apply to the human relationship called "spiritual direction" where the focus is upon the directee's relationship with the Ultimate conceived as Person.

Because they arise directly from the helping relationship of psychotherapy, Rogers' theories of therapy, personality and interpersonal relations apply most directly to other helping relationships such as those in social work, academic counseling and guidance, medicine, and indeed, spiritual direction. Roger's work is particularly relevant for St John's theory of spiritual direction, for it adds the results of scientific research to John's naturalistic observation: for example, Rogers' research with the therapeutic conditions that promote positive personal growth enables us to appreciate even more than did John himself the importance of the interpersonal relationship in spiritual direction.

Perhaps the main value of Rogers' theories for St John of the Cross' theory of spiritual direction is that they are primarily psychological theories derived from clinical experience and research evidence. With as much scientific rigor as possible, Rogers attempts to describe the human organism as he observes it in therapy and research, independent of philosophical and theological presuppositions. His theories attempt to account for the entire complexity of human life on psychological grounds alone. Such a psychological theory enables us to understand better the human person as a natural organism when we consider the human person in relationship with God. If, for example, clinical experience and empirical research demonstrate that under certain interpersonal conditions the human organism acts in certain predictable ways, these findings ought to be taken into account when treating of the human person's journey to union with God, which is the focus of the spiritual direction relationship.

Rogers himself seems in accord with the logic of relating his psychological theories to St John of the Cross' theory of spiritual direction. Although he confines his own psychological investigations to the operational methods of empirical science, Rogers nonetheless appreciates the possibility of other realities not measurable by present psychological methods,[41] realities which seem to include the vast world of the spirit explored and described by St John of the Cross. To relate Rogers' theories to

John's may not only have valuable implications for the ministry of spiritual direction, but may in turn serve to widen the context of Rogers' client-centered approach and to extend its applications beyond human relationships to facilitating a person's relationship with God.

To relate Rogers' theories to John's, I have examined in detail two writings of Rogers—"A Theory of Therapy, Personality, and Interpersonal Relationships, as Developed in the Client-Centered Framework" and "Client-Centered Psychotherapy"—which state his major psychological theories with scientific economy and precision.[42] In this examination I ask the heuristic question: What relevance do these theories have for St John of the Cross' theory of spiritual direction as contained in the *Ascent-Dark Night*? I then establish six areas where I judge a significant relationship exists between Rogers and John and state a guiding hypothesis for investigating this relationship further. Before stating these relationships, however, it will be helpful first to review briefly those Rogerian concepts and theories with the greatest implication for John of the Cross' theory of spiritual direction.

According to Rogers, a human being is endowed from birth with an *actualizing tendency*, an "inherent tendency of the organism to develop all its capacities in ways which serve to maintain or enhance the organism."[43] When the human organism lives in an environment of *genuineness, caring* and *understanding* provided by other persons, the actualizing tendency moves the organism toward "growth, maturity, life enrichment."[44] These qualities appear to emerge in an individual as a result of *congruence* or harmony between the *experiencing* of the organism and the concept of *self*. Experiencing is "the process that includes all that is going on within the envelope of the organism which is available to awareness."[45] The self-concept may be defined as "the organized, consistent conceptual gestalt composed of perceptions of the characteristics of the 'I' or 'me' and the perceptions of the relationships of the 'I' or 'me' to others and to various aspects of life, together with the values attached to these perceptions."[46] The concept of self is formed gradually over an individual's entire life history from relationships with persons perceived as important to one's growth and development. When, in adults, the self-concept is congruent or in harmony with one's organismic experience, the individual is viewed as relatively *mature, psychologically adjusted, a fully functioning person.* On the other hand, when there is a discrepancy between one's experience and self-concept, the individual is seen to some degree as *psychologically maladjusted*, not functioning fully in accord with his inner capacities for growth. This incongruence may, however, be reduced and congruence increased though new interpersonal relationships in which the individual perceives others relating to him with genuineness, caring and understanding.

In Rogers' view of the human organism, the individual possesses within his actualizing tendency the potential for a constructive direction in life, within his organismic experiencing the potential for reliably guiding behavior, and within the organism itself the potential for forming constructive human values. The individual's potential for self-direction, behavioral guidance and value formation is ordinarily released through relationships with other persons who experience and communicate to the individual their own genuineness, caring and understanding.

As we compare these concepts and theories of Rogers with St John of the Cross, we must recall the different vantage points and linguistic expressions — the differing world views and symbol systems — of these two men. Rogers views human functioning with the eyes of a twentieth-century psychologist, using the methods and language of modern behavioral science. John views human functioning from a sixteenth-century theological perspective, using methods and language appropriate to that view. Although their perspective, method, and language differ, both St John and Rogers observe the same subject matter — the human organism in the process of becoming fully actualized, more fully a person. Realizing the unity of subject matter, but the differences of perspective, method and language enables us more easily to compare the scientifically based theories of the one with the theologically based theories of the other. Furthermore, we can more easily specify in the precise psychological terminology of Rogers many of the human processes which John expresses in theological terms. Awareness of the different perspectives, methods and terminology permits us to see more clearly the practical implications of Rogers' psychological theories for John's theory of spiritual direction.

In the six areas of comparison that follow, St John's position is stated first, followed by Rogers'. They are then compared and a hypothesis stated to guide further research. Corollaries related to the hypotheses are also indicated. Following the six areas of relationship between John and Rogers, I describe three areas in which Rogers' writings have special significance for contemporary spiritual direction.

Direction from Within

John of the Cross clearly holds that the primary spiritual director in guiding a person to divine union is God present within the person. With God as the primary director, the role of the human director is to help persons respond fully to this interior divine guidance.[47]

Rogers maintains as a central hypothesis derived from his experience and research with persons in individual psychotherapy and other forms of interpersonal relationships that the human organism contains within itself the capacity for constructive self-direction. This capacity is inherent in the organism's actualizing tendency and, given an atmosphere of interpersonal genuineness, caring and understanding, a person will naturally direct his life in personally enriching and socially constructive ways. Consequently, the role of a counselor or psychotherapist is not to teach a person how to direct his life; rather it is to provide through his or her own attitudes of genuineness, caring and understanding the conditions or the interpersonal climate in which the person's own potential for self-direction may be released.[48]

Both Rogers and St John agree that guidance for attaining

the full realization of a person's life comes primarily from within the person, rather than from outside. As a result, both see the primary role of a helping person such as a psychotherapist or spiritual director is to support and facilitate a reality already present within the person. While both agree that such helping persons play significant roles in fostering the guidance process within the person, whether conceived theologically or psychologically, they also concur that helping persons are instrumental rather than efficient causes of this guidance, their fundamental help being to remove obstacles that inhibit and to create an atmosphere that allows the inner direction process to occur.

Further research is needed to explore the relationship between John's theory of guidance as coming from God substantially present within the person and Roger's theory regarding the capacity for self-direction inherent in the actualizing tendency of the organism. The guiding hypothesis of this research is that God's interior guidance of the person to divine union is experienced psychologically in the human organism's natural tendency to develop all its capacities. This hypothesis does not limit God's guidance to the actualizing tendency of the organism; however, it does maintain that divine guidance is definitely expressed through it. The hypothesis also expresses John's contention that God guides persons to divine union through the ordinary processes of human nature, especially the light of reason and the laws of human development.[49]

The advantage for the ministry of spiritual direction in exploring this hypothesis would seem to be a better understanding of the essential factors involved in the spiritual director's fulfilling his instrumental role in disposing persons to respond more effectively to God's interior guidance. Rogers has discovered in psychotherapy that the antecedent conditions to the self-directing movement of the organism's actualizing tendency are the attitudes of genuineness, caring and understanding in the therapist. Applying this discovery to spiritual direction, it would appear that these same attitudes in the director would create the conditions most favorable to the directee's discovery of God's guidance within his or her own life. Thus, while John attributes a number of guidance functions to the spiritual director such as advice, counsel, instruction, evaluation, understanding and compassion, it may be hypothesized on the basis of Rogers' work, that the director's attitudes of genuineness, caring and understanding are the sufficient and necessary conditions which best dispose a directee to discover and respond to God's inner guidance.[50]

The Goal of Direction

In St John, the goal of spiritual direction is a person perfectly united with God through love. This goal is both theological and psychological: it implies not only the perfection of the spiritual faculties of intellect, memory and will through the theological virtues of faith, hope and charity, but also the fulfillment of the whole person. Persons united with God in faith, hope and love are interiorly free and open, at peace within themselves, esthetically sensitive, perceive reality accurately, enjoy everything, love people and work efficiently.[51]

For Rogers, the goal of psychotherapy is a fully functioning person. This is purely a psychological goal, "the ultimate in the actualization of the human organism."[52] From his experience in psychotherapy, Rogers has observed that in an interpersonal climate of genuineness, caring and understanding, the human organism grows in observable and predictable directions, exhibiting "a shift in the quality of life from stasis to process, from structure to fluidity,"[53] a shift away from facades, "oughts," meeting expectations, and pleasing others toward self-direction, complexity of process, openness to experience, acceptance of others and trust of self. This experience led Rogers to formulate the behavioral characteristics of a hypothetical person who has experienced optimal psychological growth. Such a person is one: who is open to his experiencing process and whose experiences are available to conscious awareness and can be accurately symbolized in awareness without defensive denial or distortion; whose self-concept is congruent with his experiencing and thus flexible and able to change with the assimilation of new experience; whose organismic experiencing is both the source of evidence as to values that hold meaning for him and a trustworthy guide for satisfying behavior; who accepts his own experiencing unconditionally independent of the attitude of others; who meets each new situation uniquely and creatively; whose reality testing is effective; who lives harmoniously with others experiencing fully the reward of giving and receiving acceptance.[54]

Thus, St John and Rogers both have goal-oriented views of human nature guiding their work in helping relationships. From their respective experience in spiritual direction and psychotherapy, both observe the behavioral characteristics of persons who are moving toward these goals. Both realize that these goals are not completely attainable in this life, for at any given point in one's growth a person is capable of further actualization, conceived either theologically or psychologically. Nonetheless, they both observe that the more persons move toward these goals, the more they exhibit the described behaviors.

Further research ought to investigate the relationship between John of the Cross' concept of a person perfectly united with God through love and Rogers' theory of the fully functioning person, the guiding hypothesis being that a person growing in union with God through love will increasingly manifest in behavior the characteristics of a fully functioning person.

This research would potentially benefit the ministry of spiritual direction by delineating more precisely than did St John the behavioral indicators by which a director might discern a directee's growth in union with God. One cannot measure directly the degree of faith, hope and love present in the intellect, will and memory; however, one can observe directly in a person's behavior the above stated qualities noted by Rogers as characteristic of a fully functioning person. On the basis of this observation, a director might more confidently conclude to the directee's growth in union with God. This research would also help to provide specific behavioral referents or operational definitions to such traditional words in

Christian spirituality as "sanctity," "holiness," and "perfection," thus removing from them much of their present ambiguity and rendering them more understandable to present-day Christians. Finally, this research would assure spiritual directors that helping persons toward union with God is simultaneously helping them become more fully functioning persons.

Self-Experience-Congruence/Incongruence: Explanatory Concepts in Spiritual Direction

St John explains human behavior by a person's relationship to God. When one centers his entire being—faculties, appetites, emotions—in God, one's life is well-ordered, productive and rewarding; when one inordinately invests the energies of his being in objects other than God, the result is personal disorder. For John, human well-being depends upon one's conscious relationship with God.[55]

Rogers explains human behavior by the degree of congruence existing between a person's self-concept and his organismic experience. When one's experiencing process is in harmony with the self-concept, a person is well-adjusted psychologically and moving toward full functioning; when there is discrepancy between the experiencing of the organism and the concept of self, a person is in some degree psychologically maladjusted and becoming dysfunctional. For Rogers, human well-being depends upon the degree of congruence between self and experience.[56]

Thus, St John and Rogers explain human behavior by functional relationships. In John, human well-being is a function of one's relationship to God; in Rogers, of the degree of congruence present in the organism between the concept of self and the experiencing process. Rogers' functional relationships are stated more explicitly, in scientific and psychological terms; John's are expressed more implicitly, in Scholastic and theological terminology.[57] Yet, their approaches are related; for behavioral problems which John attributes to disordered appetites, the influences of the devil, inordinately seeking joy in objects other than God and the seven capital vices[58] can be explained phenomenologically by Rogers as arising from incongruence or a discrepancy between "the self as perceived, and the actual experience of the organism,"[59] leaving the person observably tense, vulnerable, threatened, defensive, rigid and psychologically maladjusted.

Future research should explore the implications of Rogers' self-experience-congruence/incongruence model for St John's theory of spiritual direction. The guiding hypothesis of this research would be that the behavioral phenomena associated with the spiritual life and the practice of spiritual direction described by St John can be explained phenomenologically by the degree of congruence existing between a person's self-concept and his experiencing organism. The benefit of this research would be to provide spiritual directors with new conceptual tools for understanding the behavior of their directees and the optimal response to that behavior.

Consider, for example, John's description of the imperfections of beginners in the spiritual life and his advice to spiritual directors for dealing with them. Writing in Book One of *The Ascent of Mount Carmel* where he deals primarily, though not exclusively, with beginners, John states that disordered appetites leave a person "unhappy . . . with himself, . . . cold toward his neighbors, . . . sluggish and slothful in the things of God."[60] To help persons overcome these evils, John gives this advice to spiritual directors:

> . . . the chief concern of spiritual directors with their penitents is the immediate mortification of every appetite. The directors should make them remain empty of what they desire so as to liberate them from so much misery.[61]

As expressed, this advice is difficult for a director today to interpret and follow. First, what precisely does the phrase "every appetite" mean? In today's idiom, the word appetite does not convey the exact meaning given to it by St John. Even if we interpret appetite to mean, as it did for John, habitual, voluntary, inordinate attachments of the will to objects other than God,[62] a second question arises: how does the director bring about the "immediate mortification" of these attachments in his directee? By advice? Command? Instruction? Prescribing ascetical exercises? A reliable procedure for mortifying appetites in another is not given. Thus, John's advice, as stated, provides little light for today's director in understanding the condition of beginners and helping them overcome the effects of disordered appetites.

However, with the help of Roger's self-experience-congruence/incongruence theory, the director can more readily understand the behavior of beginners and his most effective response to it. Persons who are unhappy with themselves, cold toward their neighbors, and spiritually sluggish are clearly in a state of incongruence, their self-concept out of harmony with their organismic experience. This incongruence can be seen in the beginners who suffer from spiritual pride described by John in Book One of *The Dark Night*, persons not unlike many seen today by spiritual directors:

> Sometimes they minimize their faults, and at other times they become discouraged by them, since they felt they were already saints, and they become impatient and angry with themselves, which is yet another fault.[63]

In these persons, the rationalization, impatience, anger and discouragement observed by the spiritual director arise from a concept of self as being a saint which is too rigid to accommodate the experience of personal fault. Such persons are in a state of incongruence which can be readily observed and understood by the director.

Rogers' congruence model also helps the director to see his role more clearly in assisting beginners. He may be uncertain about how to mortify the appetites of others; but there is no puzzle about how to reduce their incongruence. Rogers' experience and research in psychotherapy have revealed that incongruence in a client is best relieved through a relationship with a therapist who is experiencing genuineness within himself together with caring and understanding for the client; and who can communicate something of these experiences to the client. In such a relationship, the discrepancy between self and experience decreases and the client moves gradually toward becoming a more fully functioning person.

Similarly, the spiritual director's best approach in helping beginners to overcome their disordered appetites is to provide them with a genuine, caring and understanding human relationship. According to Rogers, this kind of interpersonal relationship allows an individual to see for himself the factors involved in his own incongruence and to reorganize his self-concept, thus allowing him to move toward greater psychological adjustment. A director, therefore, best mortifies the appetites of a beginner, not by advice or instruction, but by establishing an unthreatening interpersonal climate in which the beginner can become increasingly aware of the causes of his own disordered condition and find within his own natural tendency toward actualization the ways to remedy them. In this regard, Rogers' conclusions about psychotherapy also apply to spiritual direction:

> . . . Psychotherapy is the releasing of an already existing capacity in a potentially competent individual, not the expert manipulation of a more or less passive personality. Philosophically it means that the individual has the capacity to guide, regulate and control himself, provided only that certain definable conditions exist. Only in the absence of these conditions, and not in any basic sense, is it necessary to provide external control and regulation of the individual.[64]

This position is fundamentally in accord with John's view that persons committed to seeking divine union are by nature capable of following God's guidance without the help of a human spiritual director, although they may be greatly helped by an interpersonal relationship with a human guide.[65]

Rogers' self-experience-congruence/incongruence construct applies not only to beginners, but also to persons at any point on the spiritual journey, including the advanced stages of contemplative prayer. By definition, experience includes whatever is happening in a person at any given moment which is available to awareness. Furthermore, the self is not a rigidly fixed entity, but a fluid and changing conceptual gestalt, capable of continuing alteration as the person becomes aware of new experiences.[66] Thus, as the person's spiritual journey continues, there will always be some degree of congruence or incongruence between the ever new experiencing of the organism and the ever changing concept of self indicating the person's current psycho-spiritual condition.

Two important corollaries flow from using the self-experience-congruence/incongruence relationship in spiritual direction. First, when persons strive for spiritual ideals derived from Sacred Scripture or the history of Christian spirituality, they often apply literally to themselves lessons from Scripture or examples from the saints which are not in harmony with their own organismic experience. If this happens in an exaggerated degree, a person's actualizing tendency becomes bifurcated, with part of one's energy trying to actualize a self-ideal drawn from Scripture and tradition and part trying to meet the needs of the organism which may be at odds with one's conscious desires. Because the person is attempting to actualize a self-ideal not in harmony with experience, he or she is in a state of incongruence.[67] If a director continually reinforces a directee's incongruent strivings after static models of holiness, he more likely fosters estrangement and alienation within the person rather than progress toward union with God in love. Therefore, a director must help his directees adopt models of holiness and self-ideals which are relatively congruent with their organismic experiences.

A second, related corollary involves the interpretation of the word "self" which, aside from its use by Rogers and other modern psychologists, has a prominent place in the New Testament and the literature of Christian spirituality. Jesus insists upon self-denial (*aparnēsasthō heauton*) as a condition for discipleship and the losing or hating one's life or self (*apolesē tēn psychēn autou* — MT; *ho misōn tēn psychēn autou* — JN) in this world as a condition for salvation and eternal life.[68] Inspired by these biblical passages, Christian spiritual writers like St John of the Cross emphasize self-denial, self-surrender, self-hatred, self-renunciation and death to self as essential to Christian spirituality.[69] Because a misunderstanding of these terms has serious psychological consequences, a spiritual director often spends considerable effort in helping directees interpret and apply them to their lives. Although a wide range of exegetical and devotional interpretation of this terminology already exists,[70] Rogers' self-experience-congruence/incongruence theory provides an insight that is extremely valuable in spiritual direction: for example, death to self or self-surrender may be seen as letting go of rigid self-concepts and self-ideals which are incongruent with one's lived experience. In this interpretation, self-denial involves, not the inflicting of physical or emotional damage upon one's personhood, but rather the surrendering of unrealistic self-concepts which prevent a person from being open to God's guidance as manifested in one's own organismic experience.

The Helping Relationship

In his approach to spiritual direction, John of the Cross stressed the value of the relationship between the director and directee. In theory, John maintained that a person can respond to God's guidance without the help of a human director; indeed, one is better off having no human director than an incompetent one. In practice, however, John encouraged persons to have spiritual directors for the guidance, clarification, confirmation and support provided by this relationship, enabling them to walk more securely on the road to union with God.[71]

We have already seen the importance Rogers assigns to genuine, caring, understanding interpersonal relationships for fostering a person's growth. In fact, his theory of therapy and personality change, derived from years of experience and research by himself and his colleagues with the helping relationship of psychotherapy, is the heart of his theoretical system, the most scientifically reliable portion of his theory, and the basis of his many hypotheses regarding personality, interpersonal relationships, the fully functioning person, and various other human activities such as family life, education, group leadership and conflict, and international relations; it is his most significant contribution to modern psychology.[72]

Rogers' theory of therapy hinges on the attitudes of genuineness, caring and understanding in the therapist. To understand this theory fully, let me first review these qualities to see their significance for personality change and growth in a client.

Genuineness, or congruence, in a therapist means being oneself as fully as possible in the helping relationship. This involves a continual awareness in the therapist of his own organismic experiences, especially his attitudes and feelings, which arise in the course of the relationship and the ability to communicate this awareness to his client when it is appropriate to do so, particularly when the same attitudes and feelings persist in the therapist during his relationship with the client. Genuineness in a therapist is, quite simply, being real with himself and with his client.[73]

Caring, or unconditional positive regard, is an experience within the therapist of unqualified acceptance of the client as a person. Caring means prizing or valuing a client in all his uniqueness with all his strengths and weaknesses, placing no conditions which the client must fulfill to merit the therapist's esteem. Because caring implies respectful, non-possessive, non-romantic love for the client just as he is, it is equivalent to *agape* in the New Testament.[74]

The quality of understanding is an experience by the therapist of the client's inner world of meaning as if it were his own, but without losing the "as if" character of the experience. It is the therapist's ability to see life as the client sees it, from his or her own frame of reference, and to understand accurately and sensitively the experiences and feelings of the client and the meanings he or she attaches to them. Empathic understanding enables the therapist "to get inside of the skin" of his client and to understand his or her subjective world as though it were his own.[75]

For therapeutic growth to take place in a client, these qualities of genuineness, caring and understanding must be real
organismic experiences of the therapist; they cannot be pretended or imagined. For the therapist to experience threat and
discomfort in a helping relationship and be aware only of acceptance and understanding is to be incongruent in his relationship with the client; to act as though he prizes a client when
he is aware only of deep antipathy or to believe he understands
a client when he has merely formulated a diagnosis of him is for
the therapist neither an experience of unconditional positive regard for the client nor an experience of empathic understanding of the client's inner world. Under these conditions, where
there is little or no experience in the therapist of congruence,
caring or understanding, it is unlikely that therapeutic growth
will occur in the client.[76]

In addition to the three attitudes of the therapist, therapeutic
growth also depends upon certain conditions present in the client: he or she must be both in a state of incongruence and able
to perceive the therapist's genuineness, caring and understanding. Thus, assuming contact between a therapist and client,
five conditions are necessary for the therapeutic process to begin: a client in a state of incongruence, a therapist who is genuine or congruent in the relationship and who is experiencing
unconditional positive regard for the empathic understanding
of the client, and the client's perception of the therapist's attitudes in some degree. These conditions need only be minimally
present for the therapeutic process to begin: if they are absent,
even though the therapist and client are in contact, no therapeutic growth or constructive personality growth occurs in the
client.[77]

When these five conditions are met, an observable process —
the process of therapy — naturally begins within the client.
There are many elements in this process, but the following are
the most characteristic. The client becomes increasingly free in
expressing his feelings which gradually refer more to the self
than to the non-self. He begins to differentiate more accurately
between his feelings and perceptions and their objects and his

experiencing becomes more accurately symbolized in awareness. He begins to recognize the discrepancy between his immediate experiencing and his self-concept and to experience fully this discrepancy in awareness. His self-concept begins to change and become reorganized to assimilate previously denied experiences. He recognizes that the structures by which he has guided his life are neither fixed nor outside himself, but within himself, the product of his own making and subject to his change. His defensiveness decreases. His self-concept becomes more congruent with his experience, leaving him less threatened, more able to receive the therapist's unconditional positive regard, and more free and open in his relationships with others. Increasingly, he comes to regard himself as the locus of evaluation, the source of his valuing process, reacting to his experience less according to conditions of worth imposed by others and more according to his own organismic valuing process.[78]

As this therapeutic process continues, certain relatively permanent outcomes are predictable in the personality and behavior of the client, outcomes which are implicit in the process itself. The main result is a greater degree of congruence between the client's experiencing process and his self-concept. But being more congruent, the client is also more open to his experience, less defensive, more realistic in his perceptions, more effective in problem solving, better adjusted psychologically and less vulnerable to threat. His ideal self is more congruent with his self, more realistic, more achievable. He is less tense and anxious. His self-esteem is increased. He perceives the locus of evaluation to be within himself, feels more confident and self-directing and his values are determined by his own organismic valuing process. He perceives others more accurately and realistically and experiences more acceptance from them. He is perceived by others as more mature. His behavior is more creative, more uniquely adaptive to each new situation and problem, and more fully expressive of his own purposes and values.[79]

In describing the conditions, process and outcomes of psychotherapy, Rogers follows an *if-then* scientific procedure. *If* the operationally definable conditions for therapy exist (independent variables), *then* a process of therapy with certain characteristic elements (dependent variable) naturally follows; and *if* this process (now the independent variable) occurs, *then* certain outcomes in personality and behavior (dependent variables) will be observed. Rogers thus proposes a field theory of therapy, rather than a genetic theory. His theory posits no intervening variables and makes no attempt to explain why, under certain conditions, a process begins which has a predictable outcome. The theory states only that if A (the conditions for therapy) exists, then B (the process of therapy) and C (the outcomes in personality and behavior) will follow. "B and C are measurable events, predicted by A." Moreover, speaking in terms of functional relationships, Rogers states:

> The greater the degree of the conditions specified in A, the more marked or more extensive will be the process changes in B, and the greater or more extensive the outcome changes specified in C. Putting this in more general terms, the greater the degree of anxiety in the client, congruence in the therapist in the relationship, acceptance and empathy experienced by the therapist, and recognition by the client of these elements, the deeper will be the process of therapy, and the greater the extent of the personality and behavioral change.[80]

Although Rogers formulated his theory of therapy primarily from his experience in individual psychotherapy, he maintains that his discovery of the conditions necessary for constructive personal growth applies "in a wide variety of of professional work involving relationships with people — whether as a psychotherapist, teacher, religious worker, guidance counselor, social worker, clinical psychologist."[81] Indeed, his theory has special relevance for the ministry of spiritual direction and future research ought especially to explore the significance of Rogers' work for elucidating John of the Cross' observations concerning the human relationship in spiritual direction. The guiding hypothesis of this research would be that to the degree a spiritual director can bring genuineness, caring and understanding to his relationship with a directee, to that degree does the director fulfill his role as a human instrument in God's guidance of a person to divine union.

This hypothesis holds that the director's qualities of genuineness, caring and understanding are important for helping persons at every stage of the journey to God. We have already seen how they facilitate the growth of beginners; let us now see their relevance for those experiencing both the purgative and illuminative effects of contemplation in the higher stages of the spiritual journey.

When describing the painful effects of purgative contemplation, John explains that a person undergoes excruciating interior suffering due to the pain of true self-knowledge and the fear that this pain will last forever. When one is in this condition, the advice and reassurance of spiritual directors only aggravate the person's suffering, for "he believes his directors say these things because they do not understand him and do not see what he sees and feels (*parécele que, como ellos no ven lo que ella ve y siente, no la entendiendo dicen aquello*)."[82] Instead of giving advice or reassurance, directors should rather, in John's opinion, recognize that this is

> a period for leaving these persons alone in the purgation God is working in them, a time to give comfort and encouragement (*consolidándolas y animándolas*) that they might endure this suffering as long as God wills, for until then, no remedy — whatever the soul does, or the confessor says — is adequate.[83]

Analyzing this condition in light of Rogers' theory, we can see that one of the main causes of the person's distress is precisely his perception that his spiritual directors do not experience an empathic understanding of his inner world, that "they do not understand him and do not see what he sees and feels."[84] Whereas, when one perceives that a director does understand something of his world as though it were also the director's, the person is not only supported in enduring the trials of this period, but also enabled to explore the personal meanings which these threatening experiences have for him. Clearly, a director's empathic understanding is of greater value to a directee in the throes of purgative contemplation than advice and reassurance.

Likewise, with persons experiencing illuminative contemplation, John encourages them to express their contemplative experiences to their directors for the purpose of clarification and confirmation. However, because these experiences are deeply spiritual, received without word or sensory image, they are difficult to express in ordinary language. The effort to do so often ends in vague generalities.[85] Yet, applying the discoveries of Rogers regarding empathy, even the person's perception of the director's attempt to understand these experiences as though they were his own is an incentive for trying to put these ineffable experiences into words.[86]

Thus, in cases involving both purgative and illuminative contemplation, the director's most important asset is the ability to understand empathically and accurately persons with these experiences. This quality enables the director to be an effective instrument of God's guidance even in the presence of God's direct self-communication to persons, for his empathic understanding enables persons to explore the personal meanings contained in these contemplative experiences and derive for themselves the divine guidance implicit in them. Assuming also the characteristic of genuineness and caring, it is especially the director's ability to understand empathically the directee's experiences that enables him to be at every stage of the journey to God the directee's confident companion in his or her inner world.[87]

In researching the relationship between the necessary and sufficient conditions for therapy spelled out by Rogers and John's view of the helping relationship in spiritual direction, special attention must be paid to these conditions precisely as they apply to the ministry of spiritual direction, where the focus is primarily upon growth in the person's relationship with God and only secondarily upon constructive personality and behavioral change.[88] How, for example, do we understand the condition of client anxiety or incongruence in one committed to seeking union with God? Is this condition fulfilled by the incongruence found in beginners arising from disordered appetites or by the temporary incongruence found in more advanced contemplatives resulting from purgative and illuminative experiences of God? Or again, what is the relationship between therapist genuineness or congruence and John's insistence upon personal experience in the spiritual life as a necessary condition for giving spiritual direction?[89] Does the quality of genuineness include those instances where John expects the director to be directive and confrontative with the directee?[90] Does experience in the spiritual life enable the director to perceive more accurately and without distortion the behavior of his directee?[91] Or again, is the condition of empathic understanding able to be completely realized in a director when it involves the deeply spiritual and ineffable contemplative experiences of another? And, assuming that such an experience of empathic understanding is possible, how does a director best communicate his understanding of these experiences which transcend both sense and intellection to one advanced in the contemplative life? These and similar questions, arising from John's understanding of a person's relationship with God, must be asked when investigating the relevance of Rogers' theory of therapy for John's view of the helping relationship in spiritual direction.

Several important corollaries, each in turn requiring further research, seem logically to follow from applying Rogers' theory of therapy to the helping relationship of spiritual direction. First, although John uses various images in referring to spiritual direction — a father-son, master-disciple, confessor-penitent, or a guidance relationship — the director's abiding concern, however he prefers to imagine or describe his work, must be to create an interpersonal atmosphere of genuineness, caring and understanding, since these are the necessary conditions for promoting personal growth in another. There is no one model which best characterizes the spiritual direction relationship. A director may view his role as that of a spiritual father, a teacher, a guide, a confessor, in any way he chooses; however, his effectiveness as a human instrument in God's guidance of a person to divine union always depends upon the degree of genuineness, caring and understanding he brings to his relationship with the directee.

Secondly, John saw knowledge, experience and skill in helping relationships as the necessary qualities for an effective spiritual director.[92] All three contribute to the work of direction, but the most essential is the director's skill in interpersonal relationships. Without this skill, knowledge and experience are of limited value in helping others to dispose themselves for God's guidance in contemplation; whereas the ability to form genuine, caring and understanding relationships enables others to grow in their relationship with God, even though the director himself lacks extensive knowledge and experience of the spiritual life. In psychotherapy, Rogers views the quality of the therapist's relationship with the client to be more determinative of the client's personal growth than the director's scholarly knowledge, professional training, and therapeutic orientation and techniques.[93] Similarly, in spiritual direction: the various activities of teaching, advising, instructing, discerning and evaluating, which John sees as arising out of the director's knowledge and experience, facilitate the directee's spiritual growth only to the extent that the director has an honest, caring and understanding relationship with the directee.

The third corollary pertains to the distinction between spiritual direction and psychotherapy. In theory, real distinctions can easily be drawn between these two helping modes on the basis of the purpose, goals, subject matter and setting of each; in practice, however, it does not appear necessary to insist too strongly on these distinctions. According to Rogers' theory of therapy, both psychotherapy and spiritual direction depend for their success primarily upon the attitudinal ingredients of the helping person, ingredients he describes under the headings of genuineness, caring and understanding. Since these ingredients may be found as readily in a spiritual director as in a psychotherapist, spiritual direction can begin with any person who desires to improve his or her relationship with God, even though

the person may be at a point on the continuum of human behavior which causes others to judge him or her to be "neurotic,"
incapable of spiritual growth, and in need of referral to psychotherapy. However, the degree of incongruence described by
John in beginners who have made a sincere conversion to God
and who therefore are normal candidates for spiritual direction
appears no less severe than in those described by Rogers who
seek help in psychotherapy. Moreover, in both psychotherapy
and spiritual direction, the primary concern for the helping
person is to create an interpersonal climate characterized by
genuineness, caring and understanding. If this climate is established, then a process naturally begins in the person seeking
help that has as its predicted outcome both the reduction of incongruence and continued personal growth, both psychological
and spiritual. Thus, the primary concern for a spiritual director
in his initial encounters with a directee is not whether the person is a candidate for psychotherapy or for spiritual direction
judged by some arbitrary set of external criteria, but whether
he as a helping person can form with the person a working relationship that is honest, caring and understanding. If such a
relationship can be established, then both spiritual and psychological growth can be predicted for the directee; if not, it is
doubtful if any constructive change will occur. In the latter
case, the director ought to refer the person to another helper,
not because the person is more appropriately a candidate for
psychotherapy, but because the director is unable to establish a
growth producing relationship with the person.

Fourthly, Rogers asserts that if certain conditions exist in a
helping relationship, certain positive changes may be predicted
in a client, including a more positive self-image.[94] To this pre-
diction we may also add, based on limited observations in spiritual direction, that as a person's image of self changes in a
positive direction, the person's image of God will also change
in a positive direction, normally from a long-held concept of a
rigid and condemning God to an image of God as more accepting and forgiving. Thus, it appears that positive changes in
one's view of God are related to positive changes in one's self-

concept, and that both changes are an effect of a helping relationship that is characterized by genuineness, caring and understanding.

Experience: The Subject Matter of Spiritual Direction

For St John of the Cross, the subject matter or focus of the spiritual direction relationship is the total experience of the directee, insofar as this experience manifests the directee's relationship with God. Experience includes thoughts, volitions, memories, fantasies, sensations, appetites or desires, emotions or passions, feelings and purely spiritual phenomena involving neither sensory nor cognitive processes. These psychological experiences reveal the actual state of a person's unique relationship with God and the particular way God is guiding that person.[95]

Experience is also an important concept for Rogers. In his theory, experience means "all that is going on within the envelope of the organism at any given moment which is potentially available to awareness."[96] It is primarily a psychological term, including: all that is immediately present in a person's conscious awareness as well as events of which the person is not immediately conscious, but whose effects are available to awareness; the impact of sensory phenomena, even when these are not the focus of attention; and the effects of memories and past events. In Rogers' system, experience does not include purely physiological events such as neuron discharges or changes in blood sugar, "because these are not directly available to awareness."[97]

Experience refers to the "here and now," to what is happening in the present moment of a person's life rather than to the sum total of past events. Experience implies process, the ebb and flow of whatever is occuring within a person at any given moment of his life. Rogers often uses the verbal form "experiencing" to capture the here-and-now, process quality of this concept.[98]

An important element in the experiencing process is "feeling," described by Rogers as "an emotionally tinged experience, together with its personal meaning."[99] Feelings contain both emotional and cognitive components. Feelings are not haphazard psychological events without personal consequence; rather, they are significant clues leading to the discovery of meaning and direction in one's life.

In Rogers' theory, the natural capacity for self-direction inherent in a person's actualizing tendency is directly related to the experiencing process and the meanings implicit in feelings. With growth, persons gradually rely less upon external guides such as parents and teachers for direction and more upon their own experiencing. Indeed, one of the positive changes resulting from successful psychotherapy is that a person comes "to regard his experiencing as positive, constructive, and a useful guide."[100]

Experiencing is a source, not only of guidance, but of personal values as well. As persons mature, their values emerge more from within, from an organismic valuing process rooted in experiencing, rather than from external sources; from reference to the experiencing of one's organism, rather than to outside authority.[101] Experience for Rogers is thus the ultimate source of personal meaning, guidance and values.

Future research should explore the implications of Rogers' concept of experience for John's theory of spiritual direction. The main hypothesis in this research would be that God present within the human person guides the person to union with himself principally through the person's experience. As a person becomes increasingly aware of his experiencing process and especially the personal meanings implicit in his feelings, he becomes more attuned to God's guidance in his life. Accordingly, the human spiritual director fulfills his role as an instrument of God's guidance by assisting the directee to discover the personal meanings implicit in his or her experiencing process, for these meanings reveal God's unique guidance of the directee, the way in which he guides one person to divine union differently from every other person.

This hypothesis does not posit the experiencing process as the only reliable source of divine guidance. Differing notably on this point from Rogers, who maintains that the person's inner experiencing is the primary source of personal direction and values, John holds that Sacred Scripture, Church teachings, and the judgment of competent persons are also principal sources of guidance.[102] However, this hypothesis does imply that behavioral norms arising from these external sources become meaningfully directive in individual persons only to the degree that they are verified in the person's experience. According to John, God's direction of a person to divine union is always away from what is most exterior toward what is most interior.[103] For example, the Gospel admonition to self-denial becomes personally directive only when one experiences the exhilarating inner freedom that comes with saying "no" to one's inordinate appetites. Or again, persons begin to live more in the darkness of faith only as they experience the personal rewards of relying solely on the Word of God and his providence. As the experience of Israel with God which is recorded in Sacred Scripture and the Christian interpretation of that experience become validated anew in the experience of the individual Christian believer, Scripture and tradition become living sources of guidance, not dead words or external moralism.

A first corollary of this research is the definition and extension of experience when used in discussing the theories of St John of the Cross. Experience may be defined as any activity or subjective state of the person, regardless of its origin. It thus includes not only all the organismic, visceral, psycho-physiological events denoted by Rogers' concept of experiencing, but also those mystical experiences which involve only the spiritual part of a person and are independent of sensory activity, yet are significant and often determinative human events. Experience in St John includes all human knowledge — active or passive, ordinary or extraordinary, natural or supernatural — regardless of origin. And experience includes faith which although not originating in organismic experiencing is always a human activity available to awareness and for discussion in the spiritual direction dialogue. Thus, the value of the term experience is that it can be used to include all that is happening in the human person, regardless of origin.

As a second corollary, it appears unwise to limit arbitrarily the subject matter of the spiritual direction dialogue, as, for example, to a discussion of the directee's prayer or progress in faith, hope and love. In theory, growth in one's relationship with God is intrinsically related to prayer and the theological virtues; in practice, however, prayer and theological virtue can never be separated from one's experience and behavior.[104] Spiritual direction's abiding concern is the directee's relationship with God, a God who is known more through experience (*sentir*) than through conceptual knowledge (*entender*).[105] Because this relationship is manifested in the person's experience, any sensory or spiritual experience of the person — any thought, feeling, desire, emotion, or purely spiritual movement — may reveal the nature or quality of this relationship, where one is in the journey to divine union, or how God is presently acting in one's life. Since the major variables in the spiritual direction process are God, the human person and their relationship, any experience of God, of self, or of the relationship is potential subject matter for the spiritual direction dialogue.

A third corollary involves the discernment of spirits or the determination of God's will in choosing a particular course of action. If God guides persons through the experiencing process, then this process ought to be consulted in discerning God's will in individual choices. Along with consulting such factors as the Gospel, human reason, the judgment of directors, and the potential growth in one's personal virtue and fervor toward God when considering a practical course of action, one must also clarify the personal meanings present in one's own experiencing process, for these meanings not only constitute "the wisest and most satisfying indication of appropriate behavior,"[106] but they are also a principal means for revealing God's will. In turn, a person is most likely to discover the meanings present in his or her feelings and experiencing in a relationship with an empathic person, for the empathic understanding of another (in this case, a spiritual director) provides the most conducive climate in which to discover the personal meanings implicit in one's total organismic functioning.[107]

A fourth corollary concerns the trustworthiness of human nature. How far can human experience be trusted as a guide to human behavior? Rogers' answer to this question is more optimistic than St John's. While maintaining that God is present in the human person communicating himself through the person's experience and that human reason is more reliable in discerning God's will than supernatural revelations, John also holds that in matters of faith and of the spirit the sensory part of human nature (*el sentido*) is often a source of error and little to be trusted.[108] Rogers, on the other hand, though by no means regarding the experiencing process of the organism (roughly equivalent to "sense" in St John) as infallible, maintains on the basis of thirty years of experience as a psychotherapist that the basic nature of the human being is constructive and trustworthy and the organismic valuing process is a source of personally and socially enhancing behavior.[109] In light of Rogers' experience and research, we ought to reevaluate John's position on the untrustworthiness of sense in the life of the spirit to determine whether in his theory of spirituality a development is possible that would permit a greater integration of sense and spirit in the order of behavior, thus enabling persons in their journey to union with God to maintain a "close and confident relationship" with their ongoing organismic process.[110]

Growth in Prayer and the Therapeutic Process

From his perspective as a spiritual director, John of the Cross views the human person's ascent to union with God as a journey in prayer. In the beginning of this journey, one is "unhappy with himself, . . . cold toward his neighbors, . . . sluggish and slothful in the things of God;"[111] at the end, one is transformed through faith, hope and love. It is a journey with three distinct and successive stages, the first stage being that of beginners, the second of those making progress in prayer, and the third of those whose prayer is perfect. This prayerful journey leads from meditation to contemplation, from a life centered in the senses to one centered in the spirit. The journey is often dark and disruptive, forcing persons to change in light of new insights into themselves and into God; but these changes also means profound growth. In the last stage of the journey, purified of inordinate desires for created things and united with God through the loving knowledge that is contemplation, the person transcends human laws and ways and is a "law unto himself,"[112] lives free of social expectations, is open to all creation, loves others, is healed of deeply rooted disorders, and is fully an individual. This journey in prayer thus leads not only theologically to the transformation of the person in God, but also psychologically to the perfection of the human personality.[113]

From his perspective as a psychotherapist, Rogers views becoming a fully functioning person as a process that begins with a person who is incongruent, in a state of tension or internal confusion due to the discrepancy between the self-concept and the experience of the organism, and ends with a person who has achieved harmony between self and experience, who is whole, integrated and genuine.[114] This process, involving a relationship with an honest, caring and understanding person, continues through seven distinct stages, from a "rigid fixity of attitudes and constructs and perceptions, to a changingness and flow in all these respects . . . from remoteness from experiencing to immediacy of experiencing."[115] The process is often disruptive as the self reorganizes to incorporate experiences newly admitted to awareness;[116] yet, out of this process emerges a person who is more open to his experience, more accepting of others, more trusting of self, more creative, more "that self which one truly is."[117]

Although John's viewpoint is theological, centered in prayer, and Rogers' is psychological, centered in the therapeutic relationship, both men have similar views of a person's progress toward the goal they each posit for human life. Both see this progress as a journey or process with recognizable stages of growth, involving periods of inner turmoil, leading from a rigid, conflicted style of living to one that is more existential and effective, the end result being a person who is autonomous, open, caring and free.

Further research ought to be conducted relating John's view of progress in contemplative prayer to Rogers' theory of the psychotherapeutic process. The guiding hypothesis for this research would be that both contemplative prayer and effective psychotherapy create the necessary psychological climate that enables a person's self-concept to change and broaden so as to incorporate experiences previously denied to awareness, resulting in greater congruence between self and experience and, thus, by hypothesis, a more fully functioning person, a person growing in union with God through love.

This hypothesis implies that prayer itself is primarily an interpersonal relationship, a relationship based on faith between God and the human person (analogous to the relationship between a therapist and client) which enables the person through infused contemplation to see himself more honestly and accurately, to experience himself loved unconditionally and understood in the deepest recesses of his being. As a person in prayer experiences this honesty, caring and understanding, his self-structure becomes less rigid, more open to the experiencing of the organism, more congruent, more fully functioning, and more open to God's guidance. The key relationship in spiritual direction, then, is not that of the directee with the director, but rather the directee's ongoing, ever-deepening relationship with God that continues through prayer outside of the time spent with the human spiritual director; the directee's relationship with the human director simply supports, confirms and clarifies through the director's own honesty, caring and understanding the directee's growing relationship with God.

This hypothesis further implies that the director fulfills his role as an instrument of God's guidance by being a guide in prayer. He teaches persons how to pray, supports them in their efforts to pray, and listens empathically as they describe their experiences in prayer. The director's role is to dispose persons to receive God's self-communication in contemplation, for in this communication God heals persons of their incongruence, makes them more fully functioning and brings them to union with himself. Thus, if the director is essentially a guide (the term that comes closest to expressing John's idea of a spiritual director), he is primarily a guide in prayer. Spiritual direction can thus be most appropriately called "prayer counseling,"[118] the spiritual director being an expert in prayer, one who understands it, can teach it to others and foster its growth in others.

As a first corollary to this hypothesis, it appears that the healing and growth producing factor in both psychotherapy and contemplative prayer is the knowledge of self gained in these processes. Psychotherapy enables a person to recognize and symbolize in awareness experiences of the organism — anger, hurt, fear, etc. — that previously had been repressed or denied to awareness; as the self-structure expands to incorporate these experiences, the person lives less defensively, more realistically, more existentially. In contemplative prayer, the light of contemplation enables a person to see himself — especially all his inordinate attachments to objects — as he truly is, without distortion. This self-knowledge leads to change as one gradually lets go of the inordinate attachments which cause the distorted view of self. Thus, in both psychotherapy and in contemplative prayer the person's increasing self-knowledge rather than the technique of the therapist or spiritual director causes the growth producing change in a person; the therapist and director merely establish a psychological atmosphere that helps this growth producing self-knowledge to occur.[119]

Moreover, in contemplative prayer, this growth producing knowledge also extends to God. In light of God's self communication, a person sees the inadequacy of his own understanding of God and begins to relinquish these inadequate conceptions or images and to relate to God more by unknowing than by knowing, by knowing him through "what he is not, rather than through what he is."[120] Thus, in contemplative prayer, not only is one's concept of self continually changing in light of new knowledge about self, but one's conception of God is continually changing, progressing from the known to the unknown, from particular conceptions of God to a general experience of God that transcends human conceptualizations. As a result, a person is less bound to rigid or limited concepts of self and God, more open to change in ways of thinking about existence, less defensive and more open to his experience in all areas of life — the personal, interpersonal, cosmic and transcendent.

A second corollary to our hypothesis is that Rogers' seven stage process conception of psychotherapy[121] appears useful for discerning a person's growth in contemplative prayer. If it is true, as our hypothesis maintains, that both psychotherapy and contemplative prayer facilitate a change in a person's self-structure that enables one to be more congruent with his experiencing and if in both therapy and contemplation the growth is away from rigidity to openness, from stasis to process, from fixedness to fluidity, then the stages of growth delineated by Rogers for measuring progress in psychotherapy ought also to be useful in assessing growth in contemplative prayer.

Applications: Training, Research and Contributions to Theology and Psychology

Up to this point, I have been concerned with establishing subject areas wherein the psychological theories of Carl Rogers might profitably be compared with St John of the Cross' theory of spiritual direction with a view ultimately of building a theoretical model for guiding practice and research in contemporary spiritual direction. I would now like to comment on the relevance of Rogers' work for the ministry of spiritual direction today in the areas of training, research and contributions to theological and psychological science.

1. Training

According to St John of the Cross, competent spiritual directors should possess knowledge, experience and skill in helping relationships. To be effective, training programs in spiritual direction ought to prepare trainees in each of these three areas. Academic knowledge alone is obviously insufficient preparation for the ministry of spiritual direction: the training of spiritual directors must also provide for experience in the spiritual life and the acquiring of skills in the helping relationship.

For years, training counselors and psychotherapists has been a major concern of Carl Rogers.[122] In his mind, the challenge of counselor education is not to turn out individuals skilled in counseling technique, but rather persons capable of experiencing and communicating their own realness, caring and empathy. Training should aim primarily at cultivating these human attitudes in prospective counselors and only secondarily at teaching them therapeutic technique.

The growth of spiritual direction as a modern ministry will in part depend upon the wise selection and adequate training of future directors. Based upon theories of both St John and Carl Rogers, training programs in spiritual direction ought to include at least the following four components: (1) a training atmosphere created by the staff which is conducive to the growth of trainees as persons who are honest, caring, understanding and able to communicate these attitudes to others; (2) opportunities for personal and spiritual growth experiences, including private prayer and meditation, retreats and spiritual exercises, common worship and liturgical celebrations, journal keeping, spiritual reading, psychotherapy and/or spiritual direction on an individual and/or group basis; (3) academic studies in theology, Sacred Scripture, spirituality, philosophy and psychology, concentrating on learnings in these fields which apply to the ministry of spiritual direction; and (4) opportunities to provide spiritual direction for persons desiring guidance in the spiritual life under the supervision of qualified staff members. Training programs built on these foundations should increase the number of directors who are personally, practically and theoretically qualified to guide others in the spiritual life.[123]

2. Research

As noted earlier, John of the Cross and Carl Rogers both evidence a scientific spirit in their respective approaches to the helping relationship and the study of human behavior. Living in an age previous to the development of empirical methodology, John researched the spiritual life as a participant observer, building his theories of spirituality and spiritual direction upon personal introspection and natural observation. Rogers, on the other hand, as a twentieth-century American psychologist, has used empirical procedures extensively in ascertaining the natural order present in helping relationships and in formulating his theories of psychotherapy, personality and interpersonal relationships. Utilizing such research instruments and methods as analysis of tape recorded therapeutic interviews, rating of interviews by independent judges, Stephenson's Q technique, Rank Pattern Analysis, operational definitions of theoretical constructs, psychological tests, statistical measurement, and research designs involving pre- and post-therapy evaluation of matched therapy and control groups, Rogers and his colleagues have defined many of the significant factors affecting the therapeutic relationship and the process and outcome of psychotherapy and have developed many testable hypotheses regarding personality and interpersonal relationships which have implications for education, family life, group behavior, intercultural conflicts, and other areas of human life where interpersonal relationships are involved. Writing in 1974, Rogers claimed: "No other mode of psychotherapy has been so thoroughly investigated by the methods of empirical research as client-centered therapy;"[124] indeed, this research has greatly increased the effectiveness of the client-centered approach to helping relationships and greatly enhanced our understanding of the nature of psychotherapy, personality and interpersonal relationships.

While modern psychologists have been developing objective empirical methods and instruments for researching counseling and psychotherapy,[125] spiritual directors investigate their own work relying almost exclusively upon subjective approaches such as introspection and uncontrolled observation used by St John in the sixteenth century. Current literature in spiritual direction notes the importance of research,[126] yet reports very little empirical research. The vast majority of studies in spiritual direction today either apply psychological or theological insights to the spiritual direction process or present the results of uncontrolled observation on that process: there are almost no reports of studies using objective empirical methodology.[127]

Admittedly, it is difficult to design empirical research for the spiritual direction process, primarily because the main "variables" in spiritual direction — God dynamically present in human life and the human person considered principally as a spiritual and transcendent being — defy empirical control and measurement. Nevertheless, spiritual direction also implies a human relationship, as amenable to empirical investigation as the counseling or psychotherapeutic relationship. The renewal of spiritual direction as a ministry in the Church today can be greatly enhanced by adapting empirical research methods of psychology to investigate the significant factors affecting the director-directee relationship and the process and outcome of that relationship and to develop testable hypotheses regarding a person's journey to union with God as these emerge within the direction process itself (for example, the relation of the director's spiritual life to the progress of the directee, the effects of prayer in a person's daily life, the effects of change in one's self-concept upon one's understanding of God and growth in faith, etc.). If, like Rogers, spiritual directors bring a research attitude to their work and creatively adapt available psychological methods and instruments for use in discovering the significant factors affecting the spiritual direction relationship, their understanding of their work and their effectiveness as instruments in God's guidance of persons to divine union will surely increase.

3. Contributions to Theological and Psychological Science

John of the Cross was not a professional theologian; yet, as a spiritual director he carefully observed the psychological effects of God's action in persons who consciously strive for divine union. His treatises on the spiritual life indicate that his understanding of the journey to union with God was derived both from personal introspection and from his discoveries in guiding others to God. As modern theological writings testify, John's observations as a spiritual director have contributed greatly to theological science, especially spiritual theology which treats of the person's growth to a perfect Christian life.[128]

Similarly, the major contributions of Carl Rogers to modern psychological science stem primarily from his observations as a psychotherapist.[129] His experience in the interpersonal relationship that is psychotherapy led him to postulate that the therapist's empathic understanding of the client's inner subjective world is not only a necessary condition for the client's growth, but also a valid and fruitful source of knowledge for advancing psychological science. Rogers discovered that when through his own genuineness, caring and understanding he is able to provide a non-threatening climate for his client, the client experiences the freedom to explore, discover and describe his or her own inner world — experiencing, feelings, perceptions of self, goals, beliefs, attitudes, values, motives, etc. — which previously had been largely hidden from the client's conscious awareness. By translating his client's subjective discoveries into operational terms that can be explored by more objective procedures, Rogers paved the way for building his psychological theories of psychotherapy, personality and interpersonal relationships upon a solid empirical basis. By thus using empathic understanding both as a means of facilitating his client's personal growth in psychotherapy and as a source of scientific information, Rogers has contributed to developing psychology as a truly human science, one not limited to studying only observable external human behavior, but able also to explore the vast inner world of personal meaning.[130]

As John of the Cross and Carl Rogers have both contributed respectively to theology and psychology from their experience in the helping relationship of spiritual direction and psychotherapy, so spiritual directors today and in the future can contribute to the continuing development of both theological and psychological science if, in addition to being companions with persons in their interior journey to union with God, they also attempt to share with theologians and psychologists what they observe in persons who make this journey.

Theology, of course, is the perennial "search for an understanding of our relationship to God."[131] Traditionally, the sources of knowledge about this relationship are divine revelation, Sacred Scripture, the traditions of the Church, and the writings of gifted persons like St Augustine or St Teresa of Avila who had profound personal experiences of this relationship. However, the empathic understanding which Rogers has shown to be such a fruitful means of increasing our psychological understanding of the human person emerges also as a valuable source of knowledge for increasing our theological understanding of the human person in relationship to God. Spiritual direction is a window through which theologians can observe how God is experienced by very ordinary people in their daily living.

As hypothesized earlier,[132] a director's empathic understanding of the directee's subjective world is one quality that constitutes an effective spiritual direction relationship. When this quality is present together with a director's genuineness and caring, the directee experiences the freedom to explore, discover and describe without threat of embarrassment or ridicule perhaps the most intimate of subjective experiences — his or her personal relationship with God. Directors who are companions to persons in this inner discovery are often amazed at both the depth and variety of their experience of God. By formulating their observations in terms comprehensible to theologians, spiritual directors can provide new data and hypotheses that will lead to a richer theological understanding of the human person's relationship with God. These findings when critically evaluated against traditional sources of theological knowledge and the ongoing experience of Christian persons, should prove particularly helpful to theories of prayer,[133] and grace,[134] and divine providence.[135] Thus, in addition to enabling directors to be more confident guides of persons in their spiritual journey, empathic understanding makes the spiritual direction relationship itself a fruitful source of theological knowledge for an ever deepening understanding of our relationship to God.

Spiritual directors can also contribute to psychological science, especially today in the United States when psychologists are moving beyond the limits of research established earlier by behaviorism and psychoanalysis to investigate the phenomenological, humanistic, existential and transpersonal aspects of human life. Rogers has long championed this movement: in fact, after 45 years as a clinical psychologist he has challenged his fellow American psychologists to consider "the possibility of another reality (or realities), operating on rules quite different from our well-known commonsense empirical reality, the only one known to most psychologists."[136]

Spiritual direction is a centuries-old ministry devoted to helping persons live daily in just such a reality, the inner world of human spirit, which might be aptly described in Rogers' own words as

> . . . a lawful reality which is not open to our five senses; a reality in which present, past, and future are intermingled, in which space is not a barrier and time has disappeared; a reality which can be perceived and known only when we are passively receptive, rather than actively bent on knowing.[137]

St John of the Cross described the laws of this reality with such precision that his writings continue after four centuries to be a reliable handbook for persons who live daily in this world of the spirit.[138] In this world, spiritual directors act as companions and guides for persons in their interior journey to union with God through love, the most fascinating of all transpersonal journeys. If, in addition to being guides and companions, spiritual directors today also attempt to formulate in language comprehensible to modern psychologists what they observe in persons who live in the reality of the spirit, they will contribute significantly to psychology's own exploration of the farthest reaches of human nature, and most especially into such areas as the nature of human consciousness, the mind-body-spirit relationship, behavioral self-control, and the therapeutic effects of prayer, meditation and contemplation.[139]

Rogers has commented that only a "secure scientist" aims his work toward areas of "greatest mystery."[140] Yet spiritual directors work daily with the greatest mysteries: the mystery of God, the mystery of the human person and the mystery of the human person's relationship with God. From the vantage point of their helping relationship with persons consciously living this mysterious relationship with God, spiritual directors who attempt to share their discoveries in this world of the spirit with the world of science will contribute significantly to the advancement of both theology and psychology.

Summary

This section explores the relevance of Carl Rogers' psychological theories of psychotherapy, personality and interpersonal relationships for the theory of spiritual direction found in St John of the Cross' *The Ascent of Mount Carmel* and *The Dark Night*. After a discussion of the similarities and differences between these two authors, six areas are indicated where the theories of Rogers relate to those of St John and hypotheses are stated to guide further examination of these relationships. The six areas are: direction from within, the goal of direction, self-experience-congruence/incongruence as explanatory concepts in spiritual direction, the helping relationship, experience as the subject matter of spiritual direction, and growth in prayer and the therapeutic process. The relevance of Rogers' work is also shown for the contemporary ministry of spiritual direction in the areas of training, research, and contributions to psychological and theological science.

A METHOD OF RESEARCH AND DEVELOPMENT OF MODELS IN SPIRITUAL DIRECTION

In the preceding section, I elaborated six areas of research in which the psychological theories of Carl Rogers appear to relate to St John of the Cross' theory of spiritual direction as contained in the *Ascent-Dark Night* and stated hypotheses which might serve as the bases for exploring these relationships further. It remains now to enumerate the steps necessary to carry forth this research with a view to formulating a theoretical framework or model to guide practice and research in spiritual direction.

Analysis and Synthesis of the Theory of Spiritual Direction in the
Collected Writings of St John of the Cross

Following a method drawn from biblical theology for analyzing and synthesizing themes or teachings in religious writings,
I analyzed St John of the Cross' *The Ascent of Mount Carmel-The*
Dark Night to discover both its explicit and implicit teachings on
spiritual direction. I then synthesized these teachings into eight
statements and arranged them in a logical order suggested by
the teachings themselves. As presented in Part One of this article, these logically arranged statements express St John's theory
of spiritual direction in the *Ascent-Dark Night*.

Future research must now extend this method to all the writings of St John, first analyzing their content for both the explicit
and implicit teachings on spiritual direction and then synthesizing these teachings into statements which are arranged according to a logic suggested by the teachings themselves. This
final synthetic statement would represent the complete theory
of spiritual direction as found in all the writings of St John.[141]

Heuristic Analysis of Collected Writings of Carl Rogers

To arrive at the six areas stated above in Part Two in which
Rogers' theories appear related to St John's, I carefully examined two writings of Rogers'—"A Theory of Therapy, Personality, and Interpersonal Relationships, as Developed in the
Client-Centered Framework" and "Client-Centered Psychotherapy"—which rigorously and economically express the essential components of his psychological theories, asking one
heuristic question: What relevance do these theories derived
from Rogers' clinical experience and empirical research have
for St John's theory of spiritual direction as derived from the
Ascent-Dark Night? I discovered six areas where an apparent
relationship exists between St John's theories and those of Rogers. I stated these relationships and formulated hypotheses to
guide future explorations of these relationships.

Following these same procedures, all of Rogers' writings, especially those most supported by clinical experience and empirical research, must be heuristically analyzed with the question:

How does this article, this book, this insight, this research finding relate to the theory of spiritual direction found in the writings of St John of the Cross? As demonstrated earlier, the perceived relationships between Rogers' psychological theories and St John's theory of spiritual direction are systematically formulated into hypotheses that can be evaluated in future research.[142]

Researching Relationships and Testing Hypotheses Derived from the Theories of John of the Cross and Carl Rogers

Once the significant relationships between the theories of St John and Rogers and the guiding hypotheses for researching these relationships have been formulated in the manner demonstrated in the preceding section, these relationships and hypotheses can be explored and tested according to the appropriate phenomenological, theological and empirical research procedures. Because spiritual direction relies upon both theology and psychology as upon basic sciences, these relationships and hypotheses must be open to critical examination by both theological and psychological methods. For this reason, the relationships and hypotheses must be formulated broadly enough, yet economically and operationally enough, to permit this interdisciplinary evaluation. The six areas of research already developed in this article indicate the major relationships and hypotheses which can be drawn from the theories of St John and Rogers; however, as the complete works of both are analyzed according to the steps explained above, these areas of research may increase in number.

Formulation of Theoretical Model for Guiding Practice and Research in Spiritual Direction

The results of exploring and testing relationships and hypotheses derived from John of the Cross and Carl Rogers will be formulated into a theoretical model of spiritual direction. A model is a network of concepts and relationships which to some degree represents symbolically a particular reality, but more importantly guides practice and research within that reality. Thus, the concepts and relationships that emerge from investigating the hypotheses drawn from St John and Rogers must to the extent possible be operationally defined and systematically arranged so as both to express conceptually the reality of spiritual direction and to guide actual practice and continuing research therein.

The components of this theoretical model — its basic concepts and relationships and their systematic arrangement — can be determined only as the three steps of previous research outlined above reveal them; yet, from the exploratory research already concluded the emerging structure of such a model may be tentatively outlined as follows:

1. *basic assumptions* underlying the ministry of spiritual direction drawn from theology, philosophy and psychology
2. *definition of terms* to be used in the model, defined as rigorously and operationally as possible
3. *goal* of spiritual direction
4. the *practice* of spiritual direction, expressed to the degree possible in operational terms and functional (if-then) relationships, as it pertains to
    a. the directee
    b. the director
    c. the relationship of the director and directee
    d. the process of spiritual growth
5. *research* procedures for investigating the practice of spiritual direction.

Several points may be made about this model. First of all, it is primarily an interpersonal relationship model of spiritual direction in that it places the utmost importance upon the relationship between the director and directee. However, there are other ways of understanding spiritual direction in the Church today: direction as institutionalized, direction as charismatic, direction as sacramental, direction as incarnational, and so forth.[143] Because each of these models expresses a valid truth about the reality or mystery of spiritual direction, the interpersonal model must not be viewed as describing the entirety of this reality. It presents but one aspect of the mystery of spiritual direction and must be used with the awareness that other equally valid models of direction exist.

Secondly, a theoretical model is not a dogma, but merely a useful conceptual tool for guiding research and practice. Thus, as this model of spiritual direction develops, it must never be regarded as a final statement about the reality of direction; rather, it must always be ready for reformulation to incorporate new data arising from practice and research.

Thirdly, the hypotheses from which this model is derived originate, not in the direct observation of spiritual direction as practised today, but in the reported experiences of a sixteenth-century Spanish spiritual director and the clinical and research findings of a twentieth-century American psychotherapist. The initial formulation of this model, then, while not totally a conceptual entity unrelated to the actual experience of spiritual direction or the helping relationship, is nevertheless several steps removed from the current reality it attempts to describe and, for this reason, will undoubtedly contain a large degree of error and mistaken inference. Yet even a model built initially upon deductive hypotheses related only indirectly to experience is valuable if it contributes to more enlightened practice and stimulates illuminating research. As new data arise from practice and experience in spiritual direction, the model can be reformulated to reduce its margin of error and mistaken inferences and to represent more accurately the actual experience of spiritual direction today.[144]

Finally, this model should not be conceived as St John of the Cross' theory of spiritual direction updated with the insights of Carl Rogers or as a client-centered theory of psychotherapy baptized for spiritual direction; rather, it should be thought of as an independent theoretical model to guide future practice and research in spiritual direction. Although its initial formulation relies heavily upon hypotheses drawn from the work of both St John of the Cross and Carl Rogers, the model may with continual revision according to new data arising from ongoing research and practice in spiritual direction evolve to an expression quite removed from the original theories of either St John or Rogers.

In the four successive steps stated above — analysis and synthesis of theories of spiritual direction in religious writings, heuristic analysis of psychological writings for data relevant to these theories, evaluation of hypotheses derived from these analyses and formulation of a theoretical model based on this evaluation — we have a method for constructing theoretical models for use in spiritual direction. Assuming the importance of contemporary psychology for the traditional Christian ministry of spiritual direction,[145] this method enables any reliable theory of spiritual direction (one validated in experience and theology)[146] and any reliable theory of personality and psychotherapy (one supported by solid clinical and research evidence) to be assimilated into an integrated conceptual framework useful for guiding practice and research in spiritual direction. Hopefully, developing such models will promote the renewal of spiritual direction as a relevant ministry in today's Church.

Summary

In this final section, a method is described for continuing the research reported in this article and for developing a theoretical model of spiritual direction based on the writings of St John of the Cross and Carl Rogers. This method involves four successive stages: analysis and synthesis of the theory of spiritual direction in the collected works of St John; heuristic analysis of all the writings of Carl Rogers; critical evaluation of the relationship and hypotheses derived from the theories of John and Rogers; and the formulation of a theoretical model for guiding practice and research in spiritual direction. A tentative outline for the components of such a model is presented and evaluated. The section concludes with the suggestion that this four-step method may be used for developing a variety of theoretical models of spiritual direction based on writers other than St John of the Cross and Carl Rogers.

NOTES

1. Louis J. Cameli, *Spiritual Direction for Priests in the USA: The Rediscovery of a Resource* (Washington, D.C.: United States Catholic Conference, 1977), p. 15.

2. See, for example, the following: Reginald Garrigou-Lagrange, "Special Graces of the Spiritual Director," trans. M. Timothea Doyle, *Cross and Crown*, 2 (December 1950), 413; Dorothy Dohen, "Spiritual Direction," *Spiritual Life*, 4 (September 1958), 199–204; Ernest E. Larkin, "Spiritual Direction Today," *American Ecclesiastical Review*, 161 (September 1969), 205–7; Sandra M. Schneiders, "The Contemporary Ministry of Spiritual Direction," *Chicago Studies*, 15 (Spring 1976), 131–33; Matthias Neuman, "Letter to a Beginning Spiritual Director," *Review for Religious*, 37 (November 1973), 883.

3. A systematic demonstration of modern psychology's contribution to spiritual direction may be seen in F. W. Kimper's, "A Psychological Analysis of the Spiritual Direction Given by Saint Francis of Sales" (Ph. D. dissertation, Boston University, 1956).

4. Cameli, *Spiritual Direction*, p. 14.

5. This article is based on my doctoral dissertation, "Toward a Model of Spiritual Direction Based on the Writings of Saint John of the Cross and Carl R. Rogers: An Exploratory Study" (Ph. D. dissertation, Boston University, 1979). I am particularly indebted to Professors Orlo Strunk, Jr., and Judson D. Howard of Boston University for their guidance throughout the course of this research.

6. St John wrote his major treatises — *The Ascent of Mount Carmel, The Dark Night, The Spiritual Canticle*, and *The Living Flame* — expressly for the benefit of his directees (see, for example, A, Prologue, 9; C, Prologue, 1–3; F, Title and Prologue, 1). His Letters and Minor Works derive almost entirely from his spiritual direction ministry.

7. See, for example, Bruno de Jésus-Marie, "Saint Jean de la Croix et La Psychologie Moderne," in *Les Etudes Carmélitaines: Direction Spirituelle et Psychologie* (Bruges: Desclée, De Brouwer & Cie, 1951), pp. 9–24. This article is translated into English as "Saint John of the Cross and Modern Psychology" by Jane Maddrell in William Birmingham and Joseph Cunneen eds., *Cross Currents of Psychiatry and Catholic Morality* (New York: Pantheon Books, 1964), pp. 226–43.

8. See, for example, the following: Francis X. Meehan, *Client-Centered Therapy in the Writings of Carl R. Rogers: A Theological Evaluation* (Rome: Pont. Universitas Lateranensis, 1965); Francis Colborn, "The Theology of Grace: Present Trends and Future Directions," *Theological Studies*, 31 (December 1970), 692–711; Michael R. Parisi, "Justification and the Theory of Carl Rogers," *Thought*, 48 (Winter 1973), 478–507; Howard J. Clinebell, Jr., *Basic Types of Pastoral Counseling* (Nashville & New York: Abingdon Press, 1966), pp. 27–40, 273–75; Thomas C. Oden, *Kerygma and Counseling: Toward a Covenant Ontology for Secular Psychotherapy* (Philadelphia: Westminster Press, 1966); Joseph MacAvoy, "Direction Spirituelle et Psychologie," in *Dictionnaire de*

Spiritualité, s.v. "Direction Spirituelle," Vol. III, cols. 1156–1173; Eugene C. Kennedy, "Counseling and Spiritual Direction," The Catholic Theological Society of America, *Proceedings of the Eighteenth Annual Convention* (Yonkers, NY: St Joseph's Seminary, 1964), 119–20; Pietro Brocardo, *Direzione Spirituale e Rendiconto* (Rome: Libreria Editrice Salesiana, 1966), pp. 109–112.

9. Juan de Jesús María, "El Díptico Subida-Noche," in *Sanjuanistica*, (Rome: Collegium Internationale Sanctorum Teresiae a Jesu et Joannis a Cruce, 1943), pp. 27–83. See also the "Introduction to *The Ascent of Mount Carmel — The Dark Night*" in *The Collected Works of Saint John of the Cross*, trans. Kieran Kavanaugh and Otilio Rodriguez, with Introductions by Kieran Kavanaugh (Washington: ICS Publications, 1973), pp. 43–64. References to Saint John in this article are to the Kavanaugh & Rodriguez translation unless noted otherwise.

10. A, Title, p. 68.

11. In Sigmund Koch ed., *Psychology: A Study of a Science, III, Formulations of the Person and the Social Context* (New York: McGraw-Hill, 1959), pp. 184–256.

12. In Alfred M. Freedman, Harold I. Kaplan, and Benjamin J. Sadock eds. *Comprehensive Textbook of Psychiatry-II*, 2nd ed., II (Baltimore: Williams & Wilkins Co., 1975), pp. 1831–43.

13. Other discussions of St John's theory and practice of spiritual direction may be seen in the following: Aurelio del Pino Gómez, "San Juan de la Cruz: Director Espiritual," *Revista de Espiritualidad*, 1 (Julio-Diciembre 1942), 389–410; Gabriel of St. Mary Magdalen, *The Spiritual Director According to the Principles of St John of the Cross*, trans. Benedictine of Stanbrook Abbey (Westminster, MD: Newman Press, 1951); Lucien-Marie de Saint-Joseph, "La Direction Spirituelle d'après Saint Jean de la Croix," in *Les Etudes Carméli-taines: Direction Spirituelle et Psychologie*, 173–204; Gabriel de Sainte-Marie-Madeleine, "L'Esprit-Saint et L'Eglise Visible dans la Direction Spirituelle," *Ephemerides Carmeliticae*, 5 (1951–54), 70–90; Marco di Gesù Nazareno, "Principi di Direzione Spirituale in S. Giovanni della Croce," *Revista di Vita Spirituale*, 14 (Ottobre-Dicembre 1960), 414–38; Olivier Leroy, "Quelques Traits de Saint Jean de la Croix comme Maitre Spirituel," *Carmelus*, 11 (1964), 3–43; José Vicente Rodriquez, "Magisterio Oral de San Juan de la Cruz," *Revista de Espiritualidad*, 33 (Enero-Marzo 1974), 109–24; Elisabeth Krakau, "Johannes vom Kreuz als Seelenführer: Seine Lehre den 'Dunklen Nächten,'" *Christliche Innerlichkeit*, 13 (1978), 13–23, 83–96, 161–73, 221–28, 280–86; 14 (1979), 30–34; Joel Giallanza, "Spiritual Direction according to St. John of the Cross," *Contemplative Review*, 11 (Fall, 1978), 31–37.

14. This method of deriving theories through analysis and synthesis is taken from biblical theology. See David Michael Stanley, *Christ's Resurrection in Pauline Soteriology* (Rome: Pontificio Instituto Biblico, 1961), pp. 2–4; John L. McKenzie, "Problems of Hermeneutics in Roman Catholic Exegesis," *Journal of Biblical Literature*, 77 (1958), 199; R.A.F. MacKenzie, "The Concept of Biblical Theology," The Catholic Theological Society of America, *Proceedings of Tenth Annual Convention* (New York: n.p., 1955), p. 65.

15. A, Prologue, 3; A, 1, 5, 2&8; 13, 1; A, 2, 7, 1-12: 12, 6-8; 16,4; 17, 1-9; 19, 3; 22, 5-9; 29, 1-2&6-7&11; 30, 3-4; A, 3, 2, 7-12; 13, 2-4; 23, 2-4; 35, 5; 36, 3; 42, 1-6; N, 1, 1, 1-2; 6, 5; 7, 5; 8, 3; 9, 9; 11, 3; 13, 3; 14, 5-6; N,2, 7, 3-4; 16, 8; 17, 2; 25, 2; See C, 1, 6-7; 35, 5; F, 3, 28-33, 44-46, 54, 57, 61-62.

16. A, Title, Theme, & Prologue, 1-3; A, 1, 2, 4; 5, 2; 11, 2&6. A, 2, 5, 1-8; 6, 1; 16, 15; 17, 1; A, 3, 1, 1; 2, 8-9&16; 13, 5; 16, 3; 26, 5-6; N, Title & Prologue, N, 1, 1, 1; 3, 3; 11, 4; N, 2, 2, 1-2; 3, 3; 5, 1; 6, 5; 9, 3-4&9-10; 10, 1-10; 12, 6; 13, 10-11; 16, 10; 18, 4; 29, 4; 21, 11-12; 22, 1; See C, 11, 11-14; C, 20&21, 1-19; F, 3, 24&29.

17. A, Prologue, 2; A, 1, 13, 3-4; A, 2, 5, 10; 7, 4-12; 17, 2-3&8; 21, 2-4; 22, 5-8&13-15; 24, 6; 27, 6; A, 3, 23, 2; 36, 3; 39, 2; 44, 4; N, 1, Explanation, 1; N, 1, 1, 1-2; 8, 1; 10, 2-6; 12, 1-4; 13-10; N, 2, 1, 1; 3, 3; 5, 1-4; 7, 3; 13, 11; 14, 1-3; 16, 7-8; 17, 2&8; 23, 1-3&11-13; 25, 2. See C, 13, 10; C, 14&15, 2&5&14-21&26-27; C, 25, 5; F, 3, 25, 32-34, 44, 49, 54, 59, 62, 65-67; *Sayings of Light and Love*, 19&41.

18. A, Title; A, Prologue, 3-9; A, 2, 4, 1-4; 7, 13; 12, 8-9; 17, 4-5; 18, 2-6; 19, 5&7; 20, 3; 21, 4; 22, 7-19; 26, 18; 30, 5-6; A, 3, 15, 1-2; 24, 4; 36, 5; 39, 1-3; N, 2, 18, 5; 25, 4. See C, 1, 11-12; F, 3, 29-62; *Sayings of Light and Love*, 5-11; *Letters* 10&19 to Juana de Pedraza.

19. A, Prologue, 3-7; A, 1, 12, 6; A, 2, 4, 1-7; 8, 5-7; 10, 1-4; 22, 7&12&19; 23, 1&4; 24, 4; 28, 1; A, 3, 1, 1; 2, 2-4&13-16; 16, 1-6; N, 1, Explanation, 1-2; N, 1, 1, 1; N, 2, 1, 1; 3, 3; 16, 14. See C, 1, 21; C, 2, 3; 6, 4; 14&15, 4-5; F, 3, 18-23, 38-43, 46-47, 55&62.

20. In his original Spanish, John seldom uses the term "spiritual director" (*director espiritual*), an interesting fact in view of today's discussion about the most suitable terminology for the ministry traditionally referred to as spiritual direction. See Adrian van Kaam, "Religious Anthropology—Religious Counseling," *Insight*, 4 (Winter 1966), 1-3; Larkin, "Spiritual Direction Today," 204-7; Schneiders, "Contemporary Ministry of Spiritual Direction," 122-4; Cameli, *Spiritual Direction*, p. 6. The English term which probably comes closest to describing John's view of this ministry would be *spiritual guidance*. See my dissertation, pp. 216-21.

21. A, Prologue, 1-9; A, 1, 13, 1-11; A, 2, 7, 1; 9, 5; 10, 1&4; 11, 1&3; 12, 3-15, 5; 19, 11&14; 22, 5-19; 23, 4; 26, 1; 28, 1; 29, 5; 30, 5-6; A, 3, 1, 1; 15, 1-3; 16, 1-2; 17, 2; 21, 2; N, 1, 4, 7-8; 9, 1-10, 6; N, 2, 7, 3; 16, 4-7; 21, 1-12; 22, 2. See F, 3, 30-62; *Degrees of Perfection*, 1-17; *Letters*, 10, 12, 14, 15, 19, 28.

22. A, Prologue, 2; A, 2, Chs. 16&17; 19, 1-10; 20, 6; Ch. 22; A, 3, 2, 3-4; 5, 3; 12, 1-3; 13, 1-5, 1-2. See C, Prol. 1-3; F, 3, 30.

23. A, 2, 10, 1-4; 11, 6; 15, 2; 16, 10-11; 23, 1; 29, 7. See C, 14&15, 14-15; F, 3, 30-35, 44, 48-56.

24. We distinguish here between theology of the spiritual life and "mystical theology," one of John's synonyms for infused contemplation or the experiential knowledge of God acquired through love. A, Prologue, 4-5; A, 1, 12,

6-13, 11; A, 2, 6, 1-8; A, 2, 8, 6; Chs. 12-15; 17, 3-5; A, 3, 1, 1; 16, 1; N, 1, 1; N, 2, 5, 1; 12, 5; 17, 2&6; 18, 5; Chs. 19-21. See C, Prologue, 3; F, 1, 18-26; F, 3, 31, 43-53, 56. For examples of texts in the theology of spiritual life, see Joseph de Guibert, *The Theology of the Spiritual Life*, trans. Paul Barrett (New York: Sheed and Ward, 1953), and Antonio Royo and Jordan Aumann, *The Theology of Christian Perfection* (Dubuque, Iowa: Priory Press, 1962).

25. A, Prologue, 4-7; A, 1, Ch. 3; A, 2, 10, 1-4; 13, 6; 17, 3-4; A, 3, 16, 2-6; N, 1, 1, 3; 3, 2-3; 4, 2-5; 5, 1; 6, 1-3&5-6; 7, 2-5; 9, 2-3. In response to the question raised by Cameli regarding the "exact background in psychology needed for effective spiritual direction," St John of the Cross' answer would undoubtedly be that the background in psychology for a director should be substantial (see Cameli, *Spiritual Direction*, p. 15).

26. A, 1, 8, 1-7; 11, 5-6; A, 2, 16, 14; 18, 5-6; 19, 11; 20, 3; 21, 7; 22, 7-16; 26, 14&17; 29, 4; 31, 2; 32, 2; A, 3, 19, 3-4&6; 20, 2; 25, 2-6; 26, 4; N, 1, 13, 3; 14, 6. See F, 3, 30-31, 41, 53, 57-62.

27. A, 2, 5, 10-11; 17, 5; 18, 1-6; 21, 2-3; 22, 5-19; 24, 6; 26, 18; 27, 6; 30, 5; A, 3, 25, 7; N, 1, 2, 3-4&7; 4, 3&7; 6, 3-4; 7, 3; N, 2, 17, 5. See C, Prologue 2; C, 26, 7; 29, 3; F, 3, 59; *Letters* 8, 10, 15, 19.

28. A, 2, 26, 11-14; A, 3, 30, 1-5; 31, 2-9.

29. A, Prologue, 3; A, 1, Chs. 6-14; A, 2, 12, 1-5; N, 1, 1, 1-3; 2, 3-4; 3, 1-3; 4, 1-7; 6, 1-8; 7, 2-4; 8, 3. See F, 3, 32-33.

30. A, 2, 3, 1-5; N, 1, 8, 4; 9, 1-9; 10, 2-6; Chs. 12-13. See F, 3, 31-38; *Maxims on Love*, 40.

31. A, 2, 4, 4; Chs. 8&9; A, 2, 15, 1-5; Ch. 22; 23, 4; 24, 8; A, 3, 1, 1-2, 9; 15, 1-2; 16, 1-2; 17, 2; Chs. 37-44; N, 1, 1, 1; 14, 1; N, 2, 1, 1; N, 2, 3, 3. See C, 29, 1-4; *Sayings of Light and Love*, 19, 41.

32. A, Prologue, 4-5; A, 1, 1, 3; N, 2, 1, 3-5, 1; 7, 3-4; 8, 1-2; 9, 3; 12, 4, 13, 11; 17, 3-6; 18, 3-20, 6; 21, 11-12; 22, 2; 23, 3-4&11-14. See C, 6, 1-6; 8, 2; 9, 2; 12, 9; 14&15, 30; 17, 1; F, 1, 18-26.

33. A, 2, 5, 1-11; A, 2, 26, 1-10; A, 3, 14, 1-2; N, 2, 3, 3; 9, 4; 18, 4; 20, 4; 21, 2; 24, 1-4; 25, 4. John describes this state of perfect union with God in *The Spiritual Canticle*, Chs. 22-40, and throughout the entire treatise on *The Living Flame of Love*.

34. A, 1, 4, 1-6, 4; 13, 3-4; A, 2, 5, 5; 7, 1-12; 17, 8; 22, 3-8; 29, 1-2&6&11; 30, 4; A, 3, 2, 7-12; 23, 2-4; 35, 5; 36, 3; N, 2, 4, 1-2; 7, 3; 17, 2; 20, 4. See C, 1, 10; 17, 1-9; 35, 5; F, 2, 28-30; F, 3, 40-42, *Maxims on Love*, 42; *Letters* 6, 21, 22, 23.

35. John's scientific mentality and methodology are discussed in Gabriel, *The Spiritual Director*, pp. 40-66. Rogers' scientific mentality may be seen in "Therapy, Personality, and Interpersonal Relationships" and *On Becoming a Person: A Therapist's View of Psychotherapy* (Boston: Houghton Mifflin Co.; Sentry Edition, 1961), pp. 199-224.

36. See, for example, A, 2, 4, 5; A, 3, 21, 1; 24, 4; 28, 8; 38, 2; N, 2, 18, 4; C, 9, 5.

37. "Client-Centered Psychotherapy," p. 1838.

38. *On Becoming a Person*, pp. 23–24; "Toward a Modern Approach to Values: The Valuing Process in the Mature Person," in C. R. Rogers and Barry Stevens, *Person to Person: The Problem of Being Human* (Lafayette, California: Real People Press, 1967), pp. 13–28.

39. A, Prologue, 1–2; C, Prologue, 4; F, Prologue, 1.

40. "Therapy, Personality, and Interpersonal Relationships," pp. 192–94; "Client-Centered Psychotherapy," pp. 1842–43.

41. Carl R. Rogers, "Some New Challenges," *American Psychologist*, 28 (May 1973), 385–86.

42. In my analysis, I also draw from Rogers' other writings to illuminate the theories expressed in these two articles. These other references will be cited in the footnotes.

43. "Therapy, Personality and Interpersonal Relationships," p. 196.

44. "Client-Centered Psychotherapy," p. 1838.

45. *Ibid.*

46. "Therapy, Personality, and Interpersonal Relationships," p. 200.

47. See A, Prologue, 3–6.

48. "Therapy, Personality, and Interpersonal Relationship," pp. 196–97; "Client-Centered Psychotherapy," p. 1838. See also the following works by Rogers: *On Becoming a Person*, pp. 31–33; *Client-Centered Therapy: Its Current Practice, Implications, and Theory* (Boston: Houghton Mifflin Co., 1951), pp. 19–64; "The Actualizing Tendency in Relation to 'Motives' and to Consciousness," in *Nebraska Symposium on Motivation, 1963* ed. Marshall Jones (Lincoln, Neb.: University of Nebraska Press, 1963), pp. 1–24; "The Formative Tendency," *Journal of Humanistic Psychology* 18, (Winter 1978), 23–26.

49. See A, 2, Chs. 17, 21, 22.

50. "Therapy, Personality, and Interpersonal Relationships," pp. 212–21; see "The Actualizing Tendency," pp. 1–24.

51. See A, 3, 16, 6; 20, 1–4; 23, 1–6; 26, 5–7; 29, 2–5; 32, 1–4; N, 2, 4, 1–2; N, 2, 8, 5; 9, 1–5; 11, 3–4; 13, 11; 14, 2–3; 16, 10; 22, 1.

52. "Therapy, Personality, and Interpersonal Relationships," p. 234.

53. "Client-Centered Psychotherapy," p. 1836.

54. "Therapy, Personality, and Interpersonal Relationships," pp. 234–35; "Client-Centered Psychotherapy," p. 1839; see *On Becoming a Person*, pp. 163–96; Carl R. Rogers, *Freedom to Learn: A View of What Education Might Become* (Columbus, Ohio: Charles E. Merrill Publishing Co., 1969), pp. 279–97.

55. For example, see A, 3, Chs. 16–45.

56. "Therapy, Personality, and Interpersonal Relationships," pp. 203–7; "Client-Centered Psychotherapy," pp. 1838–39.

57. "Therapy, Personality, and Interpersonal Relationships," p. 220. In John, see A, 3, 16, 4 for an example of his statement of a functional relationship.

58. See A, 1, Chs. 6–12; A, 2, Chs. 11&12; A, 3, Chs. 4&10; N, 1, Chs.

2-7; N, 2, Ch. 23.

59. "Therapy, Personality, and Interpersonal Relationships," p. 203.

60. A, 1, 10, 4.

61. A, 1, 12, 6.

62. Kavanaugh, "Introduction to the *Ascent-Dark Night*" in *Collected Works*, pp. 48-50.

63. N, 1, 2, 5.

64. "Therapy, Personality, and Interpersonal Relationships," p. 221.

65. See *supra*, pp. 99-100.

66. "Therapy, Personality, and Interpersonal Relationships," pp. 197-200; "Client-Centered Psychotherapy," p. 1838.

67. "Therapy, Personality, and Interpersonal Relationships," p. 203; "Client-Centered Psychotherapy," pp. 1838-39.

68. Mt. 16:24-26; Mk. 8:33-34; Lk. 9:23-26; Jn. 12:23-25.

69. See, for example, A, 2, Ch. 7; N, 2, 18, 4.

70. See, for example, the following: "Self-denial," *Catholic Biblical Encyclopedia: New Testament*, eds. John E. Steinmuller and Kathryn Sullivan (New York: Joseph F. Wagner, 1950), p. 582; William F. Arndt and F. Wilbur Gingrich, *A Greek-English Lexicon of the New Testament and Other Early Literature* (Chicago: University of Chicago Press, 1957), pp. 80, 211, 524, 805 & 901-902; R. S. Barbour, "Self-Surrender," in *Dictionary of the Bible*, ed. James Hastings and rev. by Frederick C. Grant and H. H. Rowley (New York: Charles Scribner's Sons, 1963), p. 895; J. O. Hannay, "Self-Denial," in *Dictionary of the New Testament*, ed. James Hastings, Vol. II (Grand Rapids, Michigan: Baker Book House, 1973), pp. 598-99; Robert Koch, "Self-denial," in *Sacramentum Verbi: An Encyclopedia of Biblical Theology*, ed. Johannes Bauer, Vol. III (New York: Herder and Herder, 1970), pp. 833-39; R. L. Scheef, Jr., "Self-denial," in *The Interpreter's Dictionary of the Bible: An Illustrated Encyclopedia*, ed. G. A. Buttrick et al., Vol. IV (New York: Abingdon Press, 1962), p. 268; Bruce Vawter; *The Four Gospels: An Introduction* (Garden City, New York: Doubleday and Co., 1967), pp. 200, 304-5.

71. See *supra*, pp. 99-100.

72. "Therapy, Personality, and Interpersonal Relationships," pp. 192-94; "Client-Centered Psychotherapy," pp. 1832-33.

73. "Therapy, Personality, and Interpersonal Relationships," pp. 213-15; "Client-Centered Psychotherapy," pp. 1835-36; Carl R. Rogers, "The Interpersonal Relationship: The Core of Guidance," in *Person to Person*, pp. 90-92.

74. "Therapy, Personality, and Interpersonal Relationships," pp. 208-9; "Client-Centered Psychotherapy," pp. 1834-35; "The Interpersonal Relationship," pp. 94-96.

75. "Therapy, Personality, and Interpersonal Relationships," pp. 210-11; "Client-Centered Psychotherapy," pp. 1833-34; "The Interpersonal Relationship," pp. 92-94; Carl R. Rogers, "Empathic: An Unappreciated Way of Being," *The Counseling Psychologist*, 5 (1975), 2-10.

76. "Therapy, Personality, and Interpersonal Relationships," pp. 213-215;

"The Interpersonal Relationship," p. 92.

77. "Theory of Therapy, Personality, and Interpersonal Relationships," pp. 213–15; "Client-Centered Psychotherapy," p. 1839.

78. "Therapy, Personality, and Interpersonal Relationships," pp. 216–17; "Client-Centered Psychotherapy," p. 1839.

79. "Therapy, Personality, and Interpersonal Relationships," pp. 218–20; "Client-Centered Psychotherapy," p. 1839.

80. "Therapy, Personality, and Interpersonal Relationships," pp. 212, 217, 220; "Client-Centered Psychotherapy," p. 1838.

81. "The Interpersonal Relationship," p. 89.

82. N, 2, 7, 3.

83. A, Prologue, 5.

84. N, 2, 7, 3.

85. N, 2, 17, 2–5.

86. "Client-Centered Psychotherapy," pp. 1833–34; "The Interpersonal Relationship," p. 93.

87. "Empathic: An Unappreciated Way of Being," pp. 2–9. For a discussion of the director as a companion, see James G. McCready, "Spiritual Direction As Pilgrim and Companion," *Review for Religious*, 36 (May 1977), 425–33.

88. See *supra*, pp. 99–100.

89. See *supra*, p. 103.

90. See *supra*, p. 100. See also A, 2, 22, 19; N, 1, 2, 3.

91. See *supra*, p. 103.

92. See *supra*, pp. 102–04.

93. "The Interpersonal Relationship," pp. 89–90.

94. "Therapy, Personality, and Interpersonal Relationships," pp. 212–20; "Client-Centered Psychotherapy," p. 1839.

95. See *supra*, p. 100. See also, A, 1, Chs. 6–12; A, 2, 4, 4; 10, 1–4; A, 3, 16, 1–6; N, 1, 7, 1; 9, 1–9; 13, 10; N, 2, 7, 7; 16, 3.

96. "Therapy, Personality, and Interpersonal Relationships," p. 197.

97. *Ibid.*

98. *Ibid.*, pp. 197–98; "Client-Centered Psychotherapy," pp. 1838–39.

99. "Therapy, Personality, and Interpersonal Relationships," p. 198.

100. "Client-Centered Psychotherapy," p. 1839.

101. "Toward a Modern Approach to Values," pp. 13–28.

102. A, Prologue, 2; C, Prologue, 4; F, Prologue, 1.

103. A, 2, 17, 4.

104. For example, see N, 2, 7, 7.

105. For example, see C, 7, 9–10.

106. "The Actualizing Tendency," p. 18.

107. "Empathic: An Unappreciated Way of Being," pp. 2–10.

108. For example, see A, 2, 4, 1–4; 21, 4; N, 2, 16, 12.

109. *Freedom To Learn*, pp. 290–91; "Toward a Modern Approach to Values," pp. 23–28.

110. "The Actualizing Tendency," p. 20. For a discussion of the need to rein-

terpret the negative and pessimistic aspects of John's ascetical doctrine, see Marilyn May Mallory, *Christian Mysticism: Transcending Techniques* (Amsterdam: Van Gorcum Assen, 1977), pp. 3–10, 20–22, 299–300.

111. A, 1, 10, 4.

112. "The Sketch of Mount Carmel," in Kavanaugh and Rodriguez, *Collected Works*, pp. 66–67.

113. N, 1, 1, 1; N, 2, 3, 1; 6, 4–5; 8, 5; 9, 1; 10, 2; 11, 3–4; 16, 10. See also C, theme, 1–2; C, 28, 7; 29, 7–8. See *supra*, pp. 100–101, 108–109.

114. "Therapy, Personality, and Interpersonal Relationships," pp. 203–7.

115. "Client-Centered Psychotherapy," p. 1836.

116. *Ibid.*, pp. 1836–38; *Freedom to Learn*, pp. 289–90.

117. *On Becoming a Person*, pp. 163–182.

118. Don Goergen, *The Christian Counselor: A Guide to the Art of Spiritual Direction*, tape 2: *Types of Spiritual Direction* (Kansas City, Mo.: NCR Cassettes, n.d.).

119. N, 1, 12, 2–6; N, 2, 5, 5: see also F, 1, 19–21.

120. A, 3, 2, 3.

121. *On Becoming a Person*, pp. 125–59; "Client-Centered Psychotherapy," pp. 1836–38.

122. Rogers' approach to the selection and training of counselors and psychotherapists may be seen in his following writings: *Counseling and Psychotherapy: Newer Concepts in Practice* (Boston: Houghton Mifflin Co., 1942), pp. 253–58; *Client-Centered Therapy*, p. 429–78; *On Becoming a Person*, pp. 273–313; *Freedom to Learn*, pp. 101–202; *Carl Rogers on Encounter Groups* (New York: Harper & Row, 1970), pp. 149–57; *Carl Rogers on Personal Power: Inner Strength and Its Revolutionary Impact* (New York: Dell Publishing Co.; A Delta Book, 1977), pp. 69–89; "The Interpersonal Relationship," pp. 102–3; "Client-Centered Psychotherapy," pp. 1832–33, 1842–43.

123. Approaches to selection and training of persons in spiritual direction may be seen in Mauricio Iriciarte, "Una Gran Preocupación de San Juan de la Cruz: la Formación de Los Directores Espirituales," *Manresa*, 3 (1942), 302–18; Van Kaam, "Religious Anthropology-Religious Counseling," pp. 1–7; Norbert C. Brockman, "Spiritual Direction: Training and Charisma," *Sisters Today*, 48 (October 1976), 104–9; William A. Barry, "The Centre for Religious Development: An Urban Centre of Spirituality," *The Clergy Review*, 62 (April 1977), 146–50; Barry, "The Prior Experience of Spiritual Directors," *Spiritual Life*, 23 (Summer, 1977), 84–89; William A. Barry and Mary C. Guy, "The Practice of Supervision in Spiritual Direction," *Review for Religious*, 37 (November 1978), 834–42. For an evaluative review of current training possibilities in spiritual direction see Alfred C. Hughes, *A Report on Some Centers Offering Professional Training in Spiritual Formation* (Brighton, Mass.: St. John's Seminary, n.d.); Religious Formation Conference, "Resources for Personal Growth in Spirituality, Giving Spiritual Direction and Giving Retreats," (Washington D.C., February, 1977).

124. "Client-Centered Psychotherapy," p. 1841. Rogers' approach to research

in counseling and psychotherapy may be seen in the following works: Carl R. Rogers and Rosalind F. Dymond eds., *Psychotherapy and Personality Change: Coordinated Research Studies in the Client-Centered Approach* (Chicago: University of Chicago Press, 1954); Carl R. Rogers et al., *The Therapeutic Relationship and Its Impact: A Study of Psychotherapy with Schizophrenics* (Madison, Wis.: University of Wisconsin Press, 1967); *On Becoming a Person*, pp. 197–270; *Carl Rogers on Encounter Groups*, pp. 117–34; Carl R. Rogers, "A Tentative Scale for the Measurement of Process in Psychotherapy," in *Research in Psychotherapy* eds. Eli A. Rubenstein and Morris B. Parloff (Washington D.C.: American Psychological Association, 1962), pp. 96–107; Carl R. Rogers, "A Study of Psychotherapeutic Change in Schizophrenics and Normals: Design and Instrumentation," *Psychiatric Research Reports*, 15 (April 1962), 51–60; "Therapy, Personality, and Interpersonal Relationships," pp. 184–256.

125. See, for example, American Psychological Association, *Research in Psychotherapy*, 3 vols. (Washington, D.C.: American Psychological Association, 1962–68); Louis A. Gottschalk and Arthur H. Auerbach eds., *Methods of Research in Psychotherapy* (New York: Appleton-Century-Crofts, 1966); Edward S. Bordin, *Research Strategies in Psychotherapy* (New York: John Wiley & Sons, 1974).

126. Van Kaam, "Religious Anthropology—Religious Counseling," pp. 4–7; Barry, "Centre for Religious Development," pp. 146–50.

127. For example, see Gregory I. Carlson, "Spiritual Direction and the Paschal Mystery," *Review for Religious*, 33 (May 1974), 532–41; William Walsh, "Reality Therapy and Spiritual Direction," *Review for Religious*, 35 (1976), 372–85; William J. Connolly, "Noticing Key Interior Facts in the Early Stages of Spiritual Direction," *Review for Religious*, 35 (January 1976), 112–21. Barry and his associates use an empirical approach to spiritual direction, doing research "based on reflection on present experience [in spiritual direction] and on the study of the tradition." (William A. Barry, "Centre for Religious Development," pp. 146; see also, "Spiritual Direction: the Empirical Approach," *America*, April 24, 1976, pp. 356–58). However, they report no controlled empirical studies. For an example of spiritual direction research employing statistical evaluation of questionnaire data, see Henry J. Simoneaux, *Spiritual Guidance and the Varieties of Character* (New York: Pageant Press, 1956).

128. See, for example, De Guibert, *Theology of the Spiritual Life*; Reginald Garrigou-Lagrange, *The Three Ages of the Interior Life: Prelude of Eternal Life*, 2 vols., trans. M. Timothea Doyle (St Louis: B. Herder Book Co., 1948); Royo and Aumann, *Theology of Christian Perfection*. St John's observations have also influenced modern psychological writing as may be seen in Roberto Assagioli, *Psychosynthesis: A Manual of Principles and Techniques* (New York: Viking Press; Compass Edition, 1965), pp. 47–48.

129. *On Becoming a Person*, pp. 24–25.

130. Carl R. Rogers, "Toward a Science of the Person," in *Behaviorism and Phenomenology: Contrasting Bases for Modern Psychology*, ed. T. W. Wann (Chi-

cago: University of Chicago Press; Phoenix Books, 1964), pp. 109-40. See also "Therapy, Personality, and Interpersonal Relationships," pp. 210-12; *On Becoming a Person*, pp. 199-224.

131. John H. Wright, "Is There an American Theology?" *Communio: International Catholic Review*, 3 (Summer 1976), 138.

132. See *supra*, pp. 115-20.

133. Barry and his colleagues, using an empirical approach to spiritual direction, have discovered the following when systematically asking the question, "What happens when people pray?": (a) the importance of a contemplative attitude "as the necessary prelude to the kind of prayer that leads to a deeper relationship with the Lord;" (b) the directee gradually becomes more real before God and God becomes more real for the directee; and (c) a heightened (rather than diminished) social consciousness in directees. These discoveries emerging from the spiritual direction relationship are crucially significant for a modern theology of prayer. See Barry, "Spiritual Direction: the Empirical Approach," pp. 356-58, and "Centre for Religious Development," pp. 146-47.

134. Findings flowing from the interpersonal relationship of spiritual direction are especially relevant to developments in the theology of grace which concerns itself specifically with our relationship with God and which today, without rejecting earlier metaphysical categories, is attempting to formulate this relationship more in personalistic, phenomenological and psychological terms, often drawing analogies from the work of American psychologists such as Rollo May, Abraham Maslow, and Carl Rogers. See Francis Colborn, "The Theology of Grace," pp. 692-711.

135. Spiritual Direction, which frequently involves persons in the process of free choice, responsible decision-making and discerning God's will, can be a rich source of data for theologians who are today attempting to reformulate the theology of divine providence in the light of new biblical interpretations, modern scientific attitudes and a historical consciousness that views history not simply as "the context for Christian experience," but also as "the process of men and women working out their destiny in interaction with the divine saving presence. . . . the progressive creation of humanity by men and women whose freedom is a decisive input into the unfolding of the future." See Bernard J. Cooke, 'American Catholic Theology," *Commonweal*, August 18, 1978, 520-24.

136. "Some New Challenges," pp. 385.

137. *Ibid.*, 386.

138. John sees the human person as both sense (*el sentido*) and spirit (*el espíritu*). "Sense" in John corresponds roughly to those areas of human life most often treated in modern psychology, while "spirit" corresponds more to the other "reality" to which Rogers refers above. While John recognizes the importance of "sense," the primary focus in his writings is upon "spirit," the other reality.

139. There is already a growing psychological literature in these areas. See, for example, Robert E. Ornstein, *The Psychology of Consciousness* (New York:

Viking Press, 1972); Robert E. Ornstein ed., *The Nature of Human Consciousness: A Book of Readings* (New York: Viking Press, 1973); Kenneth S. Pope and Jerode L. Singer, *The Stream of Consciousness: Scientific Investigations into the Flow of Human Experience* (New York: Plenum Publishing Co., 1978); Gary E. Schwartz and David Shapiro eds., *Consciousness and Self-Regulation: Advances in Research and Theory*, 2 vols. (New York: Plenum Publishing Co., 1976&1978); Richard B. Stuart ed., *Behavioral Self-Management: Strategies, Techniques and Outcome* (New York: Brunner/Mazel, 1977); Claudio Naranjo and Robert E. Ornstein, *On the Psychology of Meditation* (New York: Viking Press, 1971); William Johnston, *Silent Music: The Science of Meditation* (New York: Harper and Row, 1974); Herbert Benson, *The Relaxation Response* (New York: William Morrow & Co., 1976).

140. "Some New Challenges," p. 386.

141. Because St John's entire theory of spiritual direction appears to be contained in principle in the *Ascent-Dark Night*, it is predictable now that the results of the analysis and synthesis of spiritual direction in his other writings will further elaborate rather than substantially change the theory of spiritual direction presented here.

142. Since the heart of Rogers' clinical and scientific work is expressed in the two articles we have examined, it is predictable now that a heuristic analysis of all his writings will supplement and expand, rather than substantially change, the major areas of future research already spelled out in this article.

143. David Fleming, "Models of Spiritual Direction," pp. 351–57. The model emerging from this dissertation contains many elements of both the interpersonal and incarnational models of spiritual direction described by Fleming. While Fleming's interpersonal model is built upon the notion of spiritual friendship, mine rests more upon the helping relationship as understood in the therapeutic professions today.

144. "Therapy, Personality, and Interpersonal Relationships," pp. 188–92, 244, 249–52.

145. Our research suggests both the importance of psychology for spiritual directors and a method for exploring the relationship between psychology and spirituality. See Cameli, *Spiritual Direction for Priests*, p. 15.

146. For examples of other theories of spiritual direction, see Kimper, "A Psychological Analysis of the Spiritual Direction Given by Saint Francis of Sales;" Cirillo Di Rienzo, *La Direzione Spirituale negli Scritti di S. Teresa d'Avila* (Rome: Teresianum, 1965); Gerald Dennis Coleman, "Religious Experience as Guide of Spiritual Living: A Study in Ignatius of Loyola and Karl Rahner, His Interpreter" (Ph. D. dissertation, University of St.Michael's College, Canada, 1974); T. K. Johnson, "The Spiritual Dialogue: Some Insights from the Practice of Spiritual Direction" (Th. D. dissertation, Pontificia Universitas Gregoriana, Rome, 1977); William A. Sutton, "An Exposition of St. Alphonsus Liguori's Doctrine on Spiritual Direction (S.T.D. dissertation, Pontificia Studiorum Universitas a S. Thomas Aquinate, Rome, 1978).

A JUNGIAN APPROACH
TO FORGETTING
AND MEMORY
IN ST JOHN OF THE CROSS

Russell Holmes, O.C.D.

Father Russell Holmes has the Diploma from the Jungian Institute in Zurich, Switzerland. He now is applying his studies there to his work as a Jungian Analyst in Boston.

INTRODUCTION

> . . . I grew
> Uncultivated and now the soil
>   turns sour,
> Needs to be revived by a power
>   not my own.
> Heroes enormous who
> do outstanding deeds —
> Out of this world
>
> Patrick Kavanaugh, *A Personal Problem*

This article represents an attempt to relate the spirituality of St John of the Cross and the psychology of C. G. Jung in an area that is important to both: forgetting and memory.

This study may be of interest to contemporary spiritual theologians and psychologists, and an invitation to further study and research in the area of spirituality and psychology. Hopefully, it will affirm the reality of inner experience whether this be at the hour of prayer or at the hour of therapy.

Contained here is a brief summary of St John's works and a comparative study of the personalities of St John and C. G. Jung structured after Jung's theory of psychological typology and attitude.

Finally, there is the subject of forgetting and memory, amplified as an archetype,[1] a component of the human psyche. The final part of this article deals with forgetting and memory in the mystical tradition of Greek Religion and in the Christian spirituality of John of the Cross.

THE WORKS OF ST JOHN OF THE CROSS

> the obscure reveries
> of an inward gaze
>
> Ezra Pound, *Hugh Selwyn Mauberley*[2]

The writings of St John of the Cross comprise approximately twenty poems and ballads and three major treatises on mystical theology. The treatises are attached to and flow from three major poems as commentaries on them; they bear the titles of the poems and are: *The Ascent of Mount Carmel — Dark Night/Noche oscura*; *The Spiritual Canticle/Cantico espiritual*; and *The Living Flame of Love/Oh llama de amor viva!*

His poetry is most original yet he wrote eclectically and derivatively from Spanish, Portugese and Hebrew sources. The best known mystics of the Iberian Peninsula, as distinguished from their German counterparts, such as Eckhardt, Tauler and a Kempis, were important literary as well as religious figures. Among these were Judah Halevi, 1085–1140; Ibn Arabi, 1165–1240; Raimondo Lulli, 1233–1315; and St John's contemporaries, Luis de Leon and Teresa of Avila. Lulli is the author of the famous poem, *Cantico del amigo del amado*, which is similar to John's *Cantico* in that the common imagery which they use shows the rich sensual nature of the Arabic style. Another important source of mystical-literary authors of Spain was Jewish mysticism, a key document being *Dialogui d'amore*, 1535, of Leon Hebreo. The book is Neoplatonic in nature, and reveals the thoughts of Ben-Gabriel, Maimonides and the *Cabala*; it is a philosophy of love as a means to union with God.

Spanish literature of the sixteenth century derived a great deal also from beyond its borders, from Neoplatonism, Indian Brahminism and Persian Sufism. But all the literature is perhaps most revealing of Platonic philosophy from which its fundamental motives are drawn. For example, Plato's basic separation of mind from matter, his concept of the immortality of the soul (*Phaedo*), of human love (*Symposium*), of the various levels of cognition (the divided line concept in the *Republic*), and the oneness of absolute truth, beauty and good, which one may attain only through powers above the level of reason — all these are primary assumptions of the mystic. Plato also made clear that a knowledge of absolutes can never be fully conveyed even in dialogues; he uses the allegory of the cave as a useful method of suggesting the ineffable; the stunning and blinding lights of the sun's illumination, he claims, cannot be fully explained: to know it, one must have experienced it.

The difference between St John's poetry and that of a number of his religious poetic contemporaries is this: where many of them recast images *a lo divino*, rendering convoluted Christian messages, he does not. His images are left as they originated, in archetypal form, below and for the most part unhampered by the collective religious tradition to which he belonged. This symbolic purity may be the reason for his poetry's universal appeal. As such, his poems have deep meaning for human lovers, for the prayerful and for the analytical psychologist, as they are the expression of the dynamic organs of the human soul and concentrate on the fundamental process of rebirth of the soul through the union of opposites.

In terms of Jung's observation on poetry, we may apply both his categories of extroverted "naive" and introverted "sentimental" to St John's poetry. In the former instance John was moved by the creative force, as a subject reacting to the poetic archetypal urge, with his consciousness not being identified with the creative process.[3] This is obvious from the purity of the archetypal motifs, as well as their being completely opposed to St John's conscious mystical theology which demands total *mortificatio* of the sensory parts of the soul:[4] it is the death of the conscious standpoint which leads to life in the unsconscious at the beginning of the "ascent of the mount," and affirms the reality of the transcendent or spiritual life.

In the instance of introverted "sentimental" poetic form, we know that St John worked on his poetry, so this category can also be applied to his major poems without its losing archtypal quality. When a nun asked him if the words of the *Spiritual Canticle* were given to him by God, he answered: "Sometimes God gave them to me; at other times I looked for them myself."[5] The difference between the clearly cut naive and sentimental products is easily noticeable in the poem, *I Entered into Unknowing/ Entréme donde no supe*, a poem he wrote after an ecstasy and a lovely poem for sure, but one without the timbre of the "naive" *Noche oscura* or *Llama de amor viva*.

In the context of Jungian psychology, St John's poetry demonstrates a decisive relationship with the archetypes of the collective unconscious, and the exercise of active imagination. Though it may be argued that he insisted in his mystical theology on the mortification of the imagination, seen in the proper perspective, this component of his teaching is understandable.[6] Whereas modern man needs prodding in the use of his imagination or "imagining" in James Hillman's terms, this was hardly the case for the sixteenth century Christian; the sixteenth century imagination was, especially in religious matters, untamed. For example, there was at the time of St John a nun in Lisbon, Maria de la Visitación, a young and beautiful woman who was said to have miraculous powers. In rapture she was surrounded by lights, she healed the sick and finally developed the stigmata. All were convinced of her genuineness to a degree that, when the Armada set sail, it passed her convent so she could bless it. Contrary to all opinions, John of the Cross thought she was a fraud while his confreres were quite taken up with her and held pieces of cloth stained with her blood. A few years later John was vindicated when it was discovered that her "wounds" were painted on and washed off quite easily.[7] The purification of the imagination prescribed by St John was for such cases and there were many like the religious mysteries — especially those of the suffering of Christ — which were highly constellated.[8] In his profession as spiritual guide, St John would have to make means available for curbing the passive imaginations of the souls in his care in the same sense that Luther criticized the abuse of relics and religious symbols. In both cases, there was an attempt to direct souls to inner reality and away from clinging to the externals of a very cluttered Christianity. But by the same token, John appreciated and approved the use of religious symbols; his poetry is filled with them.[9]

John of the Cross wrote the commentaries on his poems for friends who inquired into the meaning of the verses. They were written between 1578 and 1591, the last fourteen years of his life, between his thirty-fifth and forty-ninth years. From a literary point of view, the prose commentaries leave much to be desired. They are, in the main, didactic and often discursive especially in the *Ascent of Mount Carmel-Dark Night*. He made no attempt to phrase ideas gracefully, thus it is unpolished and cluttered with repetitions and ambiguities. We have the remarkable example in a recent Spanish translation of his works in which one sentence is buttressed with fifty commas, four semi-colons, two uses of parentheses and a dash. There are particular passages, however, which are outstanding for their beauty, power and originality.

The first commentary on the poem, *Ascent of Mount Carmel-Dark Night*, was written between 1579 and 1585, while John was the confessor to the Carmelite nuns at Beas. It is the longest of the commentaries and fearsome for its radical demands for motification. It was written for those "who are on the road to the high state of perfection."[10] It is not written for all "but for some who are on the path leading up this mount."[11] Accompanying this treatise is a sketch of the mount and the paths leading to the summit. The sketch is similar to Guilio Camillo's memory theater. Camillo was a contemporary of St John of the Cross.[12]

The substance of the teaching in the *Ascent-Dark Night* concerns the "active" and "passive" nights of the soul. The active night represents the soul's conscious entry into the process and subsequent efforts to be faithful to the demands made on it for the direct ascent of the mount. The passive night represents the soul's surrender to God who directs the purification process by faith in the intellect, hope in the memory and love in the will, the spiritual parts of the soul. The sensory parts of the soul include the five senses, the imagination and fantasy.

St John says that the sources of his teaching are in the sciences, experience and the Sacred Scriptures, the latter being the most important because the Holy Spirit speaks through Scripture. Considering the times in which he wrote, it was courageous of him to use the Scriptures, especially the Old Testament. This is impressive because he interprets the Scriptures symbolically and not literally. Again, men had been burned at the stake for less. His manner of amplification by the use of scriptural passages is a good example of symbolic thinking.

The process he proposes leads through the *via purgativa, via illuminativa* and to the *via unitiva*; this final "way" is for St John perfect union with God through love; it is the summit of Mount Carmel.[13] The union he speaks of is not the essential union by which God preserves his creatures in existence, but the total permanent union according to the substance of the soul and its faculties; it is a union of likeness, to the extent that, where the soul maintains its uniqueness, it "seems to be one with God." He uses the allegory of the sun shining through a window, God being the sun, the soul the window. When the window is clean, it is invisible and cannot be distinguished from the sun. The "nights" are the cleaning process.[14]

The *Spiritual Canticle* is one of St John's prison poems. He later rearranged stanzas to make them fit chronologically into his teaching and added several stanzas also.[15] He wrote this commentary in 1586 and revised it in 1589. He wrote it for Ana of Jesús, a Carmelite nun of Beas, about whom I shall say more later.

He describes the poetic experience of the *Spiritual Canticle* as being utterances of love arising from mystical understanding.[16] The tone of this commentary is markedly different from that of the *Ascent-Dark Night*. The soul is now united with her elusive lover. Here the sensory and spiritual parts of the soul are reunited in a transformed state. The *coniuntio* takes place at the deepest center of the soul in climactic waves as the bride and bridegroom flow together in the "inner wine cellar."[17] He says that it is impossible to describe the experience of the poem:

> Since these stanzas were composed in a love flowing from abundant mystical understanding I cannot explain them adequately, not that it is my intention to do so. I wish only to shed some general light on them. It is better to explain the utterances of love in their broadest sense so that each may derive profit from them according to the mode and capacity of his spirit. As a result, though we may give some explanation of these stanzas, there is no reason to be bound by this explanation.[18]

As I have suggested above, John's use of scriptural passages to amplify his poetic images is similar to Jung's amplification of dream images with mythological material. For example, commenting on the word "waters" in the *Spiritual Canticle*, he writes: "'waters' denote the emotions of sorrow which afflict the soul for they enter like water. David, referring to them, says to God, 'Salvum me fac, Deus, quoniam intraverunt aquae usque ad animam meam.'"[19] For St John, the poetic images are ineffable and need such amplifications and can be discussed only with their aid. He says that the communications of God to the soul are as "imperceptible as footprints on the water."[20] His understanding of the symbol-making process fits Jung's description of the same: "A view which interprets the symbolic expression as the best possible formulation of a relatively unknown thing, which for that reason cannot be more clearly or characteristically represented, is symbolic."[21] In this sense, John's poetic images are psychological, in that they express mystical and poetic facts which are relatively unknown, but are known to exist by the one who experiences them.

The final treatise is contained in the commentary on the poem, the *Living Flame of Love*; it was composed between 1582 and 1585. Both the poem and the commentary were written for Doña Ana de Penalosa, a Segovian widow.[22] The substance of the treatise is commentary on the stanzas of the poem which treat of the very intimate and qualified union and transformation of the soul in God.[23]

Again, John disclaims the capability of writing understandably of the experience: "understanding that everything I say is as far from reality as is a painting from the living object represented."[24]

Briefly, there is in this commentary an explanation of a number of important matters relating to the mystical experience: the cause and mode of "death" of those who have reached the transformed state; the purifying aspect of the "flame," and the spiritual gifts of God to the transformed soul. He also includes in this treatise an interesting and still applicable exhortation to the spiritual director which is surprisingly similar to Jung's comments on the analyst and his shortcomings in his essay, "The Psychology of the Transference."[25] Most importantly, St John urges the reader of his treatise not to feel that the experiences he describes are exaggerated, because God had one desire only and that is to exalt the human soul: "Since there is no way in which he can exalt her (the soul) more than by making her equal to himself, he is pleased with her love, for the property of love is to make the lover equal to the object loved."[26]

The one final "work" of St. John I would mention is his drawing of the crucified Christ, the inspiration of Dali's *Christ of St John of the Cross*. René Huyghe of the Louvre has made this comment on it:

Some people imagine that seeing is merely a matter of opening one's eyes. Seeing is a technique, a science which makes slow progress from century to century. And there is a technique in vision just as much as in execution. John of the Cross escapes right out of those visual habits by which all artists form part of their period. He knows nothing of the rules and limitations of contemporary vision and he is not dependent on the manner of seeing current in his century. He is dependent only on the object of his contemplation.[27]

ST JOHN OF THE CROSS AND C. G. JUNG: MEN OF HIGH DEGREE

> Fabled by the daughters of memory. And
> yet it was in some way if not as memory
> fabled it. A phrase then of impatience,
> thus of Blake's wings of success. I
> hear the ruin of all space, shattered
> glass and toppling masonry, and time
> one livid final flame.
>
> James Joyce, *Ulysses*[28]

In this third chapter, I should like to dwell on the high degree of consciousness and the transformation of consciousness to the transpersonal level as it is demonstrated in the lives and personalities of St John and C. G. Jung. I have taken the term, "men of high degree," from Prof. A. Peter Elkin, the Australian anthropologist, who has done extensive work and research with the Aboriginal medicine man. He defines the term in this way:

Men of high degree are those who have taken a degree beyond that taken by most adult males — a step which implies discipline, mental training, courage and perseverance. They are men of immense social significance and the psychological health of the group often depends on them. The psychologies attributed to them must not be too readily taken for primitive magic or "make-believe," for many of them have specialized on the working of the human mind and the influence of mind on body and mind on mind. The mystery of death and rising by which they

receive their knowledge includes and causes a deep psychological experience. Finally, as long as they observe the customary
disciplines of their "order," this experience continues to be a
source of faith to themselves and their fellows. In brief, men of
high degree are a channel of life.[29]

Between Jung and St John of the Cross, there is a gap of
almost three-hundred years, the Reformation and the Alps,
barriers which in St John's day might have been insuperable,
though not in C. G. Jung's and certainly not in ours. Physical-
ly, St John and Jung were very different. John was a small "half
a friar," thin, oval-faced with long aquiline nose and receding
hairline. Outstanding was his smallness which St Teresa of
Avila speaks of with frequency.[30] Until his final illness, there is
no reference to ill health in St John's life, with the exception of
residual pains suffered as a result of his prison beatings. Jung
was tall, of muscular build and, other than his accounts of his
symptomatic childhood "eczema and fainting," Jung, too, enjoyed general good health. Jung lived 86 years; John, 49.[31]

Using the Alps as a line of division between the two, John of
the Cross was on the hot, sunny, Catholic side, and though introverted, grew in a cultural setting that was strongly extroverted among countrymen who sang love songs in the street
and danced to the lively rhythm of the Andalusian Gypsies'
flamenco; in a country ruled by a neurotic Catholic king, Phillip
II.[32]

Jung's side of the Alps was considerably different, especially
in a family heavily laden with Reformed pastors, in a land of
hard-working farmers, the Rheinfalls, Fastnacht — the annual
days of extroversion; in a country that was nearly a perfect
democracy.

From the beginning of their conscious lives, both Jung and
St John loved solitude.[33] We can presume this in the life of St
John who as a young boy preferred working in the sacristy of
the church to printing and carpentry. This predilection for
quiet and aloneness must have caused him pain in the common
setting of an orphanage, and later as he worked in a busy city

hospital where the poorest of the poor came for care and to die.[34] At an early age Jung and St John would have experienced what Jung describes so well in his insight into his childhood village of Klein-Hunigen: a world of immeasurable beauty but also a world which was filled mostly with "old age and death."[35] For both men this initial awareness of suffering was a prerequisite for their respective works: St John's "dark night," and Jung's "shadow." The recognition of the shadow of conscious life for Jung led him ultimately to the shadow of God which appeared in his childhood as "terrible, vulgar and ridiculous, and also a diabolical mockery."[36] John of the Cross had recognized the same in his experience and describes it in his theology as the *spiritus blasphemiae*.[37] For Jung, this other side of God experience eventually led him outside the religious tradition of his family which he describes as falling out of the faith, the Church and everybody's faith: "I could no longer participate in the general faith but found myself involved in something inexpressible in my secret which I could share with no-one — God alone was real, an annihilating fire and an indescribable grace."[38] St John also described God in these terms, that is, as an annihilating fire, in his commentary on the poem, the *Dark Night*. Here he uses the analogy of the soul as a wooden log, God being the annihilating-transforming fire: ". . . by heating and kindling it from without, the fire transforms the wood into itself and makes it as beautiful as it is itself for it possesses the properties and performs the action of the fire . . ."[39]

The comparable exit from the established religious setting for St John was his meeting with St Teresa of Avila and his subsequent involvement in her reform. This was John's surrender to the "God alone was real" of C. G. Jung, along the lines of "annihilating fire and indescribable grace," which was the substance of his teaching and the essential component of Jung's as well.

Having established what appear to be some meaningful historical parallels in the personal myths of Jung and St John, I should like now to move to some deeper parallels. By way of introduction to the deeper levels of their souls, I cite a similar incident from their childhoods. It appears significant because it is common to both, and both remember it in detail. There was an incident in the childhood of St John which led to his memory of being rescued from a muddy pond by a person who appeared at first to be the Virgin Mary. Jung remembers a similar incident that occurred when he was saved by a maid from falling into the Rhein from a bridge. St John interprets the experience as being saved from distress, as he was from prison; Jung interprets the experience in his life as possibly a suicidal urge or resistance to life.[40] I would interpret the incident symbolically in the light of their later development. As such, it indicates an unconscious attraction they had in childhood for the inner realities, an attraction subsequently confirmed by their life work which each followed to its conclusion.

I should now like to concentrate on this work along the lines of general typology, introversion and the integration of the inferior function. One of the first and most valuable contributions Jung made to depth psychology was his psychological typology.[41] He completed this work in 1920.

There are disadvantages to applying a man's psychology to himself, and every analyst knows the difficulties and dangers of applying a rigid typology to any individual; Jung was the first to recognize this.[42] It seems constructive and important in this comparative section of my study to risk an examination of the similarity of function and attitude of the subjects, for on this basis a number of other parallels follow.

Considering their interests, relationships and works, it appears that Jung and John of the Cross can be considered introverted rational types.[43] In writing about this general category, Jung makes a number of remarks which relate to his own psychology and also to St John's mystical theology. He says that introverted rational types make their judgments (rational) on the subjective (introverted) factor. This principle is demonstrated in both their writings. Jung's psychology presents not only a very obvious subjective attitude, but the subjective factor is Jung's psychology, his way being the way of the individual.[44] In his alchemical studies his frequent citation of the "secrecy of the art" underscores the subjective attitude and the unique quality of each man's process of individuation.[45] Likewise in St John the subjective principle holds true. What he writes is not for everybody, not even for all Carmelite friars and nuns but "for certain persons whom God favors by putting them on the path leading up this mount," or for "Christians who want to attain mystical union."[46] Without disclaiming mystical understanding in general and his own soul in particular, St John leaves the way open for others to interpret their interior experiences according to their own mode and capacity. And his reverence for each person's soul and the freedom of God to act subjectively—that is, not along the lines of his teachings—is nowhere so clearly stated as when he says:

> God grants these favors of mystical union to whom he wills and for what reason he wills. For it may come to pass that a person will have performed many good works, yet that he will not give him these touches of his favor; and another will have done far fewer good works, yet he will give him them to a most sublime degree and in great abundance.[47]

Possibly supporting this attitude of John of the Cross are his numerous references to David; he could not have been unaware that David did not follow the *via negativa*.[48] Like Jung also, St John avows the "secrecy" of the whole process of the transformation of the soul:

> On that happy night—in secret;
> no one saw me through the dark—[49]

Jung writes of the misunderstanding the introvert must endure, attributing it to the general extroversion of the Western world.[50] The punishment the introvert must suffer for his compromise with extroversion, he says, is a feeling of inferiority. Neither Jung nor St John compromised, so neither suffered the sanction of inferiority. Consequently, they were and are misunderstood in terms of Prof Elkin's remark about men of high degree: "that their psychologies must not be too readily dismissed as primitive magic or 'make-believe'." Both men worked in the shadows of highly extroverted historical moments in fields of service which presumed an introverted posture, but which had become encrusted with professionalism. From men in these fields, and from men of ordinary degree in general, the sixteenth and twentieth centuries called for extreme extroversion. In the sixteenth, there was the discovery and settlement of the new world, the telescope and "universal doubt"; in the twentieth, there has been the discovery of atomic energy, outer space and existentialism.[51]

Regarding the introversion of Jung and St John, I mention it not to elicit sighs of horror at the lack of it; to do so would be to miss the whole point of Jung's psychology of attitude and the entirety of his and John of the Cross' teaching. Neither wished to squeeze extroverts into introverted molds or vice-versa. I wish merely to state that it is the gift of the introvert to live close to the subjective factor, in the personal and collective underworld so to speak, and when they are rational types, to speak of the experience to others. This is undoubtedly the charism of Jungian psychology and the mystical theology of John of the Cross. In this regard, Prof Elkin's remark concerning the men of high degree rings very true: "They are men of universal social significance and oftentimes the psychological health of the group depends on them . . ."[52]

Looked at from the outside, the works of Jung and St John are here, in the religious and psychological health of the group, by the operation of their introverted thinking. But on the unconscious side of both, there was also the irrational function, their auxiliary function, intuition. This was the instrument of St John's poetry and Jung's fascination with symbols. In the intuitive state, they became creative, having left the known for the unknown.[53] Once adapted in the use of this function, the inferior function, that furthest from consciousness, comes into play. For both men, this function was that of feeling, which I will comment on later in this part.

Jung wrote the treatise on typology during his "fallow period," between 1913 and 1918, when he was attempting to define how his ways differed from Freud and Adler.[54] It was then that he surrendered to his own introversion which accounts for the turn his own personal work took at the time, the fruit of which would be: *Symbols of Transformation, Psychological Types*,[55] his own drawings of unconscious material and his discovery of parallels of psychic and alchemical processes.[56]

It was his separation from Freud and the fact of World War I which led Jung into the "fallow period." Likewise, St John's separation from traditional patriarchal religious life in favor of eremetism led him, free-spirited, down the path of introversion. Regardless of the political climate of the Psychoanalytical movement and the Counter-reformation, for Jung and St John personally, the separation from established institutions coincided with their own natural energy which moved within and toward the center. Externally, it involved a sacrifice of well-being for the sake of salvation, and included the abandonment of promised security from the institutions they had served faithfully and in whose soil they had grown well. Neither abandoned the field of origin—in the words of Prof Elkin, "they observed the customary disciplines of their 'order,'"—but both, by reverencing their individual natures, extended the field's subject to new depths and arrived at a deeper understanding of its object.

In the process of their introversion, Jung and St John invited their own "deaths." Again, in the words of Prof Elkin, "The ritual of death and rising by which they receive their knowledge causes a deep psychological experience." D. H. Lawrence expresses this mode of death in his poem, *The Ship of Death:*

> Oh lovely last, last lapse of death, into pure oblivion
> at the end of the longest journey
> peace complete peace!
> But can it be also that it is procreation?
>
> Oh build your ship of death,
> Oh build it.
> Oh, nothing matters but the longest journey.[57]

Both entered, by this separation, a "dark night" or "night-sea journey" which was complicated on the outside by the rejection and resentment of their colleagues, and on the inside by their own determination to stay with the subjective factor, that is, to actively pursue the darkness, an experience which led them to an encounter with their own shadows and the paradoxical tangle of opposites: dark-light, spirit-matter, and ultimately their own contrasexual part, the *anima*. G. Bachelard has written on the importance of the soul's encounter with inner duplicity:

> A matter which does not elicit a psychological ambivalence cannot find its poetic double which allows endless transpositions. It is necessary to have a double participation of desire and fear, participation of good and evil, peaceful participation of black and white for the material element to involve the whole soul.[58]

The *terminus ad quem* of the introversion of Jung and St John is the union of opposites, dark-light, spirit-matter, human-divine, male-female. The fusion of opposites is represented by a new conscious attitude, the rebirth of the *ego* and the death of the "old man."[59]

Thus in their writings, the discovery of the inner opposite is of paramount importance and represents a peak of inner experience. In their personal lives, I feel we can attribute their search and discovery of the contrasexual part to their initial experiences of the feminine, their personal mothers.[60] In both their histories, the mother archetype remained dominant, a condition which Erich Neumann sees as one of the fundamental constellations of the creative process.[61] Again, I would see this constellation as related to their use of the auxiliary function, intuition, and further, as a bridge to the feeling function, their inferior function. For an intense relationship with the *anima*—as Jung prescribes in the process of individuation, and as seen through St John's poetry in the *Spiritual Canticle*—the inferior function would have to be dealt with.

It is very likely that both men experienced an abandonment by their personal mothers. Jung speaks explicitly of this in his *Memories, Dreams and Reflections*:

I was deeply troubled by my mother's being away (his mother had gone for a rest cure) . . . and from then on I was always mistrustful when the word "love" was spoken. The feeling I associated with "women" was for a long time innate unreliability.[42]

In the case of St John of the Cross, he was placed in an orphanage probably before the onset of puberty. There is no way we can discover how he felt about this in his own words, but for a delicate introverted child, it cannot have been easy, nor could he have escaped feelings of abandonment by his mother. This constellation, though neither "fell sick" with it, would nonetheless have made the affective dimension of life very painful.[63] It is at precisely this point where Jung and St John meet, where the transformations take place and where their teachings are most creative.

For St John the whole process is an affective one.[64] Jung deals most directly with the affective in the "Psychology of the Transference," a work he dedicated to his wife.[65] Before dealing with the affective aspect of their teachings, however, I should like to trace briefly the personal *anima* constellation in their histories.

John of the Cross' departure from the "Calced" Carmelites was precipitated by his meeting with St Teresa, a woman twice his age exactly and who, throughout her life, was referred to as *la madre*.[66] St Teresa from that time on nurtured John's love of "desert" life, and it was because of his relationship with her that he was imprisoned. His prison poems became the nucleus of his mystical theology. The relationship was particular in the extreme, so much so that no full understanding of sixteenth century mysticism is possible without a study of the two.[67] As St John's life evolved, there were two other women too who became very important to him. One of them was Ana de Jesús, a close associate of St Teresa and contemporary of John; the other was Ana de Peñalosa, a Segovian widow and benefactress of the Carmelites. For the former, John wrote the commentary on the *Spiritual Canticle*; and the poem and commentary, *The Living Flame of Love*, for the latter.[68]

In the case of Jung, his separation from Freud sent him

directly into the unconscious, the archetypal mother. In writing of this period of his life, Jung states, "Since I knew nothing at all, I shall simply do whatever occurs to me . . . thus I consciously submitted myself to the impulses of the unconscious."[69] In Jung's conscious life, the mother and *anima* components were carried by his wife, Emma, the mother of his children and collaborator in his work.[70] Jung also enjoyed a relationship with Miss Toni Wolf, a relationship which has been discussed by Barbara Hannah in her recent biography of Jung.[71] The importance of the search for the inner feminine in Jung and St John may also be substantiated by the fact that neither had close sustained relationships with men. The majority of the Psychological Club, the first association of Jung's followers, were women. In the case of St John, I come to this conclusion by the absence of any mention of male friends in the biographies. The one exception may have been his secretary, Juan Evangelista. It is noted, however, that he was attractive to women, as was Jung.

These relationships may not have been essential to the teachings of Jung and St John, though it is difficult to imagine anyone's teaching removed from the *Sitz im Leben* of the teacher. As background material, it provides a basis for the discussion of the affective aspect of the transformation through union of opposites in the teachings of both.

From the beginning of his work, St John speaks of the affective nature of the transformation of the soul: "Fired with love's urgent longings . . ."[72] The "longings" according to this commentary are "mixed" because the soul is not detached from the longing of the lower sensory appetites; these appetites would be analogous to Jung's alchemical lower waters, "Fiery Mercurial waters," *aqui Saturni*. In this form, Mercurius says of himself, "If you do not know me, I will devour your five senses."[73] For St John these lower appetites are recognized, renounced, and in the process of the "dark night," transformed. In his essay on the psychology of the transference, Jung speaks of the lower fire giving way to the higher. He wrote this work in 1945 and it is interesting to note that in his earlier work, *Symbols of Transfor-*

mation, written in 1913, he has this to say about fire and mysticism (in a commentary on the *Revelations of Mechthild of Magdeburg*): "There is an almost inexhaustible catalogue of light and fire attributes which can only be compared with the endless vociferations about 'love' in Christian mysticism."[74] Considering the treatment of the same symbol in his essay on the transference, it appears that Jung's thought and/or experience changed.

The same symbols are found in the works of both men in the work of transformation, that is, the Holy Spirit on the higher level and the devil or Mercurius on the lower. The Holy Spirit makes himself present from the beginning of John's work: "My help will be the Sacred Scripture. Taking Scripture as our guide, we do not err, since the Holy Spirit speaks to us through it."[75] The devil is present through the process also, a protagonist of the "darkness" in which the light is found. In the darkest period, "the angel of Satan appears in the form of three lower spirits: *spiritus fornicationis, spiritus blasphemiae* and *spiritus vertiginis*."[76] In the last work of St John, where he deals with the subject of mystical union, it is the higher spirit which is personified in the living flame:

> The flame of love is the Spirit of its (the soul's) Bridegroom, the Holy Spirit. The soul feels him within not only as a fire which has consumed and transformed it, but as a fire that burns and flares within it.[77]

At this point the soul is experiencing its substance; the senses and the spirit have been transformed. The Word awakens. St John describes it: ". . . it seems to the soul that all virtues, perfections, substances and graces of every creature glow and make the same movement all at once."[78] Though the soul has reached perfection in this state, the shadow is still part of it, as St Teresa notes: "Sometimes Our Lord leaves such souls (those who have experienced mystical union) to their own nature, and when that happens, all the poisonous things in the environs and mansions of the castle seem to come together to avenge themselves on them . . ."[79]

In the essay on the transference, Jung refers to the *coniuntio* in terms of the mystic marriage.[80] Disavowing a personalistic observance of the transference, he outlines the archetypal meaning of it using an alchemical model, a series of drawings from the *Rosarium Philosophorum* (1550). He sees both parties being changed in the transference, "in the transformation of the third." It may be well to keep in mind, despite Jung's protestations about a personalistic attitude toward the transference, that both Jung and John of the Cross wrote their works while they had full practices of analysis and spiritual direction respectively.

In the series of drawings, the symbol of the Holy Spirit is very prominent. In figure 2, the dove carries the symbol of reconciliation of opposites; the olive branch and the art itself, says Jung, is a *donum Spiritus Sancti*.[81] It is in connection with this symbol of the Holy Spirit that Jung introduces the affective: "As regards the psychology of this picture, we must stress above all else, it depicts a human encounter where love plays the decisive part."[82] And "on the instinctive level, this love represents the lower instinct of incest. This is symbolized in the drawing by the joined left hands."[83] Transpersonally, however, the incest represents instinctual drive to relate to oneself, one's own inner opposite; it is the instinct for rebirth and new life of the personality. St John's "bride" expresses it this way:

> Deep in the wine vault of
> my love I drank, and when I came
> out on this open meadow
> I knew no thing at all,
> I lost the flock I used to drive.[84]

It is in his psychology of the transference that the wealth of Jung's theory of transformation in revealed and its transcendent character felt. He amplifies his theory further by citing John Layard: ". . . by the introduction of this incest wish, the soul comes full circle out of the biological into the spiritual."[85]

In his own words Jung describes it this way: "Here the incest wish shows itself to be an instinctual force of a spiritual nature and regarded in this light, the life of the spirit on the highest level is a return to the beginnings so that man's development becomes a recapitulation of the stages that lead ultimately to the perfection of life in the spirit."[86]

Here Jung and St John meet face to face. Their professional work and personal relationships may have influenced their understanding of the transformation process but their meeting at this point verifies their discovery of the "secrecy" and subjective essence of the process. Jung states:

> Relationship to the Self is at once relationship to one's fellowman, and no one can be related to the latter until he is related to himself. Individuation is primarily an internal and subjective process of integration.[87]

Let us return to the symbol of the Holy Spirit. As the process continues in Jung's treatise, the higher spirit becomes the uniting principle, "spiritus qui unificat."[88] And again, Jung underscores the affective aspect of the process by noting that the dove symbol of the Holy Spirit is the attribute of the goddess of love, and as mediator a symbol of union, thus a symbol of loving union. Commenting on figure 4 of the series, he says if there is no bond of love, there is no soul.[89] What Jung discovered in the dynamics of the transference, John of the Cross found in the exercise of contemplative prayer and his practice of spiritual direction. And he expresses it poetically:

> O lamps of fire!
> In whose splendors
> The deep caverns of feeling,
> Once obscure and blind,
> Now give forth, so rarely, so
> exquisitely,
> Both warmth and light to their
> Beloved.[90]

ARCHETYPAL ROOTS OF FORGETTING
AND MEMORY

> Be still a moment . . . there's something
> here. You are afraid of it, but I know
> it. Somewhere, perhaps, in an old dream,
> I have seen this place or perhaps felt
> the feeling of this place. This is holy
> — this is old.

John Steinbeck, *To a God Unknown*[91]

In this part I should like to review the memory experience as we know it from conscious life and its archetypal roots. For the sake of completeness, however, I shall begin by citing briefly an experiment, a philosophy and a modern physical therapy which may point to a pre-human and cosmic faculty of recollection.

Clive Baxter, an American psychologist, has done experiments on the "recollective powers" of metals and plants. He has discovered that metals attached to sensitive electronic devices respond to positive and negative stimuli, and in consequent experiments "remember" which is which. This kind of memory on the part of inanimate objects may be supported by ghostly appearances and extrasensory happenings marking the deaths and traumas of persons by physical responses in dusty attics, squeaky stairs and thresholds on the anniversary of such events. In similar experiments with plants, a "memory" for positive and negative stimuli is also noted. Baxter's experiments were the beginning of a collective acceptance of this phenomenon which was the basis for the "speak to your plants" movement of the 1960's.[92]

This discovery of a kind of consciousness in lower forms of life is found in the philosophy of Teilhard de Chardin in his concept of the "within" of things, what he calls, "cosmogenesis."[93] Approaching the human experience, the therapy of Ida Rolf proves almost indisputably that our own human bodies also have memories of their own. By the Rolfing technique of massage, the body is shown to retain "memories" of traumas, often if not always associated with the conflicts of psychic growth. In this therapy such experiences are collected and relived cathartically and with therapeutic value. This experience is, I might add, supported by the unconscious in dreams.[94] From these above matters, we may draw a principle: That which collects data, has the faculty to recollect. Possibly, with further experiments we will be able to add: everything has the power of collecting data.

Memory is the faculty of recollection. Clinically, it is presented as a tri-function. Its first function is to record, to add new information to the store of facts. Its second function is to retain, to hold on to the new facts; this function includes the reserve of all that is stored, lasting deposits which can enter consciousness requested or unrequested. The third function of memory is to recall, to have access to the deposit of remembered material in circumstances where such deposits are needed by the *ego*. In the Tavistock Lectures, Jung defines the *ego* as an awareness of the body and its existence, and your memory data, an idea of having been, a long series of memories.[95] So in a sense, consciousness is memory and memory is consciousness.

In our times the importance of memory and its function is hardly recognized. With computer centers, television, tape recorders, photography and a number of other memory aids, memory need not be emphasized. In a way, we are not unlike pre-historic man who needed to think only of the very present needs. Memory aids give us the same freedom, a freedom to concentrate on the present, and of leaving the connection of past with present and future to cue cards, index cards, tape recordings, computer tapes, radios, bells and alarm clocks. Our cultures and civilizations may be losing value for us as more and more of our stuff goes out of inner storage into outer technical storage. It is difficult to imagine that the fund of myths, legends, doctrines and teachings, fairy-tales, and even music — the foundations of Western and Eastern culture — was preserved originally in the memories of men and women. The relative unimportance of memory was demonstrated by an article appearing in a popular American magazine in 1977. The title of the article was "A Hundred Things a University Graduate Should Know." It consisted of six pages of data divided into seventeen categories, only one of which required memorization; that was a list of parts of ten poems which should be committed to memory "along with the authors!"[96]

It is generally agreed upon by psychologists from Freud to the present that we tend to remember pleasant experiences and forget the unpleasant. "Pleasure" and "pain" are very much alive in the memory function. Man's affects influence very much the memory function, as Jung proved in his studies on word association.[97] And, again, in the Tavistock Lectures, Jung says that memory can be voluntarily controlled only to a certain extent "like a bad horse that cannot be mastered."[98] In terms of Jungian psychology, we might also add that typology and attitude also influence the memory function. The sensate, for example, will remember the texture and color of an object or event, while the intuitive will remember the atmosphere and possibilities. Regarding the attitude, Jung's memories are a good example of the introverted memory function. He says:

> Recollections of the outward events of my life have largely faded or disappeared; but my encounters with the "other" reality are indelibly engraved on my memory. In that realm, there has always been a wealth and abundance, and everything else has lost importance by comparison.[99]

Extroverted memory is exemplified in the *Life* of St Teresa of Avila, where she wrote in a quite different vein: "It happens at times that I find myself becoming unwrought because I want to be wholly where the greater part of me is (in prayer); but I know this to be impossible; memory and imagination make such turmoil within me that they leave me helpless."[100]

Complexes are also capable of distorting memory as a personal recollection of my own demonstrates. In 1970, I was called to the scene of a murder to administer the last rites of the Church to the murder victim, the murder having transpired in the street in front of the monastery where I then lived. I anointed the body of the victim, returned to the monastery and forgot the incident. Several weeks later a lawyer for the defense of the murderer came and asked me about the details of the incident. He asked me especially where I saw the body of the victim and I took him to the spot where I remembered the body lay. A month later I was subpoened by the court to appear and give testimony. I was the star witness for the defense because if the body lay where I remembered it, the wife of the victim could not have seen the murderer (whom she had identified). It was only when the testimony of other State witnesses was presented to disprove mine that I realized that my memory had deceived me by arranging the murder scene in keeping with my defenses. And even then, the memory image of the incident did not change. It was only later, after much thought, that I realized the connection between the distortion of the scene by my memory and my personal affects. Several persons in my family were terminally ill at the time and I had reason to bring the image of the dead man closer to the monastery where I was, somehow, and feel protected from facing the death of my relatives.

Man's memory evolved with the increase of responsibility, the development of community and the practical exigencies of society: ". . . our ancestors learned to share their food and skills in an honored network of obligation."[101] It is not difficult to understand how primitive man would associate his memory function with a power greater than himself who would remind him of the changes in season and the attendant obligations to family or tribe. With the recognition of such a power, there came religions, rituals and traditions which had to be remembered and passed on to the younger generation. There were also memorials, tombs, sacred memorial places and the like. When a man had no offspring, the memorial became even more important as we see in the life of Absalon, David's son. He set up a pillar in the King's Vale as a memorial to himself, and said, "I have no son to carry my name." He named the pillar after himself, and to this day it is called Absalon's monument.[102]

In the classical periods of Rome and Greece, memory systems were instituted for the preservation and presentation of drama, oratory and literature. Cicero in *De Oratore* traces his memory system, which became the model for Medieval and Renaissance memory systems, to Simonides of Ceos and this incident. Simonides was invited to a banquet by a magistrate. At the banquet he gave a speech about the twin healing gods, Castor and Pollux. When he had finished, the magistrate told him he would receive only half his stipend; the other half would be given to the gods as an offering. A steward came at that moment and told Simonides that there were two young men outside waiting to see him. When Simonides got outside there was no one there but at that instant the banquet hall collapsed, killing all the banqueters and leaving their bodies so mangled that they could not be identified by the next of kin. Simonides was able to help identify the victims because he remembered where the victims had sat at table.[103] From this tale, Cicero developed a mechanism of memorization which depended on placing (*Loci*) images (*Imagines Agentes*) to be remembered in an order, so that by remembering the place, one could remember the image. The mechanism endured and became the basis of the more elaborate memory systems of the Middle Ages as seen in Albertus Magnus, Thomas Aquinas, Boncompagno de Signa and Raimondo Lulli; and in the Renaissance, as seen in Guilio Camillo, Giordano Bruno and Robert Flood. The *loci* and *im-agentes* to the design and decoration of theaters. The system at the Renaissance, external *loci* were transformed to internal *loci* and to combinations of well known, well ordered truths, such as the virtues, signs of the Zodiac, the hierarchy of being and so on. This development led to the painting and drawing of symbols of the same on the inside of buildings where sermons, speeches or dramas were presented. In buildings today, such as churches and court houses, town halls and theatres, we still see remnants of this memory system in the decorative embellishments of the architect. The memory systems reached their peak in the Renaissance with the application of the *loci-imagines agentes* to the design and decoration of theaters. The system at this time became very complicated. Every inch of the building took on symbolic meaning in addition to drawings or statues of as many classical figures as was possible — all placed in order and thematically — to assist the actors to remember their lines. Then another dimension in the memory systems evolved: by the use of symbols and the conscious effort to contain the "whole" of known truth, magic and occult powers of the unconscious were constellated. Frances Yates, in her historical survey of the art of memory, expresses it in these terms: ". . . the within — the within of the psyche was established, that is, the return of the intellect to unity through the organization of significant images."[104] The archetypal images in the systems came alive and had the power of drawing the artists and the audience into the collective unconscious. But most of all, the designers of theaters and arrangers of the symbols became fascinated with the power of the images and projected on their theater design a process not unlike the process of alchemy; they were indeed accused of being alchemists. In his *De La Causa*, Giordano Bruno defines the effects of this process: "(This is) . . . a most solid foundation for the truths and secrets of nature, for you must know that it is by one and the same ladder that nature descends to the production of things and the intellect ascends to the knowledge of them, and that the one and the other proceeds from unity and returns to unity, passing through the multitude of things in the middle."[105]

The ladder of descent and ascent, referred to here by Bruno, was a common image at the time of the bridge between the higher and lower regions of the soul. St John of the Cross uses it — descending — in his poem, the *Dark Night*:

> In darkness and secure,
> By the secret ladder and disguised,
> O Blessed venture!
> In darkness and concealed,
> My house in sleep and silence stilled.[106]

With the emergence of the archetypal aspect of the memory theaters, a distinction was made between "artificial" and "real" memory. The former denotes a training of the faculty of recall to carry out tasks — ordinary life tasks of words and deeds. But the system led to real memory, the memory of the wholeness of the primitive psyche or preconscious wholeness. Artificial memory began and belonged essentially to the rhetorical tradition. It was in the practice of artificial memory that real memory emerged; this belonged to the mystical tradition and, by association, to psychology and theology.

In ancient Greece, memory was represented by the goddess, Mnemosyne, the daughter of Gaea, the primordial goddess of the earth, and Uranus, the primordial god of the heavens, both Titans. Mnemosyne was the mother of the Muses, by Zeus. It was commonly believed by the Greeks that their poets produced their works not by intellectual acumen, but that the works of the poets were recollections of what they had been told by the Muses — a memory. And it is with the Muses that memory's counter interdependence with forgetting is established, for the Muses have the effect of making men forget their sorrows and cares. Forgetting is further and more specifically represented by Lethe, one of the rivers dividing the upper and lower worlds. Personified, she became Lesmosyne or Oblivion. Those traveling to or from Hades had to cross this river and sometimes to drink its water. One must exist principally in one or the other world but not in both: the Lethe provided a forgetting of what went before and beside the Lethe. In the Lethian fields was a spring of Mnemosyne, a further indication of the twin nature of forgetting and memory. The problem or challenge associated with this spring so placed was how much water to drink from it, or how much to remember of the underworld experience. In modern psychology this problem arises with the condition of the *ego* in deep mystical experiences or numinous descents in analysis. Too much water from the spring of Lesmosyne would leave the *ego* in an unconscious state; too much from the spring of Mnemosyne might allow the memory of unconscious contents to predominate the *ego* tasks of everyday life.

If we use Jung and John of the Cross as prototypes of ascent-descent experiences, we have to conclude that a genuine descent, directed by God or the Self, carries with it a protection of the *ego*. If this were not so, we would not have their teachings, for they would never have returned and would exist now on the list of some hospital register, possibly labeled as "schizophrenic." Both were, however, conscious of the dangers associated with climbing down the "ladder." They stress the dangerous aspect of inflation or pride, the identification with the archetypes or archetypal experiences.[107] Their precautions are to protect the *ego* if not to prevent the abortion of the whole process, an experience which, symbolically, would leave the soul in trauma with the *anima* childless and the *ego* dead. Hesiod, the Greek poet who shepherded his flocks in the fields of Boetia, speaks of two springs there, one of Mnemosyne and one of Lesmosyne. Perhaps this is the solution, a sip from both, but always in the right measure to be accompanied by the memory that Hades is such a wise, intelligent, charming benefactor and that, as such, he is not taken leave of.[108]

Anyone who risks analysis or a life of interior prayer must encounter these springs of forgetting and memory and discover, by experiment, the right measure to be taken from both. This poem, which I quote with the permission of the author, represents a return from the descent:

> See the paths, read the signs
> Excited feeling.
> Selfish love, good times
> Soaring, tumbling reeling.
> Which road? Which way?
> The one that leaves a taste
> Of power sweet you say!
> Savoured, relishes.
> Soul's abhorrent vice replenished.
>
> Retreat alone, silently reflecting.
> Painfully rejecting.
> To understand the way of Hades
> So blatantly taken.

Happiness forsaken.
Deserter. Absconder.
No Love. No Hope. No Giving.
No Living.
Nightmare.
Paralysed.
Screaming Screaming Screaming!
Wake up
WAKE UP
STOP DREAMING.   (unpublished)

Forgetting is the counter-pole of memory. In clinical psychology, it falls into disturbed memory or *amnesia*. It is observed in a number of psychopathic syndromes, both organic and functional. In the less radical *amnesias* we see that the loss of memory serves the purpose of preserving the integrity of the *ego*. Even in alcoholism and drug addiction, ego-consciousness regresses to where it feels safe, to uroboric comfort. Archetypally, the drinking and drug problem may be interpreted as a Dionysian escape from time to pre-time security. Plutarch calls Dionysus the son of Lethe. In this sense, the addict prefers to remember the past and forget the present and future. This condition is solidified in Korsokof's syndrome. The same backward flow of memory can be observed in senile psychosis as well. As the function of recall degenerates, there is an increase in the vividness of recollections of the past. I have had the privilege of knowing a person who went down the ladder of descent in this way. With the progress of her condition, childhood memories increased and finally took over consciousness. Her hallucinatory system made her family the family of her childhood, so that present family disappeared and past family came alive. She told them that she was not ready to go away with them. Finally, however, she was discovered packing a suitcase and getting ready. She died shortly thereafter.[109]

Amnesias following physical or psychic shock also protect the *ego* by delaying the consciousness of a loss or accident after which life will necessarily be different.

In terms of the Self, by its regulating function, in all the above references from the analysand who forgets a dream or portion thereof, to the accident victim who might face the loss of limb, we can observe right measures of waters from the psychic springs of Mnemosyne and Lesmosyne being administered.

Freud speaks of forgetting in terms of "repression," the function of rejecting and keeping out of consciousness something that threatens defense mechanisms.[110] In his earlier works, Jung supports Freud in this regard. Forgetting and memory were the substance of the early psychoanalytic movement in the process of "chimney-sweeping." Jung showed a particular interest in this contrapuntal faculty of the psyche as early as 1902 when he wrote his doctoral thesis, his studies in word association in 1904, and an early article on cryptomnesia in 1905.[111]

These early studies of Jung were the seeds of his discovery of the collective unconscious. In the Tavestock Lectures (1935), Jung stated that memory was an "endopsychic" function of consciousness, a conscious function with its roots in the unconscious, the "ladder" of Giordano Bruno and John of the Cross, "descending to the production of things."[112] Jung also expands Freud's view of the repression of childhood memories and states that such failures of memory are "merely symptoms of a much greater loss, a loss of the primitive psyche that lived and functioned before it was reflected by consciousness."[113]

There are a number of myths in various traditions which support the affirmation of a pre-existent wholeness in man implied in Jung's Tavestock statement. In the Jewish tradition, the poetic author of Genesis presents the garden of Eden as the beginning of creation which was sacrificed by the first parents for the sake of consciousness. Symbolically, the loss of Eden sets off a process, through increasing consciousness and continued sacrifice, of restoration. In the Christian myth, the loss of this wholeness becomes the "felix culpa" bringing the God-man into the flesh, with him coming from the state of wholeness.[114] Modern de-mythologizing scripture scholars, without a belief in pre-conscious wholeness, interpret the garden as a reverse projection of desired post-existent wholeness.[115] Also, in the Jewish mystical tradition of the *Cabala*, there is found the myth of the "formation of the child."[116] Before each birth, the child is brought before the throne of God where it is decided what the child will become. The child is then taken by an angel and taught the knowledge of all things. A second angel then takes the child and teaches him to forget all the things the first angel taught him; he is then born to earthly existence. A rabbi of Memphis was asked the reason for the angel of forgetting. He answered that if man did not forget his wholeness he would think only of death and fail to get on with the tasks of life, a pattern I have noted in the context of clinical addiction above.

In the *Tibetan Book of the Dead*, the four conditions for the embryo's entrance into the womb are detailed. Here too a combination of forgetting and memory in the context of knowing and not-knowing can be observed.

> Brethren, in this world, one cometh into existence in the mother's womb without knowing, remaineth in it without knowing, and cometh out from it without knowing: this is the first.

> Brethren, one cometh into existence in the mother's womb knowingly, remaineth in it without knowing and cometh out from it without knowing: this is the second.

> Brethren, one cometh into existence in the mother's womb knowingly, remaineth in it knowingly, and cometh out from it without knowing: this is the third.

> Brethren, in this world, one cometh into existence in the mother's womb knowingly, remaineth in it knowingly and cometh out from it knowingly: this is the fourth.[117]

In these myths we can see the twins, Mnemosyne and Lesmosyne, at the archetypal roots of mankind.

Finally, we may associate forgetting-memory with one other common human experience, that of *le sentiment du déjà-vu*. This is the feeling of having been there before; such a feeling breaks in in a flash in any given circumstance. The sudden recollection can never be explained by recourse to consciousness. It is as if some ancient and long short-circuited wire came alive for a moment and exposed the present as something that was known in the past, when the present was future. In his article on syncronicity, Jung gives two explanations for *le sentiment du déjà-vu*. First, it could be a sudden memory of circumstances that were dreamt but not remembered at the time. Secondly, it could be a breaking through of a timeless foreknowledge, a simple coincidence of *ego* and Self.[118] Henri Bergson uses *le sentiment du déjà-vu* as an example of "pure memory." This is a breakdown of the brain's inhibitory function which is absent in sleep and death, but which is needed in conscious life to sustain the *ego* and its conscious functioning.[119]

THE GREEK MYSTICAL TRADITION AND FORGETTING AND MEMORY IN ST JOHN OF THE CROSS

> In these days during the migrations, days
> Freshening with rain reported from the
>   mountains,
> By loss of memory we are reborn,
> For memory is death; by taking leave,
> Parting in anger and glad to go
> Where we are still unwelcome, and if we
>   count
> What dead the tides wash in, only to make
> Notches for enemies, on northern ridges
> Where flags fly, seen and lost, denying
>   rumor
> We battle proof, speakers of a strange
>   tongue.
>
> W. H. Auden, *Paid on Both Sides*[120]

The springs of Mnemosyne and Lesmosyne which seem to belong to the permanent fund of Greek Mythology were not known in the classical period. These springs are characteristic of the non-classical period; it was the musings of the mystics of the post-classical period which first created the spring of Mnemosyne, as a counterpart of forgetfulness, the river Lethe, Oblivion. Historically, not even the river of Lethe is classical. Classical Greek Mythology speaks only of the "house of Lethe," or "fields of Lethe," where the dead disappear. And what is a facile "forgetting" to us in our approach to Lethe, was for the Greeks a state of "being hidden," "to hide oneself," "not noticing that which is hidden," and applied mainly to the dead who were finally and irrevocably "hidden."[121]

It was then a mystical tradition that created a meaning for the forgetting-memory process of "noticing and not noticing that which is hidden" in Western thought. The dynamic of not noticing what is hidden may have a parallel in modern psychology which deals with the forgetting process of human suffering by labeling it abnormal or psychopathic, and treats such experiences as a matter of religion and mysticism. Religion, from its beginning, has included the hidden and forgotten. Even Freud's "religion is the opium of the people" supports this task of religion, if we interpret it to mean that religious belief assists man to forget the temporal and spatial in favor of eternal verities.[122] And although Freud concerned himself with the forgotten details of his patients' lives, in recollecting them he was able only to relate the memories to the external and biological facts of life, and failed entirely to notice the internal springs of life and death in the psyche.

It is in the "unmystical" and "mystical" traditions of forgetting and memory in Greek Mythology that we find the foundations of forgetting and memory in later religious traditions. They are the archetypal rungs of the "ladder of descent and ascent."

In principle, contact with the original energy of life, whether from a pre- or post-existent standpoint, is related to those two springs of Mnemosyne and Lesmosyne, and the proper amount of water taken therefrom. But given human ambivalence, this is not a simple procedure. This is demonstrated by the varieties

and shades of meaning that can be seen in the writings on this
subject in Socrates, Plato, Homer, Hesiod, Heraclitus,
Pausanias and Vergil. Their interpretations of the springs and
the waters from these springs include: birth, death, sleep, inspiration of the Muses, thirst for death, will to life, carrying the
waters in leaky vessels and so on.[123] Kerenyi summarizes the
varieties:

> It is only both the elements (memory and forgetting) that make
> up the entire being of the goddess whose name comes solely
> from the positive side of her field of power. This union of op-
> posites, under the power of the positive, characterizes that older
> Greek religiosity which must, if one disregards the natural
> mysteries, appear "unmystical." It was another sort of mysti-
> cism which gave the split into two not easily re-united possibil-
> ities for men: a divine state with Mnemosyne, and another state
> which was deadly yet unceasing, whereby one flows away with
> the stream of Lethe.[124]

In the light of the teaching of John of the Cross, we are concerned with the experience of the split, the suffering of which
renders a *coniuntio*, "in the divine state with Mnemosyne," when
the "solve" and "coagula" are completed. Both ends of the process share the common symbolic form of water, fluidity. In the
Christian myth, this can be associated with the basic fluidity of
Jesus Christ who calmed rough waters, walked on water, and
from whose side blood and water flowed in death. Outstanding
in the context of the Gospel is the fluidity demonstrated by the
acts of Jesus in his conversation with the Samaritan woman at
the well, and his changing water into wine at Cana. The former
event shows Jesus in a highly flexible posture culturally and
symbolically. First, he is speaking with a woman which was not
acceptable; and the woman was also a Samaritan. Jesus then
"remembers" for the woman her marital history and gives her
the living waters which will never run dry, a gesture already
symbolized by her history and his attitude.[125] The latter event
is equally impressive in terms of fluidity. In the setting of a *coniuntio*, the wedding feast, Jesus changes the water into wine,

that is, into spirit. For Heraclitus, the changeable basic substance of all appearances is not water but fire. In Jung and St
John, fire is associated with the Holy Spirit and is the transforming element *par excellence*; but the fire, though fire, maintains its fluid aspect and, as such, is poured out.[126] So in the
wedding feast at Cana, we see the whole process of transformation by union of opposites, and also symbols of birth by water
and the spirit.[127] John of the Cross has expressed this mystery
poetically, using the same symbols, in his "Ballad on the Psalm,
'By the Waters of Babylon.'"

> By the waters of Babylon
> I sat down and wept,
> and my tears
> watered the ground,
>
> remembering you,
> O Zion, whom I loved.
> Your memory was sweet
> and I wept more.
>
> I took off holiday robes,
> put on working clothes,
> and hung my harp on a green
> willow
>
> Laying it there in hope
> of the hope I had in you.
> There love wounded me
> and took away my heart.
>
> I asked it to kill me
> since it had stabbed me so.
> I leaped into its fire
> knowing it would burn me,
>
> and forgave the young bird
> dying in the fire.

I was dying myself
and breathing only in you

I died within for you
and for you I revived;
your memory gave and took
away life.

Those strangers were glad,
they who were my captors,

and asked me to sing
what I sang in Zion:
"Sing us a hymn from Zion,
let us hear the song!"

I said how can I sing in
a foreign land where I weep,

How can I sing of joy
I felt in Zion.
I would be forgetting her
if happy in a strange land.

May the tongue I speak with
cling to my palate
if I forget you in this land
where I am.

Zion, by the green branches
that Babylon gave me,
let my right arm be forgotten
(which I cared for
only when I was with you)

If I do not remember you
who made me happy,

> or celebrate a day
> from which you are gone.
>
> O daughter of Babylon,
> in misery and doomed!
>
> I trusted him who came blessed
> who will punish you with your own hand
>
> He will bring his little ones
> to me; he wept for you
> at the rock which is Christ.
> I left you for him.[128]

In the alchemical process, fluidity indicates the *solutio*, the decomposition of the original matter into elements such as we observe in the gospel stories, cited above, and this poem of St John. In each of these products water plays the important part, the flowing of which establishes contact between the inner and outer realms which is the function of Mnemosyne and Lesmosyne.

The combination of water and fire, *via* Heraclitus, is of the Greek mystical tradition; the house or fields of Lethe were stifling hot and dreadfully torrid. This condition drove those waiting for birth or return to the upper world to drink from the spring of Mnemosyne. John of the Cross has a poem which depicts this spring very well in the context of Christ as the source of the living waters. The repeated phrase "in black of night" fits well into the *ego's* dark waiting condition in the stifling fields and the *nigredo* of alchemy:

> How well I know that flowing spring in
>   black of night.
>
> The eternal fountain is unseen.
> How well I know where she has been
>   in black of night.

I do not know her origin.
None. Yet in her all things begin
   in black of night.

I know that nothing is so fair
and earth and firmament drink there
   in black of night.

I know that none can wade inside
to find her bottomless tide
   in black of night.

Her shining never has a blur;
I know that all light comes from her
   in black of night.

I know her streams coverage and swell
and nourish people skies and hell
   in black of night.

The stream whose birth is in this source
I know has gigantic force
   in black of night.

The stream from but these two proceeds
yet neither one I know precedes
   in black of night.

The eternal fountain is unseen
in living bread that gives us being
   in black of night.

She calls on all mankind to start
to drink her water, though it dark,
   for black is night.

   O living fountain that I crave

in bread of life I see her flame
in black of night.[129]

It is in religious experience that forgetting and memory find
their deepest meaning as we observe in these two poems. In
Buddhism, too, the individual must remember all his previous
lives — lest he forget the lessons learned therefrom — before he
reaches the state of freedom, Nirvana.[130] This dynamic is
demonstrated in the psychoanalytic movement where unconscious complexes are depotentiated by exposing them to the
light of consciousness. Analytical psychology goes a step further in recognizing the archetypal nucleus of the complexes and
the healing power which is constellated by following the nucleus
to the Self. Energetically, the healing power is reached by forgetting the personal component and becoming conscious of the
eternal component. According to Jung, this is the purpose of
the complexes, a purpose which makes neurosis the source of
radical healing. St John expresses this poetically:

O sweet cautery,
O delightful wound!
O gentle hand! O delicate touch
That tastes of eternal life
And pays every debt!
In killing you changed death to life.[131]

The memory and forgetting process can be observed more
closely in the context of healing in the incubation rites of the
healing ritual of Trophonius. Before descent into the cave where
the god dwelt in the form of a snake, the incubant drank from
the springs of Mnemosyne and Lesmosyne which were nearby.
This made the incubant forget his previous concerns and
remember what he heard and saw in the manifestation of Trophonius. When the incubant returned to the surface, he was
seated on the throne of Mnemosyne in order to remember the
experience and give witness of it to the priests of Trophonius.
C. A. Meier, in his work on this subject, recognizes in this
ritual the archetypal form of modern psychotherapy and em-

phasizes the healing dimension of *amnesia*. This is also the archetypal pattern of prayer. He cites St Paul: ". . . but this one thing I do, forgetting those things that are behind, and reaching forth to those things that are before."[132] Meier concludes with this statement:

> *Amnesia* is an essential condition if the patient is to give himself up completely to the experience of incubation; this is in direct contrast to the high valuation of consciousness which prevails elsewhere in medicine. Here an *amnesis* applies exclusively to the unconscious experiences which are visualized during incubation and its purpose is to make them accessible to consciousness and reality and also to make it possible to utilize them.[133]

John of the Cross' concept of forgetting and memory, as the poetry I have quoted indicates, follows the archetypal structure of the Greek mystical tradition, and it follows the energetic inward flow to the healing fountain of the Self of Jungian psychology as seen here in Meier's interpretation of the incubation rites of Trophonius. For St John, the source of the healing spring is Christ, the "rock," from whom the waters flow, or the Self.

In order for this to take place, the *ego* must let go of the outer and even the inner attractions. In contemporary theological terms, this would be "the leap of faith," or the "courage to be."[134] In Jungian terminology, we would say that the soul has turned from the collective path to the individual. St John expresses this well in his *Spiritual Canticle*:

> If, then, I am no longer
> Seen or found on the common,
> You will say that I am lost;
> That stricken by love,
> I lost myself and was found.
>
> Now I occupy my soul
> And all my energy in his service;

> I no longer tend the herd,
> Nor have I any other work
> Now that my every act is love.[135]

In the underworld venture of the dark night of the soul, the *ego*, according to St John of the Cross, suffers "sharp trials in the intellect," "dryness and distress in the will," and "burdensome knowledge of one's own miseries in the memory."[136] And at the same time, the soul's "spiritual eye"—the vision from the center—gives the soul a very clear picture of itself. This inner vision is defined in a number of places in the poetry: it is the eye that sees things from within; sees things separate and joins them; it is the light in the dark night "which guided me more firmly than the noonday sun."[137] In the *Spiritual Canticle* we can observe the function of the spiritual eye. Here it appears on the surface of the water, suggesting the spring. The use of the word "scars" in connection with the eye suggests the memory of preexistent wholeness:

> O crystal brook, if on
> the silver surface of the water
> you instantly might form
> the eyes I most desire!
> I feel them in me like a scar!
>
> When first you looked my way,
> your eyes imprinted a grace on me
> And made me feel a woman
> And so my eyes could love
> All things which they observed in you.[138]

The sight of the inner eye reveals the shadow, personal and archetypal. This confrontation with inner darkness, the other side of the soul, says St John, resembles what Job said about God in his misery: "You are changed to be cruel toward me."[139] The personal shadow is experienced in this way:

Now with the light and the heat of the divine five, the soul feels and sees those weaknesses and miseries which previously resided within it hidden and unfelt, just as the dampness of the log of the wood was unknown until the fire being applied made it sweat and smoke and sputter . . .[140]

The soul also feels the pull of the opposites at this point:

> . . . for the contraries rise up at this time against contraries — those of the soul against those of God . . . and, as the philosophers say: one contrary when close to the other makes it more manifest.[141]

By the light of the inner eye all that is hidden becomes available to the *ego*. The suffering of opposites causes excruciating pain for the soul. In terms of the metaphor of the log of wood, the soul "smokes, sweats and sputters," an image which is reminiscent of the old king in the Lambspring Alchemical drawings.[142] In this drawing, the king is depicted sweating out the swallowing of his son, the new life and potential transformation. It is at this stage, or in this state of being, that the *ego* is in the greatest danger of being lost, carried away in the rapids of the river Lethe, and practically speaking by despair.

To prevent the loss of the *ego*, St John prescribes a vessel for the waters of oblivion, that is, Hope. He knows very well of the need for this vessel as he identifies the suffering of the soul with Job: "The soul is withering within itself and its inner parts being without hope."[143] The virtue of hope is most appropriate as a vessel for this journey because it preserves the unknown quality of the object, that is, union with the totally other, God. This is true because hope applies to something that is unpossessed. For John of the Cross, the knowledge of God is never possessed except in the center of the soul where it is unknown as far as the natural faculties of the soul are concerned. The virtue of hope has another purpose too: it is the thread that related the *ego* to time and space, to history in terms of Emil

Brunner's theology.[144] Hope, in the teachings of St John, is not unlike the star of the Holy Spirit which appears in the immersion process in the *Rosarium*, which the royal pair cling to as they go under the water.[145]

Finally, in his treatise on the purification of memory, St John insists on forgetfulness of all sensible and spiritual images, with the exception of those that awaken the knowledge and love of God in the soul.[146] Thus it would seem that the purpose of the contemplative prayer experience of St John of the Cross is revealed as a journey within which the *ego*, armed with hope, in the process of self-knowledge, is to establish a relationship with the center of the soul, with God or the Self. By referring to this encounter as a "scar," St. John's poetry establishes the fact that the acquired union with God is a memory and to protect the relationship of the *ego* and this Memory, all else is to be forgotten. In the manner of Greek mysticism, the *ego*, by its encounter with Lesmosyne and Mnemosyne, has suffered death and has returned with the memory of "that which is hidden."

CONCLUSION

> Think of nothing. Not of cabinet and
> catholon, think of the clown who
> weeps in the bath, and whose coffee
> drips into his slippers.

Heinrich Boll, *The Clown*[147]

Heraclitus says that it is death to the soul to become water.[148] As mythology would have it, regardless of the danger involved, it is man's destiny to approach liquifaction, or the *solutio* of alchemy if he is to be born, live, grow and be reborn. Christian life begins in the waters of baptism. As the unconscious of one of my clients has stated after a series of snow and ice dreams: "but snow and ice melt." In the service of the internal-external, vertical-horizontal flow of vital energy, and at its essence, are the springs of Mnemosyne and Lesmosyne, memory and forgetting. From the beginning of life and before, memory and forgetting play their part by their presence — sometimes rude — and remind us that the *ego's* participation in external reality and its attention to the procession of archetypes reveals something that is fluid as in the springs of Mnemosyne and Lesmosyne.

A major task of the *ego* in the first half of life is to remember. To remember its numbers and letters, to remember the rules of home and school, and what time it is and where I should be now. The pressure in early life is to remember, and future achievement is based on the ability to recall what is learned from parental figures. Remembering too little in the first half of life may indicate an interference of the unconscious, the personal unconscious in cases where personal or family problems are severe; in turn, this may constellate archetypal unconscious memories of uroboric comfort which permits isolation or withdrawal to the very secure Garden of Eden. This is exemplified in youthful drug addiction or alcoholism as I have mentioned above.

On the other hand, total recall in the extreme is also a memory disturbance as Jung has demonstrated in his experiments in word association.[149] In this case, there is no flow between conscious and unconscious. If the non-remembering subject is too fluid and carries his energy in a sieve, the super-remembering subject carries his in a brittle vessel and may well be driven by compulsion or an Adlerian "will to power" and achievement.

Because of a split between thinking and feeling, the hysteric, controlled by chaotic feelings, takes flight in *amnesia*: the memory of the real world can be dealt with only by the ingestion of massive doses of Lethian waters. In cases of depression, however, it is the memory of the reality of the lost object or person which causes the hellish torment known only to the depressive. It is in the second half of life that we observe the radical disintegration of memory in Pick's and Alzheimer's Diseases, a condition which is premature and appears at the end of life in older subjects, an example of which I have given above.[150] In both the first and second halves of life, in the natural progress of time, the individual struggles with all the above disturbances in varying degrees within the broad margin of "normality." As I have stated above, the memory is effected by any number of internal and external components, as Nietzsche has remarked: "Memory declares that I did this; I could not have done this, says my pride, and memory loses the day."

It is in the encounter with the unconscious or inner reality that memory and forgetting take on a deeper meaning as in prayer or the analytical experience. In this experience one is expected to remember his or her prayer experience or dreams.[151] In most cases, the cooperation between conscious and unconscious is quickly and firmly established in this regard. Where it is not, forgetting is equally significant as is the forgetting of one dream or a part thereof of an analysand who ordinarily remembers. In the spiritual director's analyst's role too, a great deal of his tools are those in his memory store, the meaning of prayer experiences, of symbols, mythology and so on. And he is expected to remember the details of the conscious and unconscious material of his clients. Most important in these roles is the ability to forget what lies outside the vessel of the direction or analysis in order to avoid contaminating the process with his own material — especially shadow material. This is a discipline which can easily be labeled "forgetting," and calls for a long draft from the spring of Lesmosyne.

In the matter of transference-countertransference, memories of feelings, sensations, thoughts and intuitions constellated during spiritual direction or analysis are very significant and oftentimes painful for both the subject and director. They are forgotten with the dawn of transpersonalization, spiritualization, in the rebirth of the personalities of both, though this may take a number of years. In this complicated dynamic, an awareness of the fluid dimension of memory and forgetting may be helpful in the endurance of the conflict between time and space *versus* the timeless and spaceless aspect of inner healing.

In the therapeutic analytical experience as such the analysand recollects his woundedness and discovers that wounds are irradicable, but discovers that what inflicts the wounds can be, and is, finally and irrevocably forgotten. In this process of remembering and forgetting, a relationship is established with the collective unconscious and the archetypes which carry a healing as well as a wounding function. This process reverses the regressive-neurotic energy flow in the Buddhist sense of remembering in order to forget. In the first half of life, the analytical work awakens the memory of the task to build the new Jerusalem, and the painful separation from Paradise, a state not easily forgotten.

In the second half of life, the energy released from neurotic knots moves toward the center and toward a release of imprisoned inferior parts in all that was neglected in the first half of life. Here we can observe a return to the matrix, the eternal womb, to be born in and by the spirit. Birth pains in this "dark night," or "night-sea journey," include the forgetting of the old and secure way, the endurance of which would be impossible without God or Self which directs and regulates the rebirth process through the presentation of healing symbols. Establishing a relationship with the Self is a recollection of a union that existed before the formation of the ego-complex; it is a Memory, and the end of prayer and Jungian analysis. According to Jung, this task is a religious task and, as such, is consonant with the mystical theology of St John of the Cross. In the context of the dialectic between forgetting and memory, he expresses it this way:

> I died within for you
> and for you I revived;
> your memory
> gave and took away life[152]

Summarily, the path of the inward flow of energy ending in self-transcendence, as exemplified in the lives and teachings of St John of the Cross and C. G. Jung, can be seen as a path illumined by Memory, the memory of preconscious wholeness, the Self, or in the words of St Augustine, *Memoria Dei.*[153]

Establishing a relationship with God or Self, the *ego* enters a "mystic" state, that is a secret and unique condition at the center of the soul where the opposites are combined. To leave this state is to leave the "presence of God, Thrones and Dominations, the original energy of life."[154] The center is arrived at by the function of forgetting and memory, and contact with it is maintained by remaining fluid in the sense of being able to recall the original energy of life and being able to forget the personal in favor of what transcends it. This makes the words of Matthew Arnold ring archetypally true:

> We forget because we must
> and not because we will.[155]

NOTES

1. The word "archetype" comes from two Greek words: "arche" which means origin, beginning, primordiality, chief; and "typos" which means a seal and the blow by which it makes an imprint producing a form or image, a "typos." Thus it means a primordial image — a typical human situation, or image of such a situation. The recurring motifs of mythology all over the world are archetypal and originate in the collective unconscious, that is, they arise in the form of images out of the very depths of the human psyche, that deposit of man's ancestral experience of life and meaning, which all men share. See Jung, *Collected Works*, Vols. 7 and 9i.

2. Ezra Pound, *Selected Poems.*

3. Jung, *The Spirit in Man, Art and Literature*, Vol. 15 *Collected Works*, p. 7455.

4. A, 1.

5. Gerald Brennan, *St John of the Cross: His Life and Poetry* (Cambridge: Cambridge U. Press, 1973), p. 118.

6. A, 2, 12. See also Henri Corbin, "Mundus Imaginalis," *Spring*, 1972.

7. Brennan, *Ibid.*, pp. 61–2. For another example of hysterical religious phenomenon, cf. Aldous Huxley, *The Devils of Loudon* (London: Chattox-Windus, 1952).

8. For the historical background of the popularity of the sorrowful mysteries of Christ, see Jurgen Moltmann, *The Suffering God* (New York: Herder and Herder, 1977).

9. A, 2, 35.

10. A, Prologue.

11. *Ibid.*

12. See I.C.S. ed., pp. 66–7; also, Frances Yates, *The Art of Memory* (London: Penguin, 1966) ch. 6, "Renaissance Memory: The Memory Theatre of Guilio Camillo."

13. A, 2, 5.

14. See M. L. von Franz, *Number and Time* (Evanston: Northwestern, 1974), for further material on the window allegory in the Middle Ages, "fenestra aeternitatis," p. 260.

15. This is not to say that there is necessarily a chronological progression in the process; it has, rather, a simultaneity. The rearrangement was for didactic purposes.

16. C, Prologue.

17. C, 17.

18. C, Prologue.

19. C, 20; and Ps 82:2.

20. N, 2 17.

21. Jung, *Psychological Types*, p. 474.

22. E. Allison Peers, *Handbook to the Life and Times of St Teresa and St John of the Cross* (London: Burns and Oates, 1954), p. 213.

23. F, Prologue.

24. *Ibid.*

25. F, 3; and Jung, *The Practice of Psychotherapy*, pp. 165–323.

26. C, 28.

27. Quoted from Père Bruno, *Three Mystics* (London: Sheed and Ward, 1952), pp. 96–98.

28. James Joyce, *Ulysses* (London, 1936), p. 30.

29. A. Peter Elkin, *Aboriginal Men of High Degree* (Sydney, 1944), p. 78.

30. See St Teresa F, 3, 3.

31. See *Memories, Dreams and Reflections* ed. Aniela Jaffe (New York, 1965), p. 30. Hereafter "MDR."

32. Eliz. Hamilton, *The Great Teresa* (London: Burns and Oates 1960), pp. 115–117.

33. MDR, p. 32.

34. Brennan, *Ibid.*, p. 65.

35. MDR, p. 24 ff.

36. *Ibid.*

37. N, 1, 14.

38. *Ibid.*

39. N, 2, 10. See also Jung, *Aion*, for Jung's quotation from *Gloria Mundi*: "that with this fire is mingled the Godhead itself, and this fire purifies," p. 130.

40. MDR, p. 9; See also Aniela Jaffe, "Creative Periods in Jung's Life," *Spring*, 1972.

41. Vol. VI of the *Collected Works, Psychological Types.*

42. See Jung's letter to Gerda Hibert, March 28, 1937, in *Letters 1901–1905* (Princeton, 1973), p. 230.

43. *Ibid*, pp. 391–393.

44. *Ibid.*, p. 448.

45. Jung, *Alchemical Studies*, p. 171.

46. A, Prologue; F, 2.

47. A, 2, 32.

48. In the *Ascent-Dark Night*, there are 62 references to David.

49. N, st. 3, (trans. W. Barstone); See also N, 2, 17, "An explanation of the secrecy of this dark contemplation."

50. *Ibid.*, p. 494.

51. Cf. Hannah Arendt's commentary on inner and outer space, "Vita Activa vs. Vita Contemplativa," in *The Human Condition* (New York, 1965).

52. *Ibid.*

53. See Aniela Jaffe, *Creative Periods*.

54. MDR, ch. 6, 7.

55. Vols. V, VI of the *Collected Works*.

56. It is interesting to note that a number of alchemical works that Jung investigated were the products of contemporaries of St John of the Cross, e.g., Arileus (1620), Theobald de Hoghelande (1500), Johannes de Rupercissa (1561), Paracelsus (1541), and a number of others. There is evidence of at least an unconscious alchemical influence in the writings of St John: this can be observed in his use of scripture — symbolic interpretation, and his overall use of symbolism: see N, 2, 1: "An explanation of the word 'disguised' and a description of the colors of the disguise that the soul wears in this night."

57. D. H. Lawrence, *Last Poems*, ed. G. Orioli, (New York, 1933).

58. B. Bachelard, *On Poetic Imagination and Reverie*, trans. G. Gaudin, (Indianapolis: Bobbs-Merrill, 1971), p. 82.

59. June Singer, *Androgyny*, (New York: Doubleday, 1977), "The Philosopher's Stone in Alchemy," p. 142.

60. See Aniela Jaffe, *Ibid*.

61. Erich Neumann, *Art and the Creative Unconscious* (Princeton, 1959), p. 144.

62. MDR, p. 8.

63. Erich Neumann, *Ibid*.

64. Kavanaugh and Rodriguez, "Introduction," p. 45.

65. Jung, *The Practice of Psychotherapy*.

66. John was 26 at the time; Teresa 52.

67. St Teresa, *The Way of Perfection*, and *Interior Castle*. In the commentary on the *Spiritual Canticle*, St John writes: Teresa "left writings about these spiritual matters, which are admirably done, and which I hope will soon be printed and brought to light." C, 13, 7.

68. E. A. Peers, *Ibid.*, pp. 116, 213.

69. MDR, p. 173.

70. Cf. Emma Jung (M. L. von Franz) *The Grail Legend* (New York, 1970), and Emma Jung, *Animus and Anima* (Zurich, 1957).

71. Barbara Hannah, *Jung, His Life and Work* (New York: Putnam's Sons, 1976), pp. 112–117.

72. A, st. 1, vs. 2.
73. Jung, *The Practice of Psychotherapy*, p. 210.
74. Jung, *Symbols of Transformation*, p. 90.
75. A, Prologue.
76. N, 1, 14.
77. F, st. 1.
78. F, st. 1.
79. St Teresa, C, 7, 4, 1.
80. Jung, *Ibid.* p. 167.
81. *Ibid.*, p. 214.
82. *Ibid.*
83. *Ibid.*
84. C, st. 17, trans. W. Barstone.
85. John Layard, "The Incest Taboo and the Virgin Archetype," *Eranos Yearbook*, 1945, p. 253 ff.
86. *Ibid.*, p. 230.
87. *Ibid.*, p. 234.
88. *Ibid.*, p. 238.
89. *Ibid.*, p. 443.
90. F, st. 3, trans. Kavanaugh and Rodriguez.
91. John Steinbeck, *To a God Unknown* (New York, 1968), p. 30.
92. Citation from unpublished lecture of Gerhard Adler, "Forgetting and Memory," *Panarion*, 1976.
93. Teilhard de Chardin, *The Phenomenon of Man* (New York: Harper-Row, 1965), p. 221.
94. Ida Rolf, *A Therapy of Structural Integration* (Boulder, 1970).
95. Jung, *The Symbolic Life*, p. 11.
96. *Esquire*, Vol. 80, Sept. 1977.
97. Jung, *Experimental Researches*, p. 72.
98. Jung, *The Symbolic Life*, p. 22.
99. MDR, Intro., p. 5.
100. St Teresa, L, 17, 6, p. 103, trans. E. A. Peers.
101. Richard Leaky, *People of the Lake*, New York, 1978, p. 69.
102. ISM, 18:18.
103. Cicero, *De Oratore*, II, 1xxxvi.
104. Frances Yates, *The Art of Memory* (London, 1966), p. 224.
105. *Ibid.* (*Dialoghi Italiani*), p. 329.
106. N, st. 2, trans. L. Nicholson.
107. Jung, *Two Essays on Analytical Psychology*, pp. 70–71; St John, A, 2, 9.
108. Plato, *Cratylus*; See *Phaedo*, 80d.
109. R.I.P.
110. Freud, *Psychopathology of Everyday Life*, (London; Penguin, 1975), p. 40.
111. Jung, "On the Psychology of So-called Occult Phenomena," "Studies in Word Association," "Cryptomnesia," Vols. 1, 7, 2.
112. Jung, *The Symbolic Life*, p. 258.
113. *Ibid.*

114. Gospel of John, Prologue.

115. See Bernhard Anderson, *Understanding the Old Testament* (Englewood Cliffs: Prentice-Hall, 1957), pp. 167–79.

116. Louis Ginzberg, *Legends of the Jews*, Vol. 5, "Birth of the Child," (Philadelphia, 1955), p. 77.

117. *Tibetan Book of the Dead*, trans. Evans-Wentz (London, 1927), p. 207.

118. Jung, *The Structure and Dynamics of the Psyche*, pp. 522–3.

119. Henri Bergson, *Matter and Memory* (Paris, 1896).

120. W. H. Auden, *Collected Longer Poems* (London: Faber and Faber, 1968), p. 21.

121. Karl Kerenyi, "Mnemosyne-Lesmosyne-Springs of Memory and Forgetting," Zurich: *Spring*, 1977, pp. 120–130.

122. Freud, *The Future of an Illusion* (London, 1962).

123. M. P. Nilson, "Die Quellen der Lethe und Mnemosyne," *Eranos*, 1943, p. 62 ff: *Opuscula selecta*, III (Lund, 1960), p. 85 ff.

124. Kerenyi, *Ibid.*

125. Jn 4:3–15.

126. Onians, *The Origins of European Thought* (Cambridge: Cambridge U. Press, 1965), p. 215 ff.

127. Jn 2:1–11; see also Jung, *Symbols of Transformation*, on the meaning of Christ's dialogue with Nicodemus, p. 225 ff.

128. Trans. W. Barnstone.

129. Trans. W. Barnstone.

130. H. W. Schumann, *Buddhism* (London, 1973), p. 173 ff.

131. F, st. 2, trans. Kavanaugh and Rodriguez.

132. Phil 3:13.

133. C. A. Meier, *Ancient Incubation and Modern Psychotherapy*, trans. Monika Curtis, (Evanston, 1967), pp. 97–100. Similar processes can be observed in the initiation rites of the shamman. See M. Eliade, *Australian Religions*, (Ithica, 1973), pp. 53, 95.

134. P. Tillich, *The Courage to Be* (New Haven, 1952).

135. C, sts. 19, 20, trans. Kavanaugh and Rodriguez.

136. F, st. 1.

137. N, st. 2, vs. 1–2.

138. C, st. 11, 23, trans. W. Barstone.

139. Jb 30:21.

140. F, st. 1.

141. *Ibid.*

142. See *Du*, no. 4, April, 1955.

143. Jb 30:16, 27.

144. E. Brunner, *Christian Hope* (Philadelphia, 1956).

145. Jung, *The Practice of Psychotherapy*, p. 242, fig. 4.

146. A, 3, 1–15.

147. Heinrich Boll, *The Clown* (London, 1974), p. 79.

148. See Jung, *The Practice of Psychotherapy*, p. 246.

149. See Jung, *Experimental Researches*, p. 426–38.

150. See p. 196.

151. See Henry Reed, "The Art of Remembering Dreams," *Quadrant*, Summer 1976.

152. *By the Waters of Babylon*, st. 6, trans. W. Barnstone.

153. St. Augustine, *Confessions*, Bk. X, ch. 11, 18. According to St. Augustine, the soul, by the help of illumination, "Pre-contains" the power of grasping every immutable truth; all knowledge is but a reminiscence.

154. Jung, *The Visions Seminars*. Zurich: *Spring* 1976, p. 387.

155. Matthew Arnold, "Absence," *Oxford Dictionary of Verse* (London, 1964), p. 12.

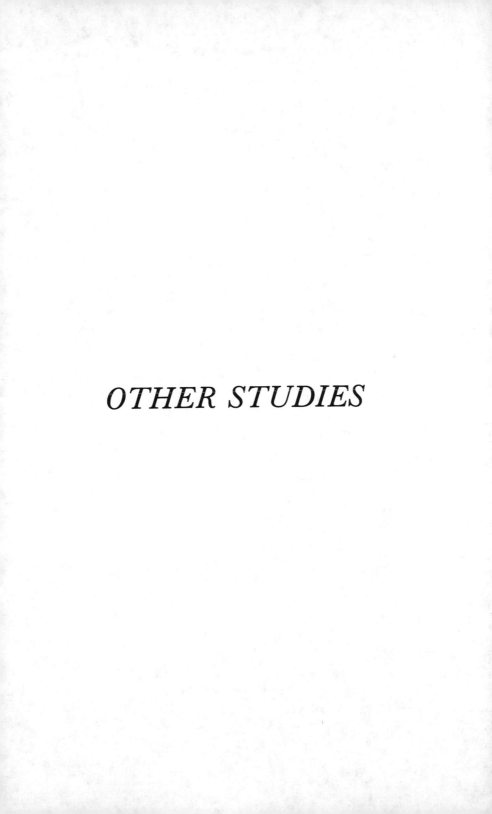

OTHER STUDIES

THE QUESTION OF FAITH IN
ST JOHN
OF THE CROSS

Karol Wojtyła, S.T.D. (Pope John Paul II)

One of the conclusions of note in this erudite article by the future Pope John Paul II is that "mystical contemplation — it seems to us — can only be understood as the highest actualization of faith, since this reveals most clearly its essential nature." His study helps one appreciate how important that "actualization of faith" was for St John of The Cross and for people today.

INTRODUCTORY REMARKS

In citing texts, reference is always to the edition *Obras de San Juan de la Cruz, Doctor de la Iglesia*, editadas y anotadas por el P. Silverio de Santa Teresa, O.C.D. in five volumes, published in Burgos 1929–1931. Citations in the notes are given in the original Spanish from this edition.

All that is set forth in this synthesis is based on long and accurate analysis of texts. Here, however, we present only the result of the examination of particular texts referring to that part of the works of the holy doctor where such doctrine is found.

THE IMPORTANCE OF FAITH IN THE WORKS
OF ST JOHN OF THE CROSS

How is the question of faith encountered in that famous tetralogy of St John of the Cross, Doctor of the Church? That is the first question of this dissertation. For as is well known, the works of this holy author, although they comprise a true and complete theological system, composed with perfect intrinsic logic, do not emphasize a speculative and abstract explanation of the problem. What prevails is a description of the mystical life in its particular phenomena, which take on a totally concrete appearance. Moreover, those phenomena are coordinated on the one hand by a great experiential knowledge of what occurs in the mystical life and, on the other hand, by certain metaphysical principles. In this way we are presented with a fullness of doctrine that simultaneously teaches us particular and concrete aspects of the spiritual life, and reveals its metaphysical and abstract side.

To the fullness of the mystical life in the human subject belong several elements which are set forth by the holy doctor in his works like a theological system. For each has its value, not only psychological and connatural to the subject in whom it exists, but also theological, because of the object to whom it opens up the human soul and its faculties. St John of the Cross has his own conception of the supernatural and mystical life, which permeates all his works. This is his conception of the union of the human soul and its faculties with God. This supernatural union, as is evident from Book Two, 5 of the *Ascent of Mount Carmel*, consists in the supernatural communication of the human soul with God according to the order of grace, whereby God is united to the soul not only as creator and preserver of its being, but by means of grace and charity offers himself to the soul supernaturally,[1] according to his divinity. Thus the supernatural union of the human soul with God in this life appears as the increasingly full actualization of the supernatural life, which is germinally present in the soul by sanctifying grace. But sanctifying grace of itself constitutes only

a habitual state, a habit of union in the substance of the soul.[2]
St John of the Cross simply presupposes such a state. He con-
ceives of the union itself in a dynamic manner. It is not simply
a question of a habitual state, in which the soul remains united
with God, but of supernatural *life*, in which the supernatural
state is habitually actualized within the soul and its faculties.
Moreover, the unitive actualization of the supernatural life is
shared by the faculties. Such actualization cannot be expected
in this life in a permanent manner, but only transiently. The
faculties themselves assume appropriate habits or supernatural
virtues, by means of which acts of supernatural union of the
human soul with God become possible.

Thus St John of the Cross introduces the question of the theological virtues, which are immediately presupposed as means
of supernatural union of the human faculties with God, and by
means of which the whole supernatural union of the soul passes
from its habitual state to successive actualizations. Thus it is
rendered dynamic and it evolves.

In this way there are ascribed to the three theological virtues
three distinct unitive functions with respect to the distinct spiritual faculties of the soul. In this trichotomy St John of the Cross
sets forth his whole doctrine concerning the supernatural union
of the human soul with God in this life. On the one hand, there
is the psychological trichotomy: the three higher, properly spiritual faculties of the soul—intellect, memory and will—to
which corresponds, on the other hand, the theological trichotomy, the three theological virtues: faith, hope and charity
(love).[3]

Only the spiritual part of the soul is capable of supernatural
union with God. It attains a habitual state of union in sanctifying grace and in the theological virtues, by whose acts it is later
rendered supernaturally alive in the divine union. This union
is perfected in stages and increases in an organic and vital manner up to the highest degree possible in this life, the so-called
"transforming union," in which the soul becomes divine by participation, even (according to St John's expression) "God by
participation" ("Dios por participación").[4]

Therefore St John of the Cross has little to say about the static and abstract concept of grace or the theological virtues. The divine union of the soul takes on a totally dynamic and vital aspect, for it evolves in the continuous actualization of the supernatural virtues. By such actualization the virtues themselves are perfected and appear more and more in their specific and native perfection. By means of the theological virtues one lives supernaturally. In the development of the supernatural life and the vital evolution of the theological virtues their own nature is manifested.

The works of St John of the Cross present to us this aspect of the problem. It seems that we must seek his doctrine concerning the nature of faith under this general aspect. When the holy doctor sets forth his system according to the above-mentioned trichotomy, he surely does not exclude all the other virtues, which cooperate in perfecting the human soul both naturally and supernaturally. St John simply centers his attention upon those whose proper task is to unite the faculties of the soul with God, that is, those which are theological by their very nature. Concerning the others, he is silent. One might be able to detect them as included in the process of union and concealed in the vital evolution of faith, hope or charity. However they cooperate, one thing remains certain: the unitive formality, that is, the theological basis of the supernatural life, can be reduced to those three.

To faith is attributed the unitive role with respect to the intellect. All that has been said thus far pertains also to the consideration of faith. For it is not treated distinctly and separately, but it has its role, along with the others, in the total union of the soul with God. It evolves along with the others and intervenes along with them in every stage of union. According to the mind of St John of the Cross, we can affirm nothing concerning faith in isolation, dead faith. Faith lives by charity and this life of faith is properly described and profoundly explained in his works. How can its proper and specific role be discerned, when in the description there are always mingled supernatural elements of the union that flow from charity and from hope, along with those that flow from faith? St John of the Cross, when he asserted that the habitual state of union with God is rooted in sanctifying grace for the substance of the soul and in the theological virtues for the soul's faculties,[5] immediately indicated the means for discerning. The means are to be found in the natural subject, that is, in the faculties of the soul, in which the theological virtues subsist and do their work. All those elements of the union which are related to the intellect find their immediate reason for being in faith, and they emanate directly from faith as from their proper root. Surely we must admit the more remote influence of charity and hope and other virtues (we will speak of the gifts of the Holy Spirit in the proper place), but nevertheless faith is indicated as the virtue to which is proximately and properly ascribed the whole unitive process of the intellect of a person in this life with God.[6] In this sense faith is posited as the means of union for the intellect and it is indicated as being the means of union throughout the tetralogy. We have, therefore, in the strictest sense, a treatise on faith as the means of union with God. Faith performs this proper and immediate function as means with respect to the intellect, while mediately it cooperates toward the total union of the soul with God.

Thus it seems that the aspect under which the whole matter of faith is dealt with in the works of St John of the Cross is functional. "Means of union" of the intellect and of the soul with God does not seem to indicate anything more. Therefore, is it possible to consider faith in the works of St John of the Cross from the point of view of its nature? Is it possible to ask: what is faith? and not simply: what does it do? or what does it accomplish? A response to the latter questions seems to be contained in the study by Fr Labourdette, OP entitled "La foi théologale et la connaissance mystique d'après Saint Jean de la Croix,"[7] in which he treats not so much of faith as such, but of the unitive role of faith. This concept corresponds directly with the character of the works of St John of the Cross and all that is explicitly treated in them concerning faith. Nevertheless, another concept seems possible, namely, that which not only explains the unitive function of faith, but also draws some conclusions concerning the nature that can be deduced from that function, indicating from the behavior of the virtue something about its essence. Such is the purpose of this present study.

The concept seems possible. Why? Because although it is based only remotely on texts, so that it can be extracted only by exact and prolonged analysis, it is nevertheless discoverable. All that is described in a particular way concerning faith in the works of St John of the Cross demonstrates for us the exercise of this virtue from the point of view of experience. All must be understood as actualizations of faith. St John of the Cross has offered us all the premises for conceiving of it in this way. The union of the human soul, and especially of its faculties, with God passes from its habitual and obscure state (see A,2,5,2) into its actualized state. St John of the Cross explicitly presupposes this. Therefore when he describes the evolution of the supernatural life by means of what is being immediately and experientially lived, then these phenomena themselves, according to this presupposition, constitute a series of actualizations, in which the unitive habits bring about the union of the soul with God. Thus, for example, when he describes particular aspects of faith as practiced and experienced, we then find actualizations of this virtue in which its very nature is revealed. So we immediately have a series of actual manifestations of the nature of faith. In this process we find some means of treating of its nature.

This means is not, however, the ultimate one. We have a still deeper basis for collecting and synthetically comparing the aforementioned actual manifestations, by which the life of faith is described. This basis is the metaphysical concept according to which the virtue of faith as means of union is treated in its most intimate aspect. To those who attentively read and investigate the works of St John of the Cross, there becomes apparent the force of irrefutable logic, which binds together the phenomena of the supernatural life. We may ask what is the real and vital root of this logical connection. In the final analysis, this root is to be found on the level of being, in the metaphysical state of the question, which, though brief, nevertheless powerfully influences the whole work of St John of the Cross, manifesting its influence precisely in this aforementioned logic.

To this ontological concept, therefore, according to which the virtue of faith is first introduced, we must now refer all particular experiences. Faith — the means of union of the soul with God in this life — is first determined and first constituted according to the principles of being whereby everything is referred to God. Beginning now to explain the doctrine of faith of St John of the Cross from this first ontological foundation, as we find it in the works of the holy doctor, we will lay the foundations for understanding the total unity whereby he makes known to us his mind on the subject.

FAITH AS AN ABSTRACT CONCEPT: THE FACULTY OF THEOLOGICAL TRANSCENDENCE

As has already been said, St John of the Cross treats of faith as a means of union of the soul with God, assigning to this virtue a characteristic unitive function with respect to the intellect of a person in this life. The assertion that "faith is the means of union of the soul with God" is found many times and in various forms in the works of the holy author. Besides many others, it seems especially appropriate to cite those texts in which the idea of means of union is more precisely expressed concerning faith. Faith is said to be a proportionate,[8] and likewise proximate,[9] proper and accommodated,[10] legitimate,[11] and adequate[12] means of union.

All those adjectives, which have a certain speculative value, seem to imply approximately the same role of mediation for faith, as is easily proved by analysis. This role is very well explained in A,2,3,2,[13] where we find the key to St John of the Cross' whole doctrine concerning faith, especially from a metaphysical and abstract point of view. The holy author introduces it very simply. Here the intellect of the person confronts God. By itself the intellect is capable of conceiving only the essence of what it perceives by means of the senses, either in itself or in an essential representation of itself. The intellect is intrinsically proportioned to know essentially all such things. This is the scope of its being and operations. Here it can serve very well as proportionate means. With respect to the divine essence, however, this natural proportion is lacking with regard to the intellect's being and operations. It cannot, therefore, by its own power form a representation of the divine essence. For, of itself, it is oriented toward creatures, in which can be found no essential representations of God. For all creatures, inferior and superior, lack any likeness to the divine essence. To be sure, according to the common opinion of theologians, they have a relationship to God in the order of being, and, in fact, constitute some trace of God that is more or less perfect according to the degree of perfection of their being. But nowhere is there found in them a likeness of the divine essence. They remain dissimilar and infinitely distant from the essence of God.[14] Therefore even the intellect, naturally oriented toward them, cannot naturally perceive in them the divine essence in some essential likeness.

Thus St John introduces the metaphysical aspect of the problem. The intentional (representational) order must be noted: essential likeness designates a likeness of the essence accessible to the intellect. The intellect, because of the limited extent of its natural object, is restricted to areas of dissimilarity with reference to the divine essence. For natural creatures, which connaturally fall within its scope, are related to God according to their manner and perfection of being (in this respect, therefore, they are capable of leading the intellect to God), but they are basically and absolutely deficient with regard to the divine essence as such. Thus the intellect's journey to God, when left to its own resources, is restricted to traces of being, to the ontological relationship, which creatures still render possible. To this incapacity of the intellect with regard to the object there corresponds its intrinsic subjective dissimilarity with respect to the divine essence. The intellect is not capable of conceiving the divine essence because of its intrinsic disproportion. It is completely incapable. The divine essence is absolutely supernatural with reference to any created nature. In this comparative sense we must understand what St John of the Cross states in A,2,5,4: it is not a question here of the natural union with God, which consists in the conservation of the "natural being" of the soul by God, but rather of that supernatural union, which consists in the communication of the "supernatural being" of God himself through grace and love. The intellect, being natural, is necessarily excluded from such unitive communication. Faith is declared to be the proportionate means of such union. For in faith is found due proportion with the "supernatural being" of God, which is called "proportion of likeness — *proporción de semejanza.*" Because of this "proportion of likeness" faith is declared to be the proportionate means of union of the intellect with God, with the divine essence as such. Proportion seems to indicate first the intentional order (for the intentional relationship of the intellect to God seeks for itself some proportion to the divine essence, as is evident from the whole context). In this sense, therefore, faith provides the intellect with an essential likeness of God, as is clearly seen in A,2,8 and still better perhaps in A,2,9. By means of faith the intellect becomes capable of a relationship to God in the order of divinity. Such a capacity is completely absent from the intellect of itself; it is infused into it by faith. Faith then merits to be designated as *the faculty of theological transcendence*, in that it causes the intellect to transcend to God not only in the order of being, but in the order of the divine essence, which is completely supernatural — in the order of divinity itself.

Such a conclusion as to the metaphysical and abstract nature of faith is not found explicitly in the works of St John of the Cross, but can easily be deduced from certain texts, especially A,2,8 compared with A,2,5. It is based, moreover, on a careful analysis of the concept of "essential likeness" and on the clear distinction that the holy doctor makes between the natural union of the soul with God and the supernatural union (see A,2,5,3-4). Natural union implies that contact with God as creator and conserver is proper to the soul, and thus is in the order of natural being. Supernatural union is conceived as being totally in the order of participating in the divinity, where the soul, according to the expression of the holy author, becomes "Dios por participación." Reducing that general presupposition to our subject of faith, we find in this virtue the same manner of participating in the divinity for the intellect. According to the strict logic of the holy doctor, we can affirm that faith causes the intellect to participate in the divinity—or makes it participatively divine. And in such an expression is explained the whole metaphysical notion of that "proporción de semejanza," proportion of likeness, which St John of the Cross teaches concerning faith.

Summarizing all this, we see the concatenation of concepts, of which the metaphysical and abstract concept of faith in St John of the Cross is constituted: faith is said to be the proportionate means of union of the intellect with God. It is declared such because of the kind of essential likeness that is enjoys with God. Essential likeness implies the intentional order because of the importance of the subject of faith, which is the intellect: faith is oriented toward the divine essence itself, the essence of divinity. This is why we have set forth the notion of the faculty of theological transcendence of the intellect to God. Thus faith, which is said to be the proportionate means of union of the intellect with him, makes the likeness of the divine essence accessible to the intellect, in that it renders the intellect a participant in the divinity.

In all of the aforesaid there seems to be borne out what we said about the metaphysical concept of the nature of faith in St John of the Cross. It is called metaphysical inasmuch as it teaches the first principles by which the very being of faith is determined—the being of faith, which is presupposed from its operations. In all of the preceding considerations we were rather explaining the "operations" of faith. This was certainly because of its function of mediating proportionately between the intellect and divinity. It fulfills that function by operating. But operation presupposes being, and St John of the Cross very clearly refers to the essential notion of the nature of faith, to the very being of faith. That notion is also included in the same concept of essential likeness (*semejanza esencial*). Just as the intellect cannot in its natural operation attain to God himself because of the intrinsic disproportion (dissimilitude) of its created nature with respect to the divine essence, so faith, which is infused into the intellect as the faculty of theological transcendence, causing it to attain to the inmost principle of divinity in God, must first have in its own being this essential likeness to God. This is expressly taught, moreover, in A,2,8,3, where faith is clearly contrasted with any created beings whatsoever in the natural order. Therefore it pertains to the supernatural order, which is the order of the divine essence as such. Faith is intrinsically constituted for participation in this essence, participation in the divinity itself. What causes the intellect to participate in the divinity must be presupposed to have this participation. Such seems to be the principle of its nature as a metaphysical and abstract concept. Likeness to the divine essence in participation of it, indeed the very participation in the divinity, constitutes for St John of the Cross the essential being of faith — fully "theological" being, in which the intellect receives the seed of its supernatural transformation, and in virtue of which it is subsequently made "divine by participation."

THE OBJECTIVE IMPORTANCE OF THE PROBLEM: FAITH CONSISTS IN PARTICIPATION IN THE DIVINITY AS ITS OBJECT

The whole preceding consideration of the metaphysical nature of faith was completely abstract in that it treated of the nature of faith entirely in the abstract, that is, apart from and independently of a psychological subject. The "theological" being of faith, considered as pure participation in the divinity, seems like something ideal and isolated. Concretely, however, that "theological" being always exists in a real connection with a psychological subject, with the intellect of a person in this life, in whom the virtue of faith subsists. In such a virtue, to be sure, its formal essence consists in that "theological" participation in the divinity, associated, however, because of the nature of the psychological subject, with many psychological elements, in which it resides and evolves in a vital manner. St John of the Cross teaches us about the unfolding of this evolution. The essential nature of faith, that is, its "theological" being, consisting as it does in participation in the divinity by the intellect, is more and more revealed as it is gradually purified of many strictly psychological elements by which it appears to be constricted. These psychological elements are not only intellectual or conceptual, but also sensory. In this gradual purification, faith itself is perfected, inasmuch as its own actualizations or acts approach more and more closely to the purely "theological" nature of this intimate participation in the divinity. Every actualization or act of faith also includes that "theological" participation in the divinity by the intellect and many accompanying psychological elements. In all this, one thing is certain: there is no actualization of faith in which the principle of divine participation is absent. There is a change, however, in the intrinsic proportion between the theological transcendence and the psychological concomitants. The theological transcendence increases, while the psychological concomitants diminish and become more passive. Thus participation in the divinity by the intellect changes the appearance of its particular actualization, that is, the appearance of its operations. In this way faith evolves in its own vital manner from within. And likewise the intellect becomes more and more deeply united with God in the order of divinity. For faith, inasmuch as it is a participation in the divinity, not only unites the intellect with God, but it contains within itself the very substance of such union. So the evolution of living faith, according to the mind of St John of the Cross, designates precisely the progress of union of the intellect with God.

This has been an anticipated projection of the whole doctrine of St John of the Cross concerning the virtue of faith. It is presented in an excellent manner, since he has a keen sense of concretization from experience. The abstract principle of the problem he sets forth with theological exactitude; the concrete he knows from experience. Moreover he knows in the same way how the theological principle is reflected in a particular type of operation and how it is actualized. Thus his whole doctrine on faith combines both elements: the exactness of the theological principle is verified by the experiential operation, by which the virtue of faith produces its actualizations or acts. Experience on the one hand confirms and verifies the abstract principle and, on the other hand, seeks to be explained by it. This becomes most apparent when he deals with the question of the object of faith.

St John of the Cross never raises this question in isolation and "ex professo." Nevertheless, we can discover it by examining his texts. In the abstract concept of faith, which we expressed in the formula "faculty of theological transcendence," the object is immediately touched upon. For when faith causes the intellect to transcend to the order of divinity in God, the proper object of this transcendence is already apparent. The very idea of transcending "theologically" to God is explained with reference to the object. Therefore the proper and "formal" object of faith is the divine essence itself, that is, the order of divinity in God.

Yet in asserting this the whole question is by no means settled. St John of the Cross had, as we presupposed, an acute sense for perceiving and verifying the metaphysical and abstract elements in a single, concrete, experiential situation. And he saw the object of faith in this way. Faith truly causes the intellect to transcend to the level of divinity in God, and then causes it to participate objectively in the divine essence. However, the process of this objective participation must be understood according to the person's manner of believing, and therefore should include the psychological role of the subject. Thus the objective participation in the divinity, which everyone understands to be the result of the essential representation of God in faith, is accompanied by an element of dissimilarity because of the psychological subject. For the latter is not essentially changed by faith, but retains its own nature and actualizes its supernatural participation in and from this nature.

That whole question, which is particularly dealt with by St

John of the Cross, needs to be more fully explained. For in the concrete human being the divine object as such begins to be participated in when there are presented to the intellect truths revealed by God, by which the hidden mysteries of the divinity are made known to it. In those truths, which are presented connaturally and in conceptual forms, the intellect learns the realities that subsist objectively in the divinity.[15] Contact with those truths means, for the intellect, an objective participation in the divinity. But how can it be called objective participation in the divinity when revealed truths are simply believed? The explanation for this is found in St John of the Cross in his exact analysis of the process of human knowledge and intellection.[16] St John delineates this process in a rather general manner. He speaks of abstraction, which is performed on the material offered by the senses and retained by the imagination. Abstraction tends toward understanding the very substance of the thing, "sustancia entendida." This "understood substance" seems to be the objective essence of the thing as conceived by the intellect in intellection. Therefore when the intellect succeeds in understanding this completely and exhaustively, it is said to be united with it. Thus the whole notion of union of the intellect with any object consists in its intellection of the essence of that object, in the intellectual assumption of its substance, which flows from the process of abstraction. Then all the accidental elements of human cognition, which consist in particular sensory representations of the object, and in which the senses, both internal and external, have thus far had an active role, now cease, and the intellect remains quiet in the intellection of the object apprehended by it.

Thus the union of the intellect with an object is conceived by St John of the Cross as the "understood substance" (*sustancia entendida*) of the thing. It is supposed, then, that the intellect naturally tends to apprehend the essence of the object. All this is clearly apparent in the writings of St John. Therefore in its contact with any object this tendency of the intellect to apprehend its essence (*sustancia entendida*) is considered completely proper and connatural to the intellect. This is called, according to the thought of St John of the Cross, the intellect's primary and unitive natural tendency. We now recognize that faith has the capacity of transcending to the divinity itself, and that this capacity is infused into the intellect. The unitive tendency of the intellect is directed toward any object. This tendency, as we saw above, in accord the thought of St John of the Cross, is primary and connatural to the intellect. In faith, however, it is rendered supernatural.

How does this come about? That is the next question. We must first note that we are no longer speaking of the sheer importance of the object in faith, but we have begun immediately with the question of the act of faith. Why so? The answer must be that it would be possible to pose the question of the object of faith from the metaphysical and abstract point of view (and this we have explained above). The Mystical Doctor, however, offers us rather a treatise on the concrete actualities of faith, in which the objective importance is not dealt with separately, but must be sought in its actualization and be judged from that standpoint. The union of the intellect with its proper object is to be found precisely in the act of faith. The act of faith is understood as being unitive because it is objective. It is unitive, indeed, with the very divinity in God, because this divinity becomes its object. It is in this unitive movement of the intellect, in seeking the very essence of the object in order to understand it, that the intellect is rendered supernatural, that is, it is supernaturally united with the supernatural divine essence itself.

How does this happen? St John of the Cross does not speak of the abstract importance of the object. Rather he teaches us about the very act of unitive participation in the object, where the supernatural object presented to the intellect is reflected in this faculty's manner of being and acting. He teaches us how the intellect lives in faith with its supernatural object. Here is the dynamic aspect of the problem. Every act—or, better still, every actualization of faith—bears within itself an intimate relationship to the divinity as to its own object and each is intrinsically formed in virtue of this essential relationship, which therefore has a share in all its acts.

The process of such supernatural objective participation is described in various places in the works of St John.[17] To the intellect, as we have already said, are presented truths revealed by God, in which many things are made known to it concerning the divine essence under a conceptual form completely adapted to the capacity of the intellect. All these things come "from hearing," and thus through the senses, in the ordinary way in which the intellect always encounters the appropriate material for intellection. As soon as the operation of the senses is completed, the intellect seeks the very essence of the thing to be understood (*sustancia entendida*) — this being the first unitive movement of the intellect. However, in the case of truths of revelation, which come to the intellect "from hearing," this ordinary way of understanding is precluded and its unitive tendency remains psychologically in a vacuum. For what is thus offered "from hearing" cannot be represented by any sensory form, nor can it be interiorly imagined according to any likeness of itself. For the divine essence does not have any such likeness in the order of creatures. It is presented as precisely itself. All concepts of revelation express it objectively to the intellect. Therefore the intellect is established in true contact with the divine essence as with its object. This unitive contact is established for the intellect by faith, the metaphysical means of union of the intellect with the divinity. At the same time the virtue of faith resides in the psychological subject and from this subject it takes on a certain psychological aspect. This psychological aspect of faith is considered by St John of the Cross as a consequence of the metaphysical presupposition that no created nature belonging to the natural order can have any likeness to the divinity. But the intellect is a natural faculty of the soul, in itself a created nature. It is therefore intrinsically incapable of offering any likeness of the divinity in the order of its own nature, that is, in the psychological order connatural to itself.

Therefore the union of the intellect with God, which faith brings about, and which is called complete from the metaphysical point of view, nevertheless is totally devoid of any psychological element and therefore lacks completeness in that sense. Such a unitive psychological element is found in the intellect's unitive contact with any object connatural to itself, that is, when the intellect by means of abstraction succeeds in apprehending the very essence of the object (*sustancia entendida*). In faith there is no such psychologically unitive element. Articles of faith, in which truths concerning God are presented to the intellect, can surely not be assimilated by the senses, because inasmuch as they present divine truths, they lack any sensory form or likeness. Nor can they be assimilated by the intellect according to their formal being, because the divinity as such totally transcends the intellect.[18] Thus, in the psychological order, any intellectual form or likeness, as well as any clear intellection (*sustancia entendida*) of the divine object is excluded. Consider once again that the proper "substance" of the revealed truths, their formal essence, is the divinity, which they present to the intellect. They present it in a conceptual form. The intellect apprehends the revealed concepts by believing. But when it seeks to understand the divine essence from these concepts, such understanding proves impossible.[19] Thus faith is declared to be, on the one hand, a truly unitive relationship between the intellect and the divinity, while, on the other hand, in a psychological sense, because it lacks "sustancia entendida," that is, understood divinity, it lacks any psychological form of union.

Thus faith as a proportionate means of union of the intellect with God because of essential likeness is shown to inhere in the psychological subject. Because of the intensity of excessive light,[20] which is infused into the intellect by faith, the intellect consents to the truths revealed, although it does not see psychologically their formal essence, namely, the very essence of God as such. On the part of the intellect as a psychological faculty, we encounter the problem of assent to revealed truths (*consentimiento*), which we will treat in due time. For now it suffices to repeat the exact words of St John: the intellect is engaged in a supernatural activity which totally surpasses and exceeds its natural power of being and operating—then, as it were, "it is conquered and overcome"[21] intrinsically by a superior, entirely supernatural light, in which it participates proportionately in the divinity itself.

In the first place, we are dealing with participation in the divinity as object. This objective participation, however, has a corresponding part in the subjective supernatural light which is infused into the intellect and by means of which it is elevated to supernatural activity. Thus there comes into play that proportion of likeness which faith, as proportionate means of union of the intellect with God, has within itself. In this proportion, which is intrinsic to itself, the intellect exceeds its natural and psychological limits. Faith acts upon the intellect, expanding its capacity and its natural range of operations in such a way that the intellect, although of itself incapable of connaturally conceiving of the divine essence from the revealed truths, nevertheless firmly adheres to them. This adherence is firm, but is at the same time "obscure," which means it is psychologically devoid of any form or likeness of the object, without its "sustancia entendida." It does not pertain to the created intellect to understand the divinity. Faith causes the intellect to transcend theologically to the divine essence as such, but faith does not enable the intellect to understand it. That theological transcendence, which the intellect possesses in faith (when it is actualized in a particular, psychological form of its activity, known experientially), cannot be called unitive in the same way that an act of clear intellection of an object connatural to the intellect is called unitive. The "infinite distance" which separates the created intellect from the divine essence as such remains also in any act of faith from the psychological point of view of the practice of that virtue. Thus faith appears as disproportion in proportion, as darkness accompanying an interior infusion of light. Here we find the inflexible logic of St John. The divinity cannot be seen by the intellect in this life. Nevertheless faith makes the intellect participate in it. This participation is called objective and, as such, unitive. Faith causes the intellect to adhere not only to the revealed truths in their conceptual form, but also to the divine essence itself. In this the native tendency of the intellect is satisfied in a totally supernatural way: the intellect cannot attain to the divinity except by faith. The intellect endowed with faith is united with God, which, in the thought of St John of the Cross, means: the intellect, in adhering firmly to the revealed truths, is united not only to their superficial conceptual form, but to the divine essence itself, which the revealed truths express. In his outline of the theory of intellectual cognition St John of the Cross is realistic. This realism, along with the intrinsic supernaturalness of faith previously affirmed in the abstract, underlies his conception of faith as means of union of the intellect with God and explains it.

The problem of the formal object is included here. Since faith is declared to be a faculty of theological transcendence, then any act of faith consists in participation in the divine object. Such union with the divine object is ultimately resolved not in a conceptual formula to be believed by faith, but in the divine essence itself to be attained by faith. Every act of faith is at the same time psychological, subsisting in the intellect, and thus in the category of a nature dissimilar to the divine essence. Any psychological likeness of the divinity in the intellect is absolutely excluded. Moreover, the more profoundly this relationship to the divine essence as the object of faith is reflected in the intellect, the more evident the aforesaid disproportion and dissimilarity becomes. There is no means of transcending from the natural to the supernatural except this obediential potency. Even then all interior participation on the part of the intellect in the divinity as object ends in the psychological darkness of the subject. This is darker as it is more profound.[22] The darkness of faith, in the thought of St John of the Cross, is not simply a concomitant of the objective participation of the intellect in the divinity. It is a true imprint of it in the subject. In its psychological darkness the intellect lives by the divine object of faith. This darkness is not simply lack of vision, of clear intellection of the divine essence as object. In this darkness the intellect, while remaining in faith, at the same time is said to be intensely recollected as it participates in the divine essence according to the proportional power of faith, in which its unitive tendency with respect to the object is supernaturally satisfied. Nevertheless, the divinity with which the intellect tends to be united does not shine in the intellect, but rather it is as if hidden in its darkness in the psychological vacuum of intellection. The darkness, or, better, the psychological vacuum of the subject serves experientially as an argument in favor of the strictly supernatural character of the object of faith: faith is dark, any psychological act of faith is dark, because its proper and formal object is the divinity.[23] The more that remains, in acts of faith, of elements psychologically satisfying to the intellect (or — still worse — to the senses, which serve the intellect in knowing), the less intensely and the less formally does it participate objectively in the divine essence. For the divine essence, when it is participated in, darkens its psychological object. It is participated in by faith — thus faith is called a "dark habit of the soul."

THE SUBJECTIVE IMPORTANCE OF THE PROBLEM: "CONSENTIMIENTO" IN THE ACTIVE NIGHT OF THE SPIRIT

From the preceding analysis we understand why St John of the Cross had this concept of faith as means of union of the intellect with God. He does not speak of knowledge of God by means of faith, but only of union. For knowledge, certain conditions of the psychological order must be present, which are totally lacking in faith. Nevertheless, there is present the objective unitive relationship with the divinity. Union in the psychological order of intellectual cognition is attained by full intellection of the essence of an object. In faith there is true union without psychologically clear intellection. This union must be understood as intentional, that is, representational: the divinity is represented to the intellect in the "darkness" of the subject. In the natural faculty the "darkness" of the subject expresses to the intellect the divine object according to the essence of divinity.

As has already been said above, the object of faith is not

treated by St John in the abstract and in isolation. It must be found in the dynamic of this virtue, in some actualization of its essence. Therefore such actualization (or actuality) of faith is directly unitive with God because of its own objective character. Moreover, the virtue of faith remains, in the objective sense, where it must be understood as a supernatural perfection of the intellect, by which it is placed in a state of union with God and thus is transformed in a supernatural manner. It is transformed gradually according to the degree of objective participation in the divinity. Such objective participation immediately evokes the idea of subjective participation. In other words, the divinity cannot be participated in objectively by the intellect without the intervention of some kind of participation on the part of the subject apprehending and knowing the divine. Is it possible, then, for faith to be defined subjectively as participation in the divine understanding and knowing? If so, how?

We repeat that we are not dealing with an abstract definition derived from the nature of the object, but rather with a concrete and experiential definition, as proposed to us by St John of the Cross in all his works. And here again the thought of St John of the Cross appears quite complete. In mystical contemplation, where the intellect experiences the divinity itself in faith, such experience seems impossible, unless the intellect participates in the experience of divine understanding.

It must then be shown whether and in what degree mystical contemplation can be understood as an actualization of faith and how it is related to other less sublime or more common actualizations.

In the first place, St John of the Cross speaks of faith inasmuch as it is the assent to revealed truths (*consentimiento*).[24] Faith, says St John of the Cross, is not knowledge but assent to revealed truths which reach the intellect "from hearing." When he says "it is not knowledge," a diligent examination of the context forces us to conclude that he is not speaking of knowledge in the Scholastic sense as cognition of a thing through rational causes in a discursive manner. The words "faith is not knowledge" indicate simply the absence, in faith, of clear intellection in the psychological sense. In this manner St John seems to exclude all those discursive processes by which one arrives at a scientific conclusion concerning the object of one's investigation. "Faith is not knowledge" simply says that in faith the "sustancia entendida" is absent. St John in this context is not referring to that evidential tendency whereby a scientific conclusion is sought in human matters, but rather to that simple perceiving tendency of the intellect by which it seeks the representational form of the object. Thus it appears from a diligent scrutiny of the context, and this meaning seems completely justified by the very circumstances of his writings and the purpose for which he wrote them. For St John wrote especially for mystics and contemplatives, not for scientific scrutiny. (Nevertheless, his works stimulated, and continue to stimulate, such analysis.)

Thus it is clear why we do not find in the works of St John of the Cross any long and exact consideration of the psychological structure of the act of faith, of the importance of the motives of credibility and of belief, of the intervention of the intellect and the movement of the will, all of which pertain to a scientific treatise on faith, especially in apologetics. All those things commonly serve to explain, in faith, the assent of the intellect to revealed truths, whose ultimate nature cannot be penetrated by any discursive process. St John does not seek to explain the assent of faith (*consentimiento*). That assent is simply presupposed. St John of the Cross had a higher experience of faith. Hence the real scope of his treatise, according to his mind, does not consist in explaining assent to revealed truths, but in describing the way of participating experientially in the divine realities. Thus even the psychological part of his doctrine concerning the nature of faith must be studied from this point of view: how and in what form can and ought the psychological faculties of the human soul be adapted to a better and more profound participation in the divine realities by means of faith?

We said above that, according to the mind of St John of the Cross, the assent of faith (*consentimiento*) does not supplant in the intellect the evidential tendency to know about God discursively by means of intellectual conclusion. It rather supplants the perceiving tendency in it, by which the intellect seeks simply to see God. For in the vision of the essence of any thing the intellect is satisfied and is united with it (see A,3,13,4: "sustancia entendida"). Such vision of the divine essence is absolutely precluded from the intellect in this life, as was fully explained above. Thus "consentimiento" (assent to revealed truths) not only indicates the simple psychological fact of faith, but—following the thought of St John—it explains the union of the intellect with the divinity itself considered as an object presented to this faculty in faith. In the assent to revealed truths the intellect not only assumes them as truths that must be believed, but also in firm adherence to them it is united to the divine essence as such and experiences in some way the infinite transcendence of the divinity in relation to itself. For this reason the "consentimiento" of faith in the final analysis cannot be explained except by the inner intervention of supernatural light,[25] whereby the intellect is intrinsically proportioned to the divinity as the proper object of faith. "Consentimiento," which is mentioned by St John only once (see A,2,3,3), is of no small importance in the vital evolution of the virtue of faith. Every act of faith is "consentimiento" (assent to revealed truths), although the psychological and experiential aspect of this assent varies greatly. For, as the superficial application of the intellect to conceptual forms of revealed truths diminishes, there opens up to the intellect an increasingly pure unitive relationship to the divinity in faith. The process of this progressive purification, which the intellect experiences in faith, is abundantly described for us, especially in the *Ascent* and *Dark Night*. When all the teachings contained in his works are diligently arranged and compared, we learn many things about the nature of faith and we are presented with a vivid concretization of what we already know abstractly under the heading of the virtue of faith.

The process of purification of the intellective faculty, in which the vital dynamic of faith is continuously evident, comprises two parts, which follow one upon the other, not in the sense of chronological succession, but resulting from their very nature.

St John calls them "nights": active night and passive night. Each night has two phases — night of the senses and night of the spirit. All the material of the *Ascent-Dark Night* treatises is arranged according to those four nights. In relation to faith, the word "night" immediately evokes the above-mentioned symbolic notion of "darkness" or "obscurity." In this respect the supernatural union of the soul with God depends upon faith and upon it alone. For faith is "night" and, as the root of union of the soul with God, it makes the whole union "night."[26] Why? Because while communicating the divinity to the soul and to the intellect, it nevertheless excludes from this unitive communication any representation connatural to the intellect in the psychological sense.

Let us explain. When St John says: "la fe no es ciencia . . . sino sólo es consentimiento," he is referring to that tendency of the intellect simply to perceive, to seek for itself the "understood substance" of the object. In revelation there are presented to this faculty conceptual formulas to be believed, to which it assents in virtue of supernatural light. In such assent it is united to the divine essence. But the unitive act itself appears as if enveloped in psychological forms, which darken the pure unitive relationship of the intellect to the divine essence and conceal it in that darkness. In this way, St John of the Cross teaches, by means of faith, in the vital evolution of this virtue, the external "darkness" of the act of faith can be progressively purified and the intellect can be introduced into a pure, unitive relationship with God, in which the proper formality of faith is most clearly apparent. This pure unitive relationship of the intellect to the divinity in no way indicates vision, but rather it indicates the perfection of faith, which is never vision (naked faith). The aforementioned "darkness" results from the mode in which the revealed truths are received. This mode is, first of all, psychological, connatural to the faculty. St John describes the purification in the course of interior prayer, in which the one praying progresses gradually from discursive meditation to contemplation. Discursive meditation is presented by St John of the Cross as a series of acts of faith and love of God. Each such act of faith "no es ciencia . . . sino sólo consentimiento." Then St John teaches us how a concrete and particular form of such "consentimiento" is actualized in discursive meditation.

In this perspective the problem of the act of faith remains very restricted. To actualize faith by praying is only one of the possible ways of actualizing this virtue. St John of the Cross chose this way and this aspect. The fact that he so chose perhaps better explains the reasons for this tendency, which is more observational than evidential in the scientific sense, that we find in St John of the Cross. It also explains the orientation of this tendency toward contemplating God. Contemplation seeks God, and then faith is opened exclusively to the divine object alone as such (it could, of course, also be oriented toward its own material object, to created things as reflections of God).

Thus the faith that we encounter in St John of the Cross is primarily a faith of transcendence — the true means of union of the intellect with God according to its activity. Thus is better explained its psychological darkness, inasmuch as its activity is especially and, as it were, exclusively directed toward contemplating the divinity. St John of the Cross practically limited the scope of his treatise on faith to this one aspect of its formal object. Only the divinity is sought there in faith, and that same divinity, which is intimately united to the intellect by faith in its assent to revealed truths, is also intimately concealed in that same assent, as the experience of discursive meditation abundantly proves. For in discursive meditation the essential assent of faith to revealed truths assumes a psychological form that is still enveloped (darkened) in sensory things. In meditating, the person praying uses his imagination and fantasy, and then the act of believing is, as it were, immersed in forms connatural to sense, and easily accommodated to the person in the senses. The intellect certainly does not imagine the divinity, since all the imaginative effort remains in the senses (principally in the interior senses). The intellect only makes this effort to apprehend more vividly the revealed truths, and in them the divinity. Thus by believing in discursive meditation very "sensitively and imaginatively," by offering its assent to revealed truths, and in them strengthening the unitive relationship of the intellect to the divinity, the intellect is marvelously prepared for faith's purifying process. For after a certain period of time all facility in discursive meditation by means of the senses, especially the interior senses, comes to an end.[27] The "night" begins. This is the first night of sense. The abundance of images concerning revealed truths recedes, and the facility in praying and meditating "sensorially and imaginatively" disappears.

Faith is easily detected in this process of "night." For what is constituted by the unitive contact of the intellect with the divinity (a contact that is purely spiritual and supernatural) cannot remain in such a sensory form in its functioning. In virtue of its supernatural object, and in virtue of the excessive light to which it is interiorly subjected, it now breaks forth from all limits of sense in its functioning, being superior to them. This takes place in what is called the "passive night of the senses" and constitutes a very important part of this night, in which phenomenon all the theological virtues concur — with faith, however, properly and formally in the intellect, purifying it from apprehending the revealed truths in too sensory and imaginative a manner.[28] In our explanation we are still within the process of interior prayer, in which the union of the soul with God is constantly being sought. As far as faith is concerned, the above-mentioned abandoning of a too sensory and imaginative manner of apprehending revealed truths results in the intellect's participating objectively in a purer manner in the divinity. The union of the intellect with God in faith in this way does not yet involve the experience of divine things, although it is more spiritual in its functioning. The concepts of revelation, which are believed in an immediate manner, are apprehended by the intellect in a more proper way, without the earlier psychological and sensory impediments. Certainly such faith, being partially purified, is clearer and more profound with regard to its functioning, although it is more obscure as far as the sensory part is concerned. For St John of the Cross, "obscurity" and "night" connote the privation of something to which the faculty is connaturally inclined.[29] The intellect is inclined toward intellection by means of a psychologically clear and distinct representation. Consequently, in the case of faith, the more deeply it operates in the soul, the darker the night is that it produces.

The process of the development of faith extends still further, in that it challenges the intrinsic strength of faith to extend its operation beyond discursive meditation, thus rendering it less sensory but more spiritual (intellectual). Let us suppose now that, with the night of sense ended, faith is operating in discursive meditation or even in the early stages of contemplation by means of conceptual representations purified of sensory images. There certainly will be great progress in interior prayer and in the whole manner of knowing God. But even here faith has not yet reached the culmination of its vital development according to the power of its nature. Even here the revealed concepts, which are believed in an immediate manner, are apprehended in a psychological way, though more perfectly psychologically, more spiritually than before. Thus even in such a degree of perfection there is not yet attained the pure unitive relationship of the intellect to the divinity which is indicated by St John of the Cross in faith. The revealed truths are believed by the intellect in an immediate way as apprehended by faith, but the intellect is not united to the revealed truths in faith, but is united by intention to the divine essence by means of the revealed truths. This cannot be contained by any intellectual likeness, by any concept.[30] Therefore another "night" is required. This is called the night of the spirit.

The active night of spirit, whose particular characteristics are described in A,2,10 to A,2,32, offers us some indications of the nature of faith according to the mind of the Mystical Doctor. In the above-mentioned chapters he analyzes several so-called "mystical phenomena," such as locutions, visions, private revelations and the like, all of which he refers to as distinct, clear and particular "aprensiones" or "noticias"[31] as opposed to the "inteligencia confusa, oscura y general," which he calls contemplation, and which is infused into the soul by faith. For the moment we will not deal with "contemplación que se da en fe" (we will treat of that later). Here we are concerned with the

above-mentioned opposition of "aprensiones." St John of the
Cross asserts and proceeds to prove from his extensive experience that any clear, distinct and particular "noticias" or "inteligencias" (or better, intellections) do not bring about union with
God under the aspect of divinity. Why? Here we encounter
that principle of the metaphysical order: the divinity as such
cannot be connaturally assimilated by the intellect, since there
is no "sustancia entendida"; true union of the intellect of a person in this life with the divinity is always psychologically devoid
of a clear representational form. This is the reason that all the
above-mentioned clear and distinct "aprensiones," that is, those
expressed to the intellect in clear and distinct psychological
forms, are not considered capable of uniting the intellect with
the divinity. Divinity is presented to the intellect only in obscurity, psychologically devoid of form or representation. As it
is in faith, so it remains in contemplation. In the active night of
the spirit all such clear and particularly distinct "aprensiones"
must be rejected in behalf of divine union.

This is of great importance to our question, for it shows the
identity and the intrinsic unity of our theme. "La fe no es ciencia . . . sino es consentimiento." The divine object of faith is
not reduced to some psychologically clear and distinct species
of intellection, connatural to the intellect. The intellect is united
to the divinity by means of faith during the night. The identity
and unity of this theme in the doctrine of faith appears precisely
in this, that the active night of spirit is governed strictly by the
same logic as the "consentimiento." As for the assent of the intellect to revealed truths which are completely devoid of any
"sustancia entendida," whose formal essence cannot be apprehended (the divinity cannot be apprehended connaturally) —
that assent is actualized in every particular act of the active
night of spirit. When the individual, clear and distinct representations (*aprensiones*) concerning revealed truths are ordered
to be rejected, including those which have come to the intellect
in a supernatural manner, then the "consentimiento" is truly
actualized according to its formal essence. This is the reason:
the divinity cannot be assimilated by the intellect, cannot be

seen (*la fe no es ciencia*). The "consentimiento" in this case properly takes the place of the perceiving tendency of the intellect. Since the divinity cannot be seen, then it cannot be expected to be seen or understood in any psychologically clear, intentionally distinct and particular representation (*aprensión*). Therefore any such representation, although it involves revealed truths and divine things, does not formally present divine things to the intellect. The formality that assimilates the intellect to the divinity is only that "obscurity" and confused, obscure, general "understanding." This is properly called contemplation in faith.

All this doctrine is based on experience. St John of the Cross was very familiar with those clear, distinct and particular "aprensiones," those intentional forms of the intellect, which come to the intellect connaturally on the way to union with God, either as a result of its own efforts or from some superior, even supernatural agent. He also knew very well how to distinguish them from the obscure "knowledge" of contemplation. Thus experience verifies the first metaphysical principle, upon which is based the inflexible logic of the doctrine: there exists no essential likeness of God in any purely natural creature; even with regard to faith, which enjoys a likeness in its essential nature, when it habitually subsists and is actualized in a "natural" psychological subject, all its actualizations, being psychological, suffer from the limitations of their subject — and therefore are "obscure," devoid of any connatural representation of the divine object. When some representation appears connaturally to the senses or to the intellect, the person is commanded to reject it, or at least not to seek it. Such is generally the tone of the active night of spirit, in which the soul will be prepared to receive a more abundant participation in the divine understanding — in which active faith is perfected according to its nature.

This active actualization of faith (which is described in great detail in A,2,10 and A,2,32), inasmuch as it is active, seems also to be rather psychological in its manner of operating. When clear "aprensiones" are rejected by faith, this is to be understood as an act of the virtue according to the psychological components of its nature. If there is question of the relationship to the proper object of faith, then the active night of spirit implies rather a negative aspect: what is properly the object of faith is not attained in the accomplishment of the act, but those things which are not properly the object of faith are rejected. The ultimate reason for rejecting them consists simply in a positive unitive relationship of the intellect to the divine essence, to which relationship all particular, distinct intellections are by their very nature opposed. To reject those contrary intellections is equivalent to strengthening the adherence to what is the proper object of faith. Faith does not adhere to any distinct intellections, because it adheres only to the divine essence as its object, and the divine essence cannot be distinctly conceived by the intellect.

Therefore in this sense the active night of spirit appears as the proper night of faith, more than the active night of sense, in which the denial of the lower part of the soul took place. For in that first night, although the ulterior reason for rejecting sensory things was to prepare the soul for union with the divine, this was, however, not the immediate reason. On the other hand, in the active night of spirit, the proximate reason for denying all kinds of spiritual satisfaction connatural to the soul and to the intellect is to foster divine union. The more all clear and distinct intellections connatural to the intellect are rejected, so much the more is the intellect strengthened in its adherence to the divine object, which it has within itself by faith. Therefore the immediate reason for this rejection is to promote participation in this object — the proper object of faith. This is the prime reason that the active night of spirit is attributed to faith.

The rejection of any connaturally clear representation (*aprensión*) in the intellect reveals to us the intentional presence of the supernatural object in this faculty. Thus the active night of spirit also reveals to us faith in relation to the formal essence of its object. Faith unites the intellect with God first because of the divinity that is presented to it as its object. Moreover, in the active night of spirit, inasmuch as it is active, we can consider faith not only as it enables the intellect to participate objectively in the divinity and itself is formally constituted by this objective participation, but also inasmuch as it is a virtue, and implies a certain manner of operating supernaturally on the part of the intellect, a certain supernatural movement. For faith as a virtue surely is not limited to a static participation in the divine object as such, but it becomes properly dynamic in this participation, enabling the intellect to operate by reason of its participation in the divinity, which is presented to it as its object. Thus the active night of spirit provides us with an abundant argument[32] in favor of participation in the divine object, which is presented only in faith and in "obscurity," psychologically devoid of intellection, without any representation.

How is this intellectual abnegation realized, which we declare takes place in the virtue of faith? Certainly the formally objective nature of faith imposes this upon the intellect: the intellect is capable of rejecting distinct and clear intellection concerning divine things, inasmuch as it remains in vital contact with the divine object, to which it is united according to the proper nature of the divinity. But how does this psychological process of abnegation develop? Here we touch somewhat upon the psychological structure of faith. According to St John of the Cross, the intellect, in realizing such abnegation, performs an act of adherence to the divine object, and performs this act as a result of the impulse and urging of the will. For neither the intellect nor any other faculty of the soul can admit or reject anything without the intervention of the will.[33] This is the case in the intellectual abnegation mentioned above. For the intellect, of itself, tends to seek rather than to reject clear intellection that is connatural to itself. For rejection to take place, it is necessary that the will intervene, along with the desire to participate in a supernatural good. All this is not taught explicitly, but is only implied in the texts under scrutiny. Likewise we cannot elaborate a formal treatise on the psychological structure of faith in St John of the Cross. One thing we can affirm immediately with certitude: in order for the divinity to be participated in by the intellect as its object, it is necessary to have the intervention of the will on the part of the psychological subject. The divinity as proper object can only be participated in by means of faith. Moreover, in faith, in the very nature of the assent to revealed truths (*consentimiento*), there is always found obscurity regarding the object to be participated in. According to St John of the Cross, in this "obscurity" there is always implied privation, abnegation.[34] Consequently the intervention of the will is definitely required. The psychological structure of faith is not explicitly described in this way, but it is nonetheless certainly implied. The difficulty here is that faith is nowhere treated separately and abstractly in the works of St John of the Cross; it is treated in the overall description of the supernatural life of the soul, in the process of supernatural union, where other supernaturally unitive virtues intervene in addition to faith. No one can assert that the aforesaid intervention of the will pertains only to the psychological structure of faith. It most certainly also proceeds from supernatural love and serves to increase this virtue;[35] for in all his works the Mystical Doctor is clearly dealing with faith animated by charity, never with faith by itself. It is for this reason that we have said that the psychological structure of faith is not defined explicitly, but is only touched upon and implied in some manner.

Generally speaking, St John of the Cross does not teach so much about the psychological structure of the interior life (although he describes very richly for us some particular aspects of mystical psychology) as about the combination of psychological conditions that are necessary in order that the supernatural participation may permeate the soul and its faculties more and more fully. Such is generally the approach in each of his works, a primarily theological approach. The divine union of the soul consists formally in participation in the divinity, which participation is fostered in each subject by some psychological element of the virtue. The more the formal participation increases for any theological virtue, the more the psychological element of the virtue practised becomes purified and the more it is adapted to richer divine participation.

This appears clearly with regard to faith. The active night of spirit teaches us about the active phase of the functioning of this virtue. Divine participation causes the intellect to act according to its objective nature. The intellect, rejecting in faith those intellections which are connatural to it concerning divine things, operates quite certainly according to the logic and measure of divine participation, operates in function of it. It is the intellect that is operating, but the logic of the operation shows that the intellect is acting not by virtue of its own nature, but in function of a higher nature in which it participates, which not only presents itself to the intellect as a supernatural object, but also interiorly influences the subjective manner of its operating. The action itself pertains to the intellect, but the manner and root of this operation appears supra-intellectual, supra-psychological, supra-natural. Thus in the active night of spirit, where faith as a virtue shows most abundantly its psychological aspect in its functioning, we find simultaneously at work its supra-psychological and supernatural elements. The psychological aspect of the virtue is evident only in function of supernatural participation.

Thus faith appears in its active phase, and thus it operates as a virtue. This virtue is the means of union of the intellect with God considered as divinity. Besides the intimate unitive relationship, which in the final analysis always underlies all the manifestations of this virtue, we can also rightly investigate the positive actualization of this unitive relationship of the intellect with God. For the whole operation of faith in the active night of spirit, although it is based on this unitive relationship to the divine object as such, nevertheless manifests a negative aspect, which consists in removing those things which act either outside of or directly against the unitive relationship of the intellect to the divinity objectively presented to it. Now we are dealing with a certain positive actualization of the aforesaid union, in which the intellect, habitually united with the divinity as its object, is also actively drawn to it, not simply by rejecting clear kinds of intellections connatural to itself, but by looking at and contemplating the divinity itself, to whom it remains intimately united in faith as its object. We are dealing, therefore, with a completely different actualization of faith, in which supernatural participation is not brought about by the psychological exercise of the virtue, but in a properly theological manner. This actualization St John of the Cross calls contemplation.

CONTEMPLATION – SUPREME ACTUALIZATION OF FAITH

The works of St John of the Cross give us every reason to conclude that the supreme actualization of faith is contemplation. Besides those texts in which he speaks of contemplation as knowledge that is simultaneously obscure, confused, general and loving,[36] and is communicated to the soul in faith, there are other passages in which he indicates how this communication takes place. Thus the actual process of contemplation is described in A,2,29,6 and under another aspect in C,13,12–14.

In A,2,29,6 we learn that contemplation is realized in faith, when the soul and the intellect are recollected in faith (not in some attempt to understand revealed truths, but in a psychologically empty adherence of the intellect by means of revealed truths to the divine essence, which is intentionally united to the intellect in them). In this recollected state there comes to the intellect a new communication of the Holy Spirit through his gifts, which, united in charity, are always waiting for this divine illumination. When this takes place, then faith becomes contemplative, then to the intellect "is communicated all divine wisdom in a general manner" (that is, without particular and connatural intellections). And this communication is described in the words of the Mystical Doctor as "the Son of God, who is communicated to the soul in faith." It is therefore necessary to understand, according to this expression and similar ones which sometimes occur in the writings of St John of the Cross, that in faith there is the communication of uncreated divine Wisdom, of the Word himself, who, since he has manifested himself to us in Jesus Christ and has revealed divine mysteries to us in his teaching,[37] by faith enters into intimate contact with every faithful soul and with every believing intellect. By causing a person to believe, he causes that person to participate in himself, namely, in that uncreated Wisdom, by which God, knowing perfectly and exhaustively his divine essence, expresses this fullness of his known infinite perfection in the person of the consubstantially and coeternally generated Word. In this sense St John of the Cross speaks of participation in the Word. This participation will become full and clear in heaven,[38] but even in this life it is essentially the same participation by faith, and it becomes experiential in mystical contemplation.[39]

This seems to sum up briefly the mind of St John of the Cross as we compare the various texts. As for faith itself, the proper role that it plays in mystical contemplation is very evident here. For it is apparent that contemplation cannot be considered the actualization of faith in the sense that contemplation is an act of faith, that is, an act of the virtue, and that it consists in the operation of this virtue as a definite perfection of its functioning. For it appears clearly in the above-mentioned text of A,2,29,6 that the very act of this contemplation, namely of obscure and general, confused and loving knowledge of God, results from the illumination of the Holy Spirit by means of his gifts. Thus it is readily understood that there is a certain passivity on the part of the psychological subject, a certain docility and obedience in receiving this divinely illuminative influence. At the same time there is indicated the great intensity both of supernatural charity, in which the gifts of the Holy Spirit remain united, and of faith, by means of which the intellect adheres not only to particular revealed truths, seeking to understand them connaturally, but to the divine essence itself, which is the formal essence of believing, and to which the intellect is united without clear, particular and distinct intellection. Therefore, in the process of contemplation, the influence of the Holy Spirit intervenes directly, whereas the theological virtues rather serve in a passive manner to assist this influence according to their nature as faculties tending to unite the soul with God. This is what faith does, inasmuch as it objectively presents the divinity itself to the intellect. From a diligent study of the text, it appears that, from a formally objective point of view, faith intervenes in the very act of mystical contemplation. And this is the reason that contemplation is called general divine knowledge, which is communicated to the soul in faith; in fact, the Word himself, who is communicated in faith to the soul.

We said above that the importance of faith in the process of contemplation consists in the fact that the formal object of faith, namely the divinity itself, is participated in according to intense supernatural influence, which comes from the Holy Spirit by means of his gifts. We have already seen how the same divinity is participated in, as the object in faith, under the influence of the believing intellect itself. This is the case in every act of "consentimiento," as is wonderfully evident in the so-called active night of spirit. We saw there that every rejection of clear and distinct intellection is undertaken for the benefit of the divinity, which, as an object presented to the intellect in faith, cannot be clearly and distinctly apprehended—and consequently demands from the intellect the rejection of any clear intellection. Thus the thrust of the intellect toward the object of faith ends in the night and produces night in the faculties. For it approaches the object of faith in an oblique manner, so to speak, not by focusing on the divinity but by rejecting non-divine things. The intellect knows what God is not, rather than what he is. As we now make a comparison with contemplation in faith, that direct influence becomes abundantly clear: the intellect, united to the divinity by faith, is carried along in faith by the same influence of the Holy Spirit, not according to any psychological plenitude of union of this faculty with its connatural object, but nevertheless according to the purity of the same unitive relationship of the intellect with God.

This subjective purity of the unitive relationship of the intellect with God as divinity, which occurs in mystical contemplation, can be called the very highest evolution of faith. It is likewise the precise reason why contemplation can be considered as the highest actualization of faith.[40] Contemplation, however, is not simply an act of faith; we saw above from A,2, 29,6 how many different virtues intervene in the act of contemplation. Nevertheless, in contemplation, and precisely in its greatest purity, we find that relationship of the intellect to the divinity as object. Faith, moreover, is called the proportionate means of such union. This purity of the unitive relationship of the intellect to the divinity as object not only coincides, but is intimately connected with the greatest intensity of participation of the intellect in divine knowledge. We saw clearly in the course of the active night of spirit how the partipation of the intellect in the divine object as such exerts a purifying influence upon the participating intellect. Moreover, according to the mind of the mystical doctor, this task of purification pertains to the essence of faith as its proper function, corresponding to the unitive function of this virtue.[41] Faith simultaneously unites the intellect with the divine object and produces a void and darkness in its psychological subject, namely the intellect. In this way St John of the Cross defines faith. Both aspects are intimately connected with each other, as we saw above. Objective participation in the divinity by the intellect produces the purification of the subject. This purification is called symbolically "night." As the subject is better and better purified through its intentionally unitive contact with the divine essence in faith, the more and more it participates in the divine object of faith. Such mutual dependence joins to each other the two functions of faith: the unitive and the purifying functions. It purifies by reason of the union, and it also purifies for the sake of the union.

From this point of view faith also cooperates efficaciously in contemplation — efficaciously though remotely. Contemplation is produced immediately by the Holy Spirit, who acts through his gifts. Remotely, however, the possibility — and, much more, the purity and perfection of contemplation — depends also upon the active participation of the intellect, which is brought about by faith. All the efforts of the active night of spirit foster this. Moreover, these efforts should be understood as acts of "consentimiento" performed with the full participation of the intellect with its inner perceiving tendency toward the divine essence itself, which, however, cannot be exhaustively and fully conceived connaturally by the intellect, nor can it be seen. This same element is found in every act of "consentimiento"—assent to revealed truths ("faith is not knowledge," and is not, because it cannot be). All actualizations of faith in the active night of spirit contain the same element in a more eminent and very explicit manner. In all of them we find the operation of the intellect intimately conditioned by the divine object that is communicated to it by faith. The intellect thus appears in function of the divine participation. Moreover, this operation of the intellect in function of the divine participation, which is brought about by faith according to the active phase of its nature, immediately produces night in the intellect. And it mediately prepares this faculty for participation in divine knowledge and wisdom, which, being obscure, general and confused, as well as loving knowledge of divine things, is properly called the contemplation of faith. In contemplation the intellect's psychological (natural) manner of operating is changed into a divinely participated manner through the gifts of the Holy Spirit. The immediate operation becomes divine. At the same time faith appears in a passive phase of its nature, in which the intellect no longer operates in function of divine participation, but is precisely passive in function of divine participation. Thus are terminated all intellect's efforts ordained in faith by means of intellectual abnegation to pursue the intimate unitive relationship with the divinity, as its proper object, according to its psychological condition, while at the same time it is established in the greatest purity of theological perfection that is possible in this life. This theological perfection of the virtue of faith, which is the properly unitive element of this virtue, seems to consist in participation in the diving knowledge, objective participation, therefore, in the divinity, and participation on the part of the subject in understanding and knowing in a divine manner. All the earlier efforts of the soul, such as we saw in the active night of spirit, contribute toward this end. Nevertheless, all of them together, inasmuch as they are psychological, and thus influenced by the natural faculty in their manner of acting, cannot provide that theological perfection of faith to the intellect experientially. All those efforts are made in function of divine participation, but they do not bring about the participation of the intellect, as long as that faculty remains active in participating. In its activity there is true participation in the divine understanding and knowledge, and indeed such activity cannot be explained other than by the aforementioned participation—nevertheless, the faculty remains conscious of its own part in it, free of its own manner of operating according to particular concepts, whose connatural clarity is constantly sought.[42] All this ceases immediately in contemplation. But it does not cease equally in every act, for contemplation admits of varying degrees according to the degree of actual purity of the intellect. The degree of actual purity in the intellect[43] is the same as the degree of habitual perfection of faith. The freer the subject is of distinct images regarding divine things, that is, the "darker" it is, the more intensely and profoundly it participates objectively in the divinity.

Such seems to be the role of faith in contemplation. The influence of the Holy Spirit comes according to the divine good pleasure, not at the will and pleasure of the believer, although the possibility of it on the part of the subject depends upon faith, and the degree of perfection of participating in it depends upon the preliminary purification of the intellect in faith. In contemplation the soul attains that perfection of supernatural union with God which St John of the Cross calls "transformation." For the intellect, such transformation properly designates the divine operation in the gifts of the Holy Spirit, when the intellect ceases to understand by operating under its own power, by its own natural light in faith, and begins to understand and to know in virtue of the divine Wisdom itself, with which it remains united in faith. See in this regard the text of N,2,4,2, where St John of the Cross speaks very clearly about this change in modality in the operations of the intellect and the other faculties of the soul. This change comes with the divine

operation, whereby faith — participation in the divine understanding — no longer functions by means of the intellect, but is
withdrawn from such modality and functions in a properly
divine manner, as a participation not only in the understanding and knowledge of God (because this can also be conceived of as the modality of the intellect, when it is itself attracted to the divinity as its proper object), but as a participation
in understanding and knowing in a divine manner. This is a
participation in divine things not only in the objective, but also
in the subjective sense. Thus faith is revealed according to the
inner perfection of its nature. For St John of the Cross, this
perfection consists in participation in the divinity, by means of
which the intellect (the subject of faith) is made divine "by participation."

Therefore the union of the intellect with the divine essence
itself (the proportionate means of this union is declared to be
faith) includes first of all an objective movement, which is actualized in each assent of the intellect to revealed truths. For in
this assent the intellect adheres in the revealed truths to the
divine essence itself, which is presented to it as an object of
knowledge. Besides the objective movement, there is also a
subjective part to this union. We have determined that this is
the participation in understanding and knowing in a divine
manner, in the divine operation itself. Experientially this participation enters into contemplation because of the illuminative
operation of the Holy Spirit by means of his gifts. And only this
can be called "transformation" of the intellect. This "transformation," as we have seen, is perfected in faith, inasmuch as in
it participation in the divine object is effected (the intellect not
being active, but reticent and passive) by the illuminative
influence of the Holy Spirit. Then the intellect, being free and
conscious of its participation in the knowing and understand of
God, is drawn directly to the object of this knowledge and
understanding, to the divinity itself, which is united to it in
faith.[44]

There still remains one question to be resolved, if the doctrine of St John of the Cross concerning faith is to be seen in its

totality. Can that subjective participation in the divine understanding and knowledge, which he explicitly states is present in
contemplation, be found in every actualization of faith, even
apart from the mystical actualization which is properly called
contemplation? Moreover, in contemplation, what precisely do
the gifts of the Holy Spirit and his influence achieve? Ought we
to attribute the whole phenomenon of participation in the
divine understanding and knowledge to the gifts, or do some
roots of this reside in faith alone, in such a way that the
influence of the Holy Spirit merely draws forth through
the actualization of faith the participation in the divine understanding and knowledge hidden there and renders the intellect conscious of them in contemplation? All things considered,
this latter concept seems to be more in keeping with the
texts of St John of the Cross and with the general line of his
doctrine. To be sure, he never teaches it explicitly. But St John
of the Cross never speaks of any virtue of the supernatural life
in complete isolation, abstracting from the others. All are connected, all evolve in a vital manner, all together bring about
the union of the soul with God. Likewise regarding any particular virtue, no distinction is made speculatively between its
objective and its subjective importance. Therefore the distinction must be drawn from an analysis of the texts and thus
asserted or sometimes offered only as probable. In this way we
present a solution to the last question we proposed above.
When St John of the Cross writes that contemplation is communicated in faith, or when he calls contemplation faith, then
he is surely conceiving of faith not according to the psychological aspect of the virtue, but from the theological point of
view of the intellect's participating in the divinity. This participation, while remaining intrinsically and intimately the
same in faith, assumes different aspects in the subject. The
seeds of contemplation lie hidden in the first assent to revealed
truths (*consentimiento*), and "consentimiento" endures into the
highest degree of contemplation possible in this life. The degree
of perfection of faith can be determined in the abstract according to the intellect's degree of participation in the divinity, both
objectively and subjectively. In a concrete situation the objec-

tive and subjective participation appear simultaneously. Therefore, in any assent to revealed truths, in any actualization of faith in the course of the active night of spirit, deep analysis leads us to assert that there is not only participation in the divine object but also subjective participation through knowing in a divine manner. This is not resolved in some positive form of activity, nor is it experienced by the faculty according to its own nature. That takes place only in contemplation under the influence of the Holy Spirit. Nevertheless, it is present in every psychological actualization of faith. St John of the Cross presents this doctrine by way of counterposition. When the intellect does not see the object (*no es ciencia*) and nevertheless assents to revealed truths (in them it also adheres to the divinity as object), and still more, when it rejects any clear and distinct intellections that are connatural to it in favor of the completely supernatural and sublime object of faith, then it is readily apparent that the intellect operating in this way above the level of its natural operation is operating in function of some higher form of understanding and knowledge, participating in it. This superior understanding and knowledge cannot exist without supernatural participation. This is very well explained by the nature of the object. Nevertheless, the participation in the divine knowledge and understanding, which surely dominates the whole process of "consentimiento," the whole operation of the active night of spirit, is, as it were, concealed in the psychological modality of its functioning. The intellect experiences it only as something negative, in "obscurity," in "night," in abnegation. It first begins to experience it in some positive manner (although always obscurely) when, under the divine influence of the Holy Spirit, it is constituted in the act of contemplation. Then the psychological modality of the act of faith ceases, and the theological substance of its operation is revealed, consisting of participation in the divine understanding and knowledge.

For this reason faith is considered by St John of the Cross as the preparation of the intellect for the beatific vision of heaven.[45] In a special way the participative "transformation" (contemplation in the sense described above) is presented as the immediate preparation of the psychological subject for clear participation in the divine object in the continuous participation of divine understanding and knowledge.[46]

FINAL CONCLUSIONS AND OBSERVATIONS

(1) We do not have in the works of St John of the Cross a complete doctrine of faith. There is rather a special aspect of this doctrine (faith as proportionate means of union of the intellect with God), in which are included, however, in an implicit manner, many things pertaining to the consideration of the nature of faith. These things should be very diligently scrutinized in the texts of his works, where we find not so much speculation on the nature of faith as vivid description of the act of faith in its functioning.

(2) In order to elaborate a genuine concept of the nature of faith according to the mind of the Mystical Doctor, two things must be taken into account: a metaphysical presupposition and the description of the particular elements of the act of faith in its functioning. With regard to both, faith is presented as the means of union of the intellect with God. From the metaphysical viewpoint we deduce the real thought of St John of the Cross by analyzing such notions as "proportionate means," "proportion of likeness" and "essential likeness," always keeping in mind the exigencies of the contexts. Thus we come to the conviction that faith, from the metaphysical and abstract point of view, is to be understood as participation in the divine intelligence. This participation constitutes its theological entity, in virtue of which it becomes capable of causing the intellect to ascend to God as divinity (the faculty of theological transcendence) and in this sense assimilates the faculty to divine things.

(3) Inquiring now into the area of operation and experience, we began our work of induction concerning the nature of faith from the many things which manifest it. And again in this area

we find the idea of participating in the divine understanding and knowledge as constitutive of the nature of faith. This appears clearly and experientially in mystical contemplation. But mystical contemplation — it seems to us — can only be understood as the highest actualization of faith, since this reveals most clearly its essential nature. Therefore this participation is included in every actualization of faith, even though it may not be mystical, and even though it takes place within the psychological modality of the intellect. As we scrutinize, according to the mind of St John of the Cross, the assent of faith to revealed truths (*consentimiento*), and especially the operations of faith in the so-called active night of spirit, we find that notion of participating in the divine understanding and knowledge as the ultimate and intimate force in any act of faith whatever.

(4) Thus the ultimate conclusions of our abstract consideration of the nature of faith and the ultimate conclusions of our induction concerning the act of faith seem to be the same. Here the abstract concept and the argument from experience coincide. The metaphysical presupposition is validated in every concrete kind of operation. Hence they verify and confirm each other.

(5) In his works, St John of the Cross presents a much more objective idea of the nature of faith than of its actualization. Faith is presented more as a virtue that unites the intellect of the person in the life with its object (which is divinely offered to the intellect by faith), than in its own actualization. The influence of faith comes ultimately from participation in the divine understanding and knowledge. In its activity, however, it takes on, from the psychological subject in which it is operating, a psychological appearance and manner of acting. In this respect there appears to be a disproportion between the objective formality, in which faith unites the intellect to the divine essence as such, and its actualization. From this is derived the "obscurity" of the intellect. For faith does not appear as a static participation of the intellect in the divine essence as its object, but rather as a dynamic participation. This totally intrinsic dynamism of faith consists in the work of purifying the

intellect. In this purification the intellect is gradually adapted to its purely spiritual and supernatural object. The purification of the intellect reveals the virtue of faith in its essential and specific strength. This is how the concept of faith proper to St John of the Cross must be understood.

(6) The psychological modality of the supernatural motivation in faith, which constantly causes obscurity, diminishes in mystical contemplation, where the intellect experiences the illuminative divine influence by means of the gifts of the Holy Spirit and thus experiences the divinity itself, which is present to it as its object.

(7) In summary, faith once more appears as the virtue that enables participation in the divine intelligence.

(8) St John of the Cross does not provide a complete treatise on the nature of faith. He shows us faith as the unitive relationship of the intellect with God—with the divine object. This is the faith of transcendence. We know, however, that this aspect is neither unique nor exclusive in faith. We know that faith also has an its proper, though not formal nor primary object, all created things according to their relationship with God. St John of the Cross says nothing about this aspect of faith, either on the part of the object or of its actualization. With him, faith appears only as a proportionate means of union of the intellect with God, and, examined from this viewpoint, he shows the supreme and formal part of its nature. (Trans. C. Latimer)

NOTES

1. ". . . aunque es verdad que . . . está Dios siempre en el alma dándole y conservándole el ser natural de ella con su asistencia, no, empero, siempre la comunica el ser sobrenatural. Porque éste no se comunica sino por amor y gracia . . . " A, 2, 5, 4.

2. "Ahora sólo trato de esta unión total y permanente según la sustáncia del alma y sus potencias en cuanto al hábito oscuro de unión porque en cuanto al acto, después diremos, con el favor divino, cómo no puede haber unión permanente en las potencias en esta vida, sino transeunte." *Ibid.*, 5, 2.

3. ". . . las tres virtudes teologales, fe, esperanza y caridad, que tienen respecto a las dichas tres potencias como propios objetos sobrenaturales, y mediante las cuales el alma se une con Dios según sus potencias . . ." *Ibid.*, 6, 1.

4. "Y se hace tal unión cuando Dios hace al alma esta sobrenatural merced, que todas las cosas de Dios y el alma son unas en transformación participante; y el alma más parece Dios que alma, y aun es Dios por participación . . . " *Ibid.*, 5, 7.

5. See the text already cited in note 2 *supra*.

6. This interpretation is also supported by the text of A, 2, (Title): "la fe es el proximo y proporcionado medio al entendimiento para que el alma pueda (llegar) a la divina unión de amor"—where St John of the Cross clearly distinguishes the unitive role of faith pertaining to the intellect from the overall work of union of the soul with God, which is performed properly in virtue of supernatural charity, which operates immediately in the will. Therefore the will is the special psychological basis of the union.

7. See Labourdette, "La foi théologale et la connaissance mystique d'après Saint Jean de la Croix" *Revue Thomiste*, 41 (1936); 42 (1937).

8. See A, 2, Tit., 1.

9. See A, 2, Title of the book; 9, Title of the chapter and 1; 24, 8; 30, 5.

10. See A, 2, 8, 1.

11. See A, 2, 30, 5.

12. See N, 1, 2, 5.

13. ". . . todos los medios han de ser proporcionados al fin, es a saber: que han de tener alguna conveniencia y semejanza con el fin, tal que baste y sea suficiente para que por ellos se pueda conseguir el fin que se pretende." A, 2, 8, 2.

14. I understand it in this way from the context of A, 2, 8, 3, having analyzed the saint's expression "divino ser." Literally it would be (in Latin): "esse Dei." Then the comparison is made between "esse Dei" (*divino ser*) and "esse creaturarum" (*ser de las criaturas*), and it is denied that there is any essential likeness (*semejanza esencial*) between them, either on the level of being, or better from the point of view of the being. Under this latter aspect, creatures are called "vestigium Dei" (*rastro de Dios*), but from a properly essential viewpoint. This is why *essential* likeness is denied, but nothing else.

15. ". . . es tanta la semejanza que hay entre ella (la fe) y Dios, que no hay otra diferencia sino ser visto Dios, o creído. Porque así como Dios es infinito, así ella nos le propone infinito; y así como es trino y uno, nos le propone ella trino y uno . . . " A, 2, 9, 1.

16. ". . . las potencias del alma no pueden, de suyo, hacer reflexión y operación, sino sobre alguna forma, figura e imagen, y ésta es la corteza y accidente de la sustancia y espíritu que hay debajo de tal corteza y accidente. La cual sustancia y espíritu no se une con las potencias del alma en verdadera inteligencia y amor, si no es cuando ya cesa la operación de las potencias. Porque la pretensión y fin de tal operación no es sino venir a recibir en el alma la sustancia entendida y amada de aquellas formas." A, 3, 13, 4. On the same subject, note also the text: ". . . el entendimiento . . . tiene por oficio formar las inteligencias y desnudarlas del hierro de las especies y fantasías" (A, 2, 8, 5), clearly referring to the intellect's task of abstracting in order to form in-

tellectual species of the object. Note also *Ibid.*, 14, 6 where the task of the sensory faculties is clearly distinguished from the spiritual faculties in the process of cognition.

17. See in this connection especially A, 2, 3, 1–4; *Ibid.* 9, and in a particular manner C, 11.

18. "La fe, dicen los teólogos, que es un hábito del alma cierto y oscuro. Y la razón de ser hábito oscuro es porque hace creer verdades reveladas por el mismo Dios, las cuales son sobre toda luz natural, y exceden a todo humano entendimiento, sin alguna proporción." A, 2, 3, 1.

19. St John of the Cross calls articles and propositions of faith "semblantes plateados." He explains his reason thus: "es de saber que la fe es comparada a la plata en las proposiciones que nos enseña, y las verdades y sustancía que en sí contiene son comparadas al oro; porque esa misma sustancia que ahora creemos vestida y cubierta con plata de fe, habemos de ver y gozar en la otra vida al descubierto, desnudo el oro de la fe." C, 12, 4. All of which is confirmed as he continues: "cuando se acabe la fe por la clara visión de Dios, quedará la sustancia de la fe desnuda del velo de esta plata de color como el oro. De manera que la fe nos da y comunica al mismo Dios, pero cubierto con plata de fe." It seems difficult to assert all this any more clearly: the conceptual formulas by which the revealed truths are presented are only the silver plating, which covers the purest gold within: the gold of the divine essence, the gold of divinity itself, which will appear clearly to the intellect in heaven. Therefore the objective reality is the same in faith and in the beatific vision: God himself in his divine essence is communicated to the intellect and to the soul in the one and in the other. When St John of the Cross says that the articles and propositions of faith contain within themselves the divine essence itself, he is speaking with respect to the intellect of the person in this life to whom they are presented, presupposing this native tendency to understand the essence itself (*sustancia entendida*).

20. "De aquí es que, para el alma, esta excesiva luz que se le da de fe le es oscura tiniebla, porque lo más priva y vence a lo menos, así como la luz del sol priva otras cualesquier luces, de manera que no parezcan luces cuando ella luce y vence nuestra potencia visiva . . . Así, la luz de la fe, por su grande exceso oprime y vence la del entendimiento; la cual sólo se extiende de suyo a la ciencia natural, aunque tiene potencia para lo sobrenatural, para cuando Nuestro Señor la quisiere poner en acto sobrenatural." A, 2, 3, 1. (Here he is speaking of so-called obediential potency.)

21. See *Ibid.*

22. ". . . la fe es noche oscura, para el alma, y de esta manera la da luz; y cuanto más la oscurece, más la da de sí." A, 2, 3, 4. Many similar statements can be found. The whole works of St John of the Cross, especially the "Subida" and the "Noche," offer us a "mystical nocturn." The words "night," "obscurity," "darkness" appear frequently. Although they are symbolic and poetic expressions, many things are implied in them which must be understood in a very strictly philosophical and theological sense. The mean-

ing of the symbol "obscurity" must be sought from the context, where reasons explaining it are clearly given. Related to faith, "obscurity" implies the transition from a metaphysical (strictly speaking, theological) to a psychological stage of the problem, in which the experience of faith on the part of the subject is ultimately resolved. It follows that St John of the Cross somehow includes in this symbolic notion of "obscurity" the noetic part of his theology. The ascent of the human intellect to the divinity itself as its object involves a comparison of the natural with the supernatural. Thus "obscurity" expresses the notion of that transcendence, not only from the ontological point of view, but also in the order of knowing, according to the strictest logic of comparison. The divinity cannot be known connaturally by the human intellect. Therefore when it is known participatively from the point of view of formal object (it is known in this way in faith, as we have seen), then the whole dynamic of such participative cognition, its whole intensity is expressed psychologically in the emptiness of the subject, who will participate all the more intensely in the divinity according as the "obscurity" is greater. In this sense we can understand the words by which St John of the Cross, in A, 2, 9, 1 explains the likeness of faith to God: ". . . es tanta la semejanza que hay entre ella (=la fe) y Dios . . . así como Dios es tiniebla para nuestro entendimiento, así ella también ciega y deslumbra nuestro entendimiento."

23. See *Ibid.*

24. ". . . la fe no es ciencia que entra por ningún sentido, sino sólo es consentimiento del alma de lo que entra por el oído." A, 2, 3, 3.

25. See A, 2, 3, 1. This text has been previously cited. See also: ". . . por este solo medio, se manifiesta Dios al alma en divina luz, que excede todo entendimiento. Y, por tanto, cuanta más fe el alma tiene, más unida está con Dios." A, 2, 9, 1. See also: ". . . la fe . . . contiene en sí la divina luz; la cual acabada y quebrada por la quiebra y fin de esta vida mortal, luego parecerá la gloria y luz de la Divinidad que en si contenía." *Ibid.*, 9, 3.

26. ". . . Dios es para el alma tan oscura noche como la fe." *Ibid.*, 2, 1.

27. See especially in A, 2, 12, where many things are said concerning the manner of discursive prayer using the imagination and phantasy.

28. See especially *Ibid.* 13, 14, 15 and the treatise N, 1.

29. "Llamamos aquí noche a la privación del gusto en el apetito de todas las cosas; porque así como la noche no es otra cosa sino privación de la luz, y, por el consiguiente de todos los objetos que se pueden ver mediante la luz, por lo cual se queda la potencia visiva a oscuras y sin nada; así también se puede decir la mortificación del apetito noche para el alma, porque privándose el alma del gusto del apetito en todas las cosas, es quedarse como a oscuras y sin nada." A, 1, 3, 1. In the case of faith, that privation and abnegation is understood as the absence or even the rejection in the intellect of any clear intellection regarding divine things (as in the active night of spirit.)

30. ". . . en este camino, el entrar en camino es dejar su camino; o, por mejor decir, es pasar al término y dejar su modo, es entrar en lo que no tiene modo, que es Dios . . . " ". . . pasar de su limitado natural interior y

exteriormente . . . en limite sobrenatural que no tiene modo alguno, teniendo en sustancia todos los modos." A, 2, 4, 5.

31. See *Ibid.*, 10, where all these concepts are distinguished with precision.

32. "Y fué, que así como la fe se arraigó e infundió más en el alma mediante aquel vacío y tiniebla y desnudez de todas las cosas, o pobreza espiritual, que todo lo podemos llamar una misma cosa, también juntamente se arraiga e infunde más en el alma la caridad de Dios. De donde cuanto más el alma se quiere oscurecer y aniquilar acerca de todas las cosas exteriores e interiores que puede recibir, tanto más se infunde de fe, y, por consiguiente, de amor y de esperanza en ella, por cuanto estas tres virtudes teologales andan en uno." A, 2, 24, 8.

33. ". . . el entendimiento y las demás potencias no pueden admitir ni negar nada sin que venga en ello la voluntad . . ." A, 3, 34, 1.

34. See similar texts: A, 1, 3, 1; A, 2, 2; A, 2, 3, 1.

35. See A, 2, 24, 8 previously cited.

36. This in very many places, See, e.g., A, 2, 10, 4; *Ibid.*, 24, 4, etc.

37. ". . . cuanto más pura y esmerada está el alma en fe, más tiene de caridad infusa de Dios; y cuanto más caridad tiene, tanto más la alumbra y comunica los dones del Espíritu Santo, porque la caridad es la causa y el medio por donde se les comunica. Y aunque es verdad que en aquella ilustración de verdades comunica al alma él alguna luz, pero es tan diferente la que es en fe, sin entender claro, de ésta, cuanto a la claridad, como lo es el oro subidísimo del muy bajo metal; y cuanto a la cantidad, como excede la mar a una gota de agua. Porque en la una manera se le comunica sabiduría de una o dos o tres verdades, etc., y en la otra se le comunica toda la sabiduría de Dios generalmente, que es el Hijo de Dios que se comunica al alma en fe." A, 2, 29, 6.

38. See *Ibid.*, 22, and especially *Ibid.*, 22, 4 ff., where St John of the Cross explicitly teaches this manifestation of the divinity in the person of Jesus Christ, to whom we must cling in simple faith, so that, believing, we may enter into the fullness of the mysteries of God.

39. "El día, que es Dios en la bienaventuranza, donde ya es de día a los bienaventurados ángeles y almas que ya son día, les comunica y pronuncia la palabra, que es su Hijo, para que le sepan y le gocen. Y la noche que es la fe en la Iglesia militante, donde aún es de noche, muestra ciencia a la Iglesia, y por el consiguiente, a cualquier alma, la cual le es noche, pues está privada de la clara sabiduría beatífica; y en presencia de la fe, de su luz natural está ciega." A, 2, 3, 5. ". . . en alguna manera, esta noticia oscura amorosa, que es la fe, sirve en esta vida para la divina unión, como la lumbre de gloria sirve en la otra de medio para la clara visión de Dios." A, 2, 24, 4.

40. Such a concept is based upon texts, especially in A, 2, 5, 2, where the holy doctor asserts that the actual union of the faculties of the soul with God does not take place in a permanent, but only in a transient manner in this life. But faith is properly the unitive virtue for the intellect, which means that the habitual union of this faculty with God must be understood from the fact of its

residing in the intellect (the habitual union is declared permanent). The actual union, however, which happens to the intellect only transiently, can be properly understood in contemplation, when this occurs in the intellect. In fact, it can be understood in no other way.

41. ". . . como las tres virtudes teologales, fe, esperanza y caridad, que tienen respecto a las dichas tres potencias (memoria, entendimiento y voluntad) como propios objetos sobrenaturales, y mediante las cuales el alma se une con Dios según sus potencias, hacen el mismo vacío y oscuridad cada uno en su potencia. La fe en el entendimiento . . . " A, 2, 6, 1.

42. ". . . todas estas formas ya dichas, siempre en su aprensión se representan, según habemos dicho, debajo de algunas maneras y modos limitados, y la Sabiduría de Dios, en que se ha de unir el entendimiento, ningún modo ni manera tiene, ni cae debajo de algún limite ni inteligencia distinta y particularmente, porque totalmente es pura y sencilla. Y como quiere que para juntarse dos extremos, cual es el alma y la divina Sabiduría, será necesario que vengan a convenir en cierto medio de semejanza entre sí; de aquí es que también el alma ha de estar pura y sencilla, no limitada ni atenida a alguna inteligencia particular, ni modificada con algún limite de forma, especie e imagen. Que pues Dios no cae debajo de imagen ni forma, ni cae debajo de inteligencia particular, tampoco el alma para caer en Dios, ha de caer debajo de forma o inteligencia distinta." A, 2, 16, 7.

43. ". . . esta noticia general . . . es a veces tan sutil y delicada, mayormente cuando ella es más pura y sencilla y perfecta, y más espiritual e interior, que el alma, aunque está empleada en ella, no la echa de ver ni la siente. Y aquesto acaece más cuando decimos que ella es en sí mas clara, perfecta y sencilla; y entonces lo es cuando ella embiste en el alma más limpia y ajena de otras inteligencias y noticias particulares, en que podría hacer presa el entendimiento o sentido . . . Y así, por el contrario, cuanto ella está en sí en el entendimiento menos pura y simple, más clara y de más tomo le parece al entendimiento, por estar ella vestido o mezclada o envuelta en algunas formas inteligibles en que pueda tropezar el entendimiento o sentido." A, 2, 14, 8.

44. See C, 13, 12–15, where the holy author describes contemplation in a different way. Contemplation occurs in the intellect as an overflowing from the experience of the "divine touch" ("el toque"). The touch itself seems to designate an intense supernatural experience, ". . . de lo cual se deriva en el entendimiento el silbo de la inteligencia." This very subtle "inteligencia" is properly experienced by the possible intellect, where it is received passively. It causes a very rich delight, the result of unitive contact with the divinity itself. The agent intellect is quiet, ceasing its operation, and therefore all the accidental elements of the process of intellectual union, all phantasms, all particular intellections also cease. The possible intellect then enjoys "sustancia entendida," not, to be sure, in a clear manner as in the beatific vision, but in the obscurity of faith, and while all particular functions connatural to the intellect cease, the "sustancia entendida" alone remains in faith. The intellection

of it is not connatural to the intellect, which simply experiences it passively (does not see it) under the influence of the Holy Spirit. Nevertheless, in such an experience faith opens up profoundly according to its objective nature. It cannot develop any further, since it has the divinity for its object, it is properly united to the divinity, and the divinity is objectively presented by faith to the intellect. Now, in such an experience as described in C, 13, the intellect attains the fullest participation in the divinity that is possible for it in this life by means of faith.

45. See, e.g., ". . . la fe . . . contiene en sí la divina luz; la cual acabada y quebrada por la quiebra y fin de esta vida mortal, luego parecerá la gloria y luz de la Divinidad que en sí contenía." A, 2, 9, 3.

46. ". . . .contemplación infusa; por cuanto es sabiduría de Dios amorosa, hace dos principales efectos en el alma, porque la dispone purgándola e iluminándola para la unión de amor con Dios. De donde la misma sabiduría amorosa que purga los espíritus bienaventurados ilustrándolos, es la que aquí purga al alma y la ilumina." N, 2, 5, 1.

MARY, THE BEES OF THE
EXSULTET AND THE
CARMELITES

John Sullivan, O.C.D.

As the liturgical nature and setting of this article suggests, the author studied liturgy at Paris' Institut Supérieur de Liturgie and obtained a doctorate from the Institut Catholique in liturgical-sacramental theology. The text is based on a paper delivered at the 1979 Eighth International Mariological Congress in Zaragoza, Spain.

THE CURRENT STATE OF LITURGICAL RENEWAL

Twenty-three years separate us from the day Pope John XXIII startled a group of Cardinals and the world with the announcement he was going to convoke a general, ecumenical council of the Church.[1] Stirred by an initial personal inspiration as unexpected by Papa Roncalli as those who were hearing the news for the first time, John XXIII had convinced himself a council would be a really efficacious means to rejuvenate the face of old Mother Church and render her beautifully appealing to a modern world suffering from a spiritual malaise that ranged from debilitating apathy and despair to open hostility to the Gospel.[2] A call went out to the Church to use the council as an opportunity for renewal and updating (or "*aggiornamento*" as Pope John liked to term it). It is neither my task to attempt

274

here, nor does the reader need either, a complete description of what transpired from that day early in 1959 until December 8, 1965 when Vatican II closed its final public session and the post-conciliar period we are still living began.

It seems evident that the council dreamed of by John XXIII and brought to term by Paul VI set underway processes in church life which have effected the broadest ever liturgical revision in the history of the Church. Whether knowingly or unknowingly, willy nilly, these two far-sighted popes were responsible for and, in the case of Papa Montini, presided over an unparalleled renovation of the ritual and devotional life of the Catholic Church. Now that we benefit from twenty years of hindsight a brief sketch of the atmosphere reigning in our time is possible in order to establish the usefulness of my consideration of one instance of devotion to Mary among the "Calced" Carmelites of the sixteenth century. This "sketch" will approach Vatican II's liturgical revisions from four points: "a real need for liturgical reform"; the "method to be used" in fostering that reform; "positive results to date"; and "some misgivings." Thereafter we will touch the points which articulate the heart of this paper on "Mary, the Bees of the *Exsultet* and the Carmelites."

A Real Need

What had been striven after by a few pioneering individuals during the early years of this century in the ferment we call the "liturgical movement" — namely, the active participation of all baptized members of the Church in the liturgy for the upbuilding of their spiritual life — is recognized by the council's very first document, *Sacrosanctum Concilium* or the Constitution of the Sacred Liturgy (*CSL*), to be the goal and aim of the renewal intended by that portentous document. But what did the *CSL* indicate as the main means to achieving that which its paragraph 14 called "full, conscious and active participation?" It designated *reform* as the way to guarantee that proper degree of participation which would unlock the liturgy's riches for the people. But reform, in turn was to be undertaken and justified for the following reason:

> The liturgy is made up of unchanging elements divinely insti-
> tuted, and elements subject to change. The latter not only may
> but ought to be changed with the passing of time if features have
> by chance crept in which are less harmonious with the intimate
> nature of the liturgy, or if existing elements have grown less
> functional.[3]

As is well known, the Council's indirect manner of speaking in
this passage ("*if* features have *by chance* crept in . . . , or *if* existing elements have grown less functional") befits the predomi-
nantly pastoral and non-condemnatory spirit adopted by the
council fathers for the council documents, but one ought not to
be mistaken: mention of "features . . . less harmonious with
the intimate nature of the liturgy" would not have been made
by the *CSL* unless this were indeed the case, and the council
was using these terms to tell us to do something about the often
sub-standard condition of liturgical practice in the Church.

Just how "sub-standard" things were at the beginning of our
century is explained for us by Dom Bernard Botte, the famous
Benedictine expert in oriental languages and monk of Mont
César Abbey in Louvain where the liturgical movement in this
century was born. He is one of those pioneers of the liturgical
movement and his *memoirs* present a fascinating, if sobering,
picture of liturgy of days gone by:

> What was the way the liturgy was celebrated at the beginning of
> the twentieth century? Young people today evidently cannot
> imagine this . . . You have to go back to the very first years of
> the century, to the time I entered secondary school. I would in-
> sist on saying that I wasn't one of those child martyrs who put
> up with high school as if it were a period of forced labor and who
> remain scarred by it for the rest of their days. Accordingly, my
> criticisms are not motivated by bitterness. I loved my old high
> school and I ended up having a good time there. Nor was I a
> precocious child whose esthetic sense could have been hurt by
> the literary and musical barrenness of the songs we had to sing.

I distinguished myself along with the others, as innocent as could be: "O Jesus, you enflame me with celestial ecstasies," or "Fly, fly, angels of prayer." My criticisms are retroactive. Hindsight helps me to try to look things over again and understand them.

Every morning at eight o'clock there was a Mass in the students' chapel. Actually, it was a large study hall in which a row of pews were placed on either side of a central aisle. Up front there was only one altar in a little apse located between two sacristies. Mass was said by an old, more or less voiceless, priest — even in the first row the only thing you'd hear was a murmur. The group rose for the gospel, but what gospel it was nobody dreamed of telling us. We didn't even know what saint's feast it was or which deceased persons were being prayed for at the Masses said in black vestments. The people's missal did not exist. You could lose yourself in any book of prayer at all, but we were pulled out of our drowsiness from time to time by the recitation out loud of a few decades of the rosary or the chanting of either a motet in Latin or a hymn in French. The only moment we would pray with the priest was after Mass when the celebrant, kneeling at the foot of the altar, recited the three "Hail Mary's" with the "Hail, Holy Queen" and the prayers prescribed by Leo XIII. Receiving Communion at this Mass was out of the question. For that matter, no one at that time seemed to notice a relationship between the Mass and Communion.

In the two parishes of my home town things weren't much better. There were some sung Masses, but they were a dialogue between the clergy and the cleric-organist. The people remained quiet and passive. Each person could follow his desire to say the rosary or lose himself in *The Most Beautiful Prayers of St Alphonsus Liguori* or *The Imitation of Christ*. As for Communion, it was distributed before Mass, after Mass or in the middle of Mass, but never at the moment indicated by the liturgy. The schedule was determinant: Communion is distributed every fifteen minutes. When a Mass began on the hour you were sure to see, as the clock struck a quarter past, a priest in a surplice come out of the sacristy, rush to the altar and interrupt the celebrant in order to take a ciborium out of the tabernacle. The celebrant then was allowed to continue the Mass until he was disturbed once again by the ciborium being returned to the tabernacle . . . Mass was no longer the prayer of the Christian community. The clergy prayed entirely in place of and in the name of the community. As a result, the faithful were only remotely involved and paid attention to their own personal devotion. Communion appeared to be a private devotion without any special link to the Mass.[4]

Undoubtedly I could appeal to recollections of similar cases related to other sectors of the liturgy previous to Vatican II, but no need: I feel most people will recognize and admit that there was a definitely "real" need for the revision aimed at by the council and its *CSL*. Now for a word about the main contours of the method suggested by the council for affecting the revision of those "elements subject to change."

Method to be Used

Here again it is enough to be brief and to touch only the essentials of a conciliar vision which has been expounded at length in entire volumes of commentary.[5]

First of all the revisions of the liturgy are to heed tradition and to flow organically out of it (*CSL*, 23). No quantum leaps are envisioned by the conciliar constitution as a result; rather, a repristinization of the best and main-line elements of the Church's communal prayer life is intended.

If interested, then, in solid prayer forms the *CSL* wants to assure that an important guiding principle is a wedding of clarity with the holy (*CSL*, 21), as well as intelligence with mystery (*CSL*, 34). Consequently, there is to be no dichotomy between the perennial nature of faith experience which catches mankind up in the holy mystery of God and the contingent expressions of that same faith experience. To use the words of the *CSL*, "in this restoration both texts and rites should be drawn up so that they express more clearly the holy things which they signify. Christian people, as far as possible, should be able to understand them with ease and to take part in them fully, actively, and as befits a community" (*CSL*, 21). This means, to choose another expression of the council's liturgy document, "the rites should be distinguished by a noble simplicity" (*CSL*, 34).

Of course, other directives can be found in the same third section of Chapter One of the *CSL* entitled "The Reform of the Sacred Liturgy," but we need not go into them so long as we realize that there is a progression inherent in any great change in liturgical practice like the one intended by Vatican II: namely, that you need to revise but must go beyond *revision* (which is limited to the texts and the ritual indications), through *reform* of both the "ways of worship" and of worshippers alike, on to true *renewal* of the liturgical piety of the Church.[6]

Now for a word or two about the fruits of the council's desiderata and principles to date. As most people are aware, public opinion on the outcome so far is divided.

Positive Results

Any attempt to be comprehensive and speak for the many sectors of the Church around the world would be futile and unrealistic. We can at least focus the perspective and point out indications of real progress afoot in the United States of America.

The National Opinion Research Center located in Chicago recently did a survey in shifts of Catholics' attitudes toward Catholic education over a ten year period which spanned the conciliar and post-conciliar phases of Church life in the United States beginning in 1963, and the results were published in the book *Catholic Schools in a Declining Church.*[7] The overall picture of Church life in general derived from their survey would best be termed "bittersweet," but the unpleasant side is not due to the changes in the liturgy. On the contrary, the liturgy in its revised form appears to be well received by a majority of American Catholics, hence attention is scarcely merited by the vociferous minority who continue to lament the loss of the Latin Mass. Many people feel "at home" in the new way of celebrating. The handshake of peace was disapproved by "only 23%" and the only new feature to fall under majority approval was lay ministers of communion which received a 45% rating of acceptance. Even though the results show a drop in Mass attendance of 21% (from 71–50%), with monthly confessions cut in half (38–17%) and devotions down (meaning activities such as retreats, days of recollection, and missions), the researchers were able to say that "the principal reasons for not going to church seem to have little bearing on dissatisfaction directed at the new liturgy."[8] And so:

> Despite the pontification from both the left and the right that "the people" are upset about the changes in the Church, we could find little evidence that any more than a minority are opposed to the "new Church." Sixty-seven percent thought the changes were for the better, only 19 percent thought they were for the worse (the rest thought the changes made no difference).[9]

Six years ago another survey, smaller in extent, was conducted by Francis Lonsway of the Center for Applied Research in the Apostolate. Though of more limited proportions, it gauged the liturgical renewal's affects on an important sector of church leadership, the junior clergy — and the results were impressive, to say the least. The sampling involved priests ordained in 1969 and who had been active in the ministry "nearly five years since their ordination."[10] As might be expected of a younger, and more idealistic, portion of the population, as many as three out of four took the trouble to answer the questionnaire sent to them. These would have been the men who, during their theological studies, could be seen on picket lines and at vigils for the end of the Vietnam War or for the Civil Rights Movement.

Aside from other significant, but general information provided by their answers, the worship role of these young men looms up as investing major importance for them. The presiding they do at the Eucharist rated the highest on the list of personal satisfactions derived from their overall ministry — 98.9, in fact, was the percentage of satisfaction. Closely aligned with it was preaching the Word of God at 96.2% and "administering the sacraments" at 95.8%. When asked to single out the *main* task that provided most job satisfaction, the Eucharist was chosen by 36.2% of the priests, followed by preaching (14.1%), counseling (11.9%) and renewing self (at 7.5%).[11] Far from alienation from liturgical actions, these men show a great deal of contentment with the revised rites they had just begun to celebrate early on in their lives as ordained ministers.

Well aware that "one robin does not make Spring," I would not conclude from these two surveys to immense success for liturgical revision, but one does notice how progress does seem to be showing up. To conclude this section I would like to quote from a man noted as much for his probity as a historian of the ancient Church as for his devotion to the cause of liturgical renewal: Canon Aimée-Georges Martimort. In his *Bilancio della Riforma Liturgica* he assures us that "the work accomplished during the years 1963–1973 in line with the directives of Vatican II surpasses in extent and in depth all the great liturgical reforms of the past, even the reforms at the end of the sixteenth century and the one attributed to St Gregory the Great."[12] And he lists six positive acquisitions of the recent reform: (1) enrichment of our doctrine of the sacraments which has been clarified in a prodigious manner; (2) pastoral enrichment; (3) changeover from Latin back to the vernacular, characterized by another great historian of the liturgy, Cyrille Vogel of Strasbourg, as the "second linguistic revolution" experienced by the Church;[13] (4) refound veracity and simplicity of rites; (5) a wonderful biblical and prayer enrichment; and (6) strengthening of eucharistic piety.[14]

Lest I appear to lack a balanced sense of realism, however, I would now direct attention to a number of voices raised against the ferment following upon the *CSL*.

Some Misgivings

Here too, in the interest of brevity, I will limit myself to the United States scene, and leave out of consideration the comments of those liturgists who have voiced a certain degree of worry over developments.[15]

Before providing an inventory of complaints, though, we should pause for a reflection of considerable importance: when faced with the unsettling reality of a "chiaroscuro" tint to the current state of liturgical affairs, we ought to remind ourselves — in case we've forgotten it — that there never has been nor will there ever be, any such thing as a "golden age" of liturgical prayer practice. This is not merely to parry the blow of the criticism leveled at the most recent contemporary attempts to provide more living forms of communal prayer for the Church, but actually as a defense of the perennial principle of *lex orandi legem statuat credendi* — in the sense that any particular prayer form of any century whatsoever, and regardless of how felicitous it might seem to the trained eye, is going to include the special "flavor" of the faith vision particular to the time in which it enters the mainstream of the prayer heritage of the "Church at Prayer."[16] As a result, most anyone will be able to point out limitations in that particular and contextualized faith vision. Every age has its limits as a result, and none is a "golden age," but we will not for that matter be authorized to dismiss out of hand the validity of that particular expression.[17] So much for the "golden age" illusion.

Criticism of the effects of liturgical revision have been present from the earliest stages of the post-conciliar reform. An adequate description of all the griefs proclaimed and solutions offered would involve a separate historical treatment in its own right, and we certainly cannot permit ourselves that here. Instead, it will be more worthwhile to indicate some of the main areas of concern for those who claim something is amiss. Liturgical language is a frequent target of the barbs of unsatisfied critics.[18] The revised *Order of Mass* often receives negative assessments.[19] Distress is registered about the abandonment and transformation of the symbols of the Catholic liturgy.[20] Music and hymnody are judged to be in a state of dismal disarray.[21] And, perhaps underlying the other complaints in all their variety, is the fear that liturgy has lost its holy dimension and that from now on we must work toward "the recovery of the sacred" since liturgical revision has tampered with it.[22]

This latter, and most crucial, misgiving deserves our attention. For, at stake is one of those methodological principles enunciated by Vatican II in the *CSL*, namely, both clarity and mystery are to be safeguarded in the revision of texts and rites "so that they express, more clearly the holy things they signify" (*CSL*, 21). One is not to be promoted at the expense of the other. What James Hitchcock of St Louis University claims, nevertheless, is that we are witnesses to a "decline of the sacred" in the past decade and a half whereby the program for a renewed liturgy has unfortunately so changed forms as to modify the spiritual content of the liturgy and has so heedlessly sought after the "chimera of relevance" as to abandon the wellsprings of Catholic devotion — thus throwing out the baby with the bath water. Hitchcock thus raises a perennially important question, even if several of his own arguments seem untenable or ought to be stated in a more nuanced way: that question concerns the symbolical adequacy of ritual actions and wordings to transmit that Sanjuanist "no-sé-qué" of the divine transcendency once they have been appreciably changed. There ought not to be any dichotomy so that devotion, considered as the interiorized *affectus cordis*, may remain intact, be respected and allowed to flourish. But that is exactly what Hitchcock and others are questionning: namely, is it in fact able to survive in our revised liturgy after Vatican II? Have there not been so many significant changes and deletions as to substantially alter the spirit of the Catholic liturgy, and leave that once revered edifice beyond recognition? Has the Church abandoned (he uses that term rather frequently), in other words, its own best treasure and drawing card? Convinced we are witnesses to a period of "deliberate iconoclasm" Hitchcock speaks for himself and others when he claims that "it is easier and less potentially destructive to add new levels of symbolism to the rite than to eliminate older ones," for "sacred ritual is a tight network of meanings in which nothing is entirely meaningless and . . . thus alterations in this network can have the effect of unraveling the whole, even if apparently trivial changes are made."[23] I personally do not agree that the whole has become unraveled in our time, but I do share his concern over results likely to follow upon excessive "abandonment" of religious symbols in the quest for renewed liturgical practice.

A whole process of discernment of what has actually happened in these past nineteen years since the promulgation of *CSL* would be necessary to prove whether Hitchcock and others like him are accurate in their accusation that things have gone too far. Time does not permit any such analysis right now, but something can be said about the opposite of abandonment, deletion and excision of symbols. Their retention bespeaks a proper conservative tendency of the liturgy, and I would like to explain how an act of retention took place in the past, during the period of revision after the other great reform council of the modern era of Church history, Trent. By understanding what happened to a small passage from the *Exsultet* found in the Carmelite Rite which expressed devotion to Mary we might be better able to calm the fears of those who have come to equate contemporary liturgical reform with getting rid of elements of our heritage.

TRENT CALLS FOR LITURGICAL RENEWAL AND CARMEL RESPONDS

Some interesting parallels can be drawn between the processes of liturgical renewal called for by Vatican II and the Council of Trent. Obviously, a univocal comparison is not possible; nor do I intend to draw up a broad-based confrontation of many instances. Just one case will serve my purposes: and it is a case which is likely to interest the disciplines of spiritual theology and mariology, as well as liturgy. I will divide my remarks into two portions: (1) Trent's Call for Renewal and (2) Carmel's Reaction to It.

Trent and Liturgical Renewal

1. Reform After the Council Itself

It is a commonplace among liturgists that when we refer to the Tridentine liturgical reform we must locate that reform in the post-conciliar period. The Council, as a matter of fact, remitted to the Pope, Pius IV, the revision of the liturgical books.[24] A commission of bishops was established to carry out the necessary work and in a certain way it could be "considered the predecessor of the Congregation" of Rites.[25]

The *Roman Breviary* was the first liturgical book to be issued as a result of this commission's work.[26] Then, two years later on July 14, 1570 the *Roman Missal* was promulgated by the new pope, Saint Pius V.[27] This edition of the *Missal* contained the Easter vigil texts which included the *Exsultet.*

2. Effects of the Tridentine Reform on Special Rites

In the bull of promulgation of the new breviary, "Quod a nobis" (July 9, 1568), the Roman Rite's usages are imposed on the Church with one significant exception. Those rites which can claim an existence of "200 or more years" need not adopt Rome's office and may retain their own texts. In the light of this obvious recommendation to embrace Rome's prayer forms, religious Orders and Congregations reacted in differing ways.

"The continued existence of the traditional rite of the (Cistercian) Order was never threatened by the reforming activities of St Pius (1566–72)," says Archdale King, but by 1618 the "repudiation of the traditional rite was consummated . . . and the general chapter formally adopted the Roman *ritus celebrandi* . . ."[28] For the Dominicans — a Mendicant Order which could claim antiquity of rite beyond two centuries — the Tridentine invitation "had little direct effect upon the(ir) Dominican rite."[29] The two branches of the Carmelites took two different routes.

Carmelite Reactions

1. Discalced Option

The Discalced Carmelite reform movement received its initial impulse in the same year the Trent breviary was promulgated. A good number of the first generation of superiors until juridical independence from the "Calced" friars of the Ancient Observance in 1586 were long since trained in Carmelite novitiates and were therefore familiar with the Carmelite rite. All the same, by 1586 their reform had adopted the Roman Rite *in toto*, thus accepting the spirit and forms of Trent's call for liturgical unity.

Some might be tempted to ascribe this complete adoption of the Roman Rite to love for the Church of Rome, just as St Teresa their foundress had always desired to be a faithful "daughter of the Church," but there were also other factors at work. As I have had the opportunity to show elsewhere,[30] the shift of the Discalced to the Roman Rite was made in order to put distance between them and the Ancient Observance, and thus assert their own identity as a separate, self-contained entity. This they did by appealing to "Quod a nobis' " 200-year-or-older clause and applying it to themselves as a reform of "more or less only twenty years" duration.[31] By September 20, 1586 the brief that established the Discalced an independent province of the Order and allowed the adoption of the Roman Rite was granted by Pope Sixtus V, and so the Discalced began to pray *more Romano* with the renewed Tridentine books.[32] Things went differently, as already hinted, for the "Calced" Carmelites after Trent; and in that difference lies a gesture which safeguarded a gem of Carmelite devotion to Mary in the Carmelite liturgy that is at the heart of this article. Now we can consider what was involved and what happened as this branch of the Order of Carmel in the sixteenth century maintained one of the quaint, though beautiful, instances of honor rendered to the "Virgo puerpera," patroness of their Order.

2. "Calced" Carmelite Awareness of Need for Change

In matters liturgical the friars of the Ancient Observance were well aware of the call to reform present in the Church at mid-century in the 1500's.[33] According to Joachim Smet, "the Order, like the Church, felt the need to reform its liturgy, and in the course of this process the rite underwent the influence of the strong Romanizing trend of the time."[34] In its main features the revision accomplished affected the following areas of the Carmelite Rite:

In Caffardi's (the Prior General) breviary and missal, as the pope notes, "doubtful and apochryphal writings are eliminated, uncertain texts of the Fathers removed, scriptural passages in the antiphons and responsories revised according to the Roman breviary, corrected by the decrees of the council of Trent." The form and order of the rubrics were completely changed, new ones introduced and many old ones suppressed. The divine office was arranged differently, the ordinary of the Mass underwent changes. The sanctoral—even in respect to Carmelite saints—was drastically reduced.[35]

We are assured by Benedict Zimmerman, however, that "one could not admire enough the good taste with which special traits of the old rite were retained and by which an important and venerable monument of medieval Christian piety was preserved intact."[36] It is my particular good fortune to have uncovered one of those "special traits of the old rite" which was affirmed and not abolished after Trent, one which testifies to the tender and unflagging devotion of the Carmelites for Mary, but—finally—one which most Carmelite scholars and writers have been entirely unaware of.

3. Mary in the "Calced" Carmelite post-Trent Version of the *Exsultet*

Upon examination the "Calced" Carmelite Missal of 1587 shows characteristics which definitely identify it as a book of the Carmelite Rite in all its particularity. And yet, a close look at the lines of the *Exsultet* in it reveals an almost exact copy of the text found in the recently reformed *Missale Romanum* of 1570. An almost exact copy, nonetheless, because there is a textual difference of six significant lines. Without any further ado I will provide here my own translation of the passage in question:

> This is the truly happy and wonderful bee,
> whom the male does not violate,
> whose progeny is not harmed by the male,
> whose integrity is not broken by its offspring,
> just like Holy Mary who conceived as a virgin,
> brought forth as a virgin and remained a virgin.[37]

Strange to say, no Carmelite mariologist has commented on

this precious gem of marian devotion hidden away in the lines of the Easter *laus cerei*. The Carmelite liturgical expert Augustin Forcadell, in a compendious article written for *Ephemerides Liturgicae* in 1950 on the Carmelite Rite, draws attention to these lines *en passant*; but in his longer series of articles on the Carmelite liturgy in the *Analecta Ordinis Carmelitarum* where he treats expressly and at length "Devotion to the Blessed Virgin Mary in the Carmelite Liturgy"—and hence would have had the opportunity to address himself to the *Exsultet* passage—he does not even mention those six lines.[38] The classic study on Carmelite mariology doesn't know they exist.[39] Study of this passage—a missed opportunity for past Carmelite mariologists and liturgists—can help us consider devotion to Mary in the sixteenth century and draw some possible lessons for our own century.

But a few preliminary remarks about the origins of this six line passage in the *Exsultet* are necessary to shed light on the importance of its presence in the post-Trent edition of the Carmelite missal, and I will divide these remarks into three points before moving on to weigh the reasons for its retention in that missal.

First of all the *Exsultet*: its nature and origins are well documented for us by historians of the liturgy. Research has established that liturgical developments in the Church from the fourth century onward had produced several versions of the Easter *praeconium* or *laus cerei*.[40] Secondly, the version which the Roman Rite adopted by the middle ages (which was not the one in its ancient Gelasian Sacramentary) was the same as the one adopted by the Carmelites when they formed their own Rite, except for the extra six lines in the "praise of the bees" section.[41] Thirdly, regarding the bees, the steps which led the early Carmelites to include the six lines about the bees escape my research—very little is known about the thirteenth century "roots" of the Carmelite liturgy—but it is certain that those lines were found in the ancient text of this Gallican version of the *praeconium paschale* and were deleted from the Roman Rite's *ordo* for Holy Saturday by the Innocentian reform of the liturgy early in the thirteenth century.[42] A study on the presence of the bees in the *Exsultet* was written about fifty years ago and may be consulted in the Belgian liturgical journal *Questions liturgiques et paroissiales.*[43]

Even though we do not at this point know the exact reasons for the early Carmelites' inclusion of the final six lines of the "praise of the bees" around the time of the pontificate of Innocent III (1198–1216), I feel I can offer some plausible reasons for the inspiration which led their spiritual heirs of the sixteenth century to retain those same lines when they reacted to Trent's call to reform.

Their motivation to conserve the passage about the bees and Mary was fed from three sources. First of all, the passage refers to *Mary*, and thus would exert a forceful influence on any liturgical revisors from an Order like the Carmelites which had so many special forms of devotion to the Blessed Mother in its liturgy. It should suffice to cite just one witness to the diffuse presence of Mary in the Carmelite Rite. The words are those of Daniel of the Virgin writing in the seventeenth century: "Among the other marks of the Order's special devotion to its most benevolent Mother is the frequent repetition, in the divine Office and Masses, of the well-known antiphon or canticle, *Salve Regina*, which has been used constantly in the Order from the most ancient times."[44]

The second is much more closely related to the special emphasis this passage gives to Mary's *virginity*. As Carmelite mariologists tell us, the earliest writings of the Order show a predilection for the virginity and the Immaculate Conception from which there grew devotion to the "virgo purissima."[45] This devotion affected the Order's interpretation of the origins of the vow of chastity, and was symbolized by the wearing of the Order's white mantle.[46] Virginity with the particular nuance of purity also reenforced the central preoccupation of all Carmelites, the pursuit of the contemplative life according to the golden words of the Order's unofficial spiritual directory, the *Institutio Primorum Monachorum*:

> In this life we distinguish a double aim: the first we attain by our effort and the exercise of the virtues with the help of divine

grace, that is, to offer God a heart holy and *purified* of all actual
stain of sin . . .

The second aim of this life is proposed to us as a simple gift of
God, that is, it consists in tasting in a certain way in our heart,
to experience in our spirit the strength of God's presence and the
sweetness of the glory from on high, not only after death but
even in this mortal life.[47]

Purity in Mary was a pre-eminent attraction for the Carmelite
contemplatives, helping them to pursue the evangelical "purity
of heart" of the first beatitude as a way to seek and see the face
of God.[48] No wonder then, that the passage of the *Exsultet*
about the bees which reached them through the transmission of
the Order's spiritual heritage and liturgical tradition was not
deleted when the changes in the liturgical books took place after
Trent. (The survival of devotion to the Virgin Most Pure
among the Discalced is attested to in the monasteries of the
Nuns in Spain where even today the usual greeting, unlike the
popular "Praised be Jesus Christ" in other parts of Europe, is
rendered "Ave Maria purísima" — with the response "sin pecado
concebida.")

The third possible reason for the survival of the passage
about Mary and the bees concerns the very *symbol of the bees.* As
Rainero Cantalamessa indicates in a recent study on Easter,
the ancients had a strange entomology which did not offer an
accurate idea of how bees generated their offspring. They believed (and the *Exsultet* passage agrees) that the bees actually
did not bring forth offspring but "collected their little ones with
their mouths from the leaves which produced them."[49] That accounts for the strange vision (to our eyes) of the first four lines
of the *Exsultet* passage conserved in the Carmelite missal. Now
to answer the question about its particular connection with the
Carmelites themselves. In his *Historia Orientalis* Jacques de
Vitry describes life on Mount Carmel in the Holy Land at
about the end of the twelfth century and likens the Carmelite
hermits there to busy bees. His description runs this way: "Others, following the example of and imitating the holy and soli-
tary Prophet Elijah, lived as hermits on Mount Carmel . . .

near the fountain of Elijah and not far from the monastery of
the blessed virgin Margaret, occupying small cells in the rocks
and like the Lord's *bees*, they made honey of an entirely spiritual
sweetness."[50] Whether or not all Carmelites were very familiar
with this passage of Jacque de Vitry's chronicles would be hard
to prove, but there is no reason to exclude some familiarity
either, and this could have guided the choice of the Carmelite
liturgists to retain the bee passage of the *Exsultet* as a welcome
embellishment of their Order's chant of that beautiful "poem
inspired with great lyricism" (Christine Mohrmann).

IMPLICATIONS OF THE SIXTEENTH CENTURY
CARMELITE OPTION FOR THE FUTURE

Well aware that there will be no practical difference at stake
for the Carmelite Rite as a result of what I am about to remark
— the "Calced" Carmelites no longer celebrate it and have given
up their right to use it — I would still like to reflect on a few lessons which derive from the sixteenth century option to retain
their Order's marian devotion contained in those six lines of the
Exsultet. At the outset I would stress that this reflection will
amount to a personal analysis, more than a refined estimate of
this historical phenomenon based on the tools of the trade of the
social sciences. It seems to me the questions can be approached
from three angles with the first related to change and cultural
differences, the second treating the interaction of liturgical
symbols, and the third addressing the matter of particularized
milieux's use of such symbols.

Change and Cultural Differences

Apart from their personal distastes for the direction taken by
the flow of things, most people today are ready to admit they
live in, or are at least witnesses to, broad changeovers in cultural patterns. So often we hear even scholarly individuals
(therefore not just popularizers) speak of a "crisis in civilization"
as it was known up until, say, the First World War.

All of us have our own list of hallmarks for this flux abroad in the land. I would propose for consideration the following pairs. *Discontinuity* seems to win out over *continuity* as attention turns more to the future than the past.[51] *Improvisation* is called for with greater insistence than just *transmission* of the wisdom of the ages. *Novelty*, and hence change itself, is esteemed more than *permanence*.[52] And, even if of late there are signs of resistance to the new scene which take the form of "back-to-basics" movements, the feeling shared by many indicates we have indeed turned a corner and will not be able to return to things as they were earlier in this century.

But, we ought not to be so caught up in the current ferment that we overestimate the imperatives of generalized transformation of all spheres of life that it appears to predicate and preach. Regardless of the proven rapid rate of social change in many sectors of society, there is no imperious hard-fast rule which can decree the abolition of particularized institutions, customs or practices. On the contrary, the more flourishing and serene particular entities are, the more the general sector will be able to depend on them and benefit from their special contribution. On occasion, this can definitely mean that sub-units hold on to those things which assure their own identity.

The "Calced" Carmelites of the sixteenth century did this very thing at a time of intense revision of the Church's liturgy in the wake of Trent; today need not be different. For, as Vatican II's *CSL* assures us, there is ample room for special usages similar to the praise of the bees in the *Exsultet* within the purview of the transformation it decreed: "Provided that the substantial unity of the Roman rite is maintained, the revision of liturgical boks should allow for *legitimate variations* and adaptations to different *groups*, regions, and peoples, especially in mission lands. Where opportune, the same rule applies to the structuring of rites and the revision of rubrics."[53] The principle is there allowing us to feel at home with the kind of affirmative operation the Carmelite liturgists performed to keep the adapted version of the *Exsultet* they possessed as a valid expression of their devotion to Mary and of their attachment to the contemplative life. A second and a third point now will address themselves to *how* that principle might be expected to operate in the future.

"Less is (not necessarily) More"

As well as being an age of "rapid social change" ours is one of dwindling resources. Because of oil shortages the cost of travel rises constantly; the situation is hardly much better in the area of food production where great imbalances continue to plague many nations. A move is afoot to convince people to do with less, to strive for conservation in order to pave the way to a more equitable distribution of the earth's wealth. "Small is beautiful" was the symptomatic title of a rather popular book in the United States.[54] Its main thesis recommends a streamlining of our demands for and use of goods and would seem to give its blessing on another popular dictum nowadays that "less is more."

While this is an altogether exemplary approach to really difficult economic decisions we need to make, it could turn out to be fairly disastrous if applied to religious practice and symbolism. When dealing with the latter, quantity has never been the ultimately determinant criterion even though liturgy is by nature quite conservative and seems to promote the accumulation of symbols over the ages. The process of initiation into the faith community enables the believer to discern relative importance and mutual resonance within a plethora of symbols connected with church life, and thus to be at ease with many verbal, performative and object symbols. As as result, one need not — and sometimes ought not — prefer "streamlined" liturgies marked by such a degree of sobriety that they fail to serve the whole person, body and soul.

Applied to the bees of the *Exsultet*, one can safely say that the *extra* passage of the Carmelite version of that great chant actually enhanced the celebration of Easter for those who conducted and/or attended the Easter vigil in their Carmelite churches. The qualitative difference appealed to that special attachment

of the Carmelite friars for Mary which justifiably depended on
something which made them, and us too, fully human: the
emotions. And we ought always to remember that in matters
liturgical, the emotions are the ever-present handmaid of faith.
Many of the difficulties of the Lefevreites or of Professor
Hitchcock with the revised liturgy today flow from an emotional bias previous to, and underlying, all their doctrinal griefs.
All the same, the sectarians of the lost Tridentine Rite, in their
yearning for emotional fulfillment, are not alone in their assess-
ment of the dryness afflicting our revised liturgy. Liturgists at a
recent symposium made much of the blandness, the verbosity,
the understatement and casualness which has creeped into the
celebration of the Roman Rite along with the introduction of
the revised rites.[55] How else does one account for so much attention being paid to popular religiosity? As the conduct of official services becomes trite and their attractive force wanes
because of a failure to cater to the emotions of individual be-
lievers, other forms of *devotio* will exert a fascinating attraction
instead.[56]

Here, too, the Carmelites' preservation of the gem in honor
of their *Virgo puerpera* in the *Exsultet* offers a precious hint at how
to move ahead. Not that one should recommend the resurrection of those six lines for actual use, but rather that we be slower
to excise similar usages from our liturgy just because they seem
too particularized, or limited in scope, or too much of an in-
cumbrance to some particular rite as it now stands. Some of
James Hitchcock's misgivings would be answered, as well.

"Different Strokes for Different Folks"

Just as individuals in the Church show needs of an emotional
nature which lie in an area beyond textual purity or precision
of execution in ritual, so too *groups* betray differing needs —
needs that require varying expressions, forms and even rhythms
which might very well be appropriate to them and them alone.[57]
The English-language expression "different strokes for different
folks" though not overly urbane-sounding offers some pertinent
advice in this regard. I might not need or relish the affection a

Neapolitan has for Our Lady of Pompeii because I am an American and not a Dominican (and also because I am much more partial to the classical beauty of the frescoes of that town by the Bay of Naples than to the flamboyant ex-voto's found in the basilica there!). Put in other words, we owe respect to valid expressions of devotion without having to accord them an un-differentiated welcome. As Vatican II states: "Even in the liturgy, the Church has no wish to impose a rigid uniformity in matters which do not involve the faith or the good of the *whole* community. Rather she respects and fosters the spiritual adorn-ments and gifts of the various races and peoples."[58]

The sixteenth century "Calced" Carmelites formed a group which decided to keep a form of liturgical prayer that did not really "involve the faith or the good of the whole community," and so they felt free to thus assert their own special emphasis and in-sight into devotion to Mary. The promotion of other special nuances in the celebration of the liturgy today is just as desir-able, if not moreso, after altogether too many people have been opting for less instead of more in their search for renewed lit-urgy. The entire Church stands to gain from initiatives like the one taken by those Carmelites in the name of a sane plurality of prayer forms. Not, however, that this would lead to automatic exportation from one religious milieu in the Church to another or to the Church at large: traditions germane to particular communities can and ought to be allowed to live lives of their own. That way, local marian shrines like the one dedicated to Our Lady of the Rosary in Pompeii, or particular group devo-tions of Orders like the Brown Scapular of the Carmelites will thrive so long as they continue to attract persons who derive some special fruit from the spirit of the particular focus of devo-tion provided by the place or object of piety. The liturgy will not fail to benefit from such healthy para-liturgical or liturgy-associated devotions, because "popular devotions of the Chris-tian people are warmly commended, provided they accord with the laws and norms of the Church."[59] And no one will have reason to blame the Church for "throwing the baby out with the bath water."

NOTES

1. "Questa festiva ricorrenza," January 25, 1959, *A.A.S.*, 51 (1959), 65–69.

2. See his programmatic discourse on the council's goals "Humanae Salutis" dated December 25, 1961 with which he convoked Vatican II in *The Documents of Vatican II* ed. Walter Abbott (New York: America Press, 1966), pp. 703–709. All the quotations of Vatican II documents to be made in this article will come from this translation.

A handy summary of expectations being voiced about the council before it started was written by Hans Küng, *The Council, Reform and Reunion* (New York: Sheed and Ward, 1961).

3. *CSL*, No. 21.

4. Bernard Botte, ch. 1 "The Starting Point," *Le mouvement liturgique: Témoignage et souvenirs* (Paris: Desclée, 1973), pp. 9–11.

5. Aside from the many specialized journals which provided paragraph-by-paragraph analyses one would do well to rely on Joseph Jungmann's "Constitution on the Sacred Liturgy," *Commentary on the Documents of Vatican II*, I (New York: Herder and Herder, 1967), pp. 1–87.

6. This fine distinction in relation to Vatican II in general is well expounded by John O'Malley, "Reform, Historical Consciousness and Vatican II's *Aggiornamento*," *Theological Studies*, 32 (1971), 573–601 and then applied to the ligurgical scene of recent years by Walter Burghardt, "A Theologian's Challenge to Liturgy," *Theological Studies*, 35 (1974), 233–48.

7. A. Greeley, Wm. McCready, K. McCourt eds., *Catholic Schools in a Declining Church* (Kansas City: Sheed and Ward, 1976).

8. See an advance-notice resume of the book's contents in S. Saldahna, Wm. McCready, K. McCourt and A. Greeley, "American Catholics—Ten Years Later," *Critic*, 33 (Jan.-Feb. 1975), 15–16.

9. Saldahna, McCredy, McCourt, Greeley, *Ten Years Later*, p. 15.

10. Francis Lonsway, "Satisfactions and Dissatisfactions in the Ministry of Young Catholic Priests, *CARA Seminary Forum*, 5 (1976), 3–8.

11. Lonsway, *Satisfactions and Dissatisfactions*, p. 5.

12. Aimée-Georges Martimort, *Bilancio della Riforma Liturgica* (Milano: Edizioni O. R., 1974), p. 13.

13. Cyrille Vogel, *Introduction aux sources de l'histoire du culte chrétien au Moyen Age* (Torino: Bottega d'Erasmo, 1975—2nd ed.), p. xi. Coll. "Biblioteca degli 'Studi Medievali,'" 1.

14. Martimort, *Bilancio*, ch. 2 "The Great Achievement of the Reform," pp. 19–39.

15. A number of leading liturgists in America have taken stock, either on the occasion of the tenth or fifteenth anniversaries of the *CSL*, of uneven progress from domain to domain of liturgical renewal and also of insufficiencies to date. See, for example, Gerard Austin, "The Constitution and the Academy: A Coincidence of Anniversaries," *Worship*, 53 (1979), 291–301 and William Leonard, "A Taste for Liturgy," *Worship*, 53 (1979), 215–20.

Mixed reviews of recent liturgical progress written by European experts are available to the U.S. reading public in the form of the following two books: James Crichton, *The Once and the Future Liturgy* (New York: Paulist Press, 1977) and Joseph Gelineau, *The Liturgy Today and Tomorrow* (New York: Paulist Press, 1978).

16. Theodor Klauser, *A Short History of the Western Liturgy: An Account and Some Reflections* (Oxford: Oxford U. Press, 1969), pp. 128–29.

17. Dom David Knowles in his "Foreword" to Albert Mirgeler's *Mutations of Western Christianity* trans. Edward Quinn (Montreal: Palm, 1964), p. vi puts the same thought this' way:

> Church historians in general say too little about the changes of cultures and of mental climates, and still less about the extravagances, ignorance and misconceptions of sentiment and devotion that have coloured or deformed the purity of the spirit in past centuries and that may well be obscuring for us now in this respect or that the full vision of revealed truth. For there is no reason to suppose that our generation is more spiritually clear-sighted than that of our forefathers, or that the Spirit of truth will not work in the future as He has worked in the past.

18. See the extensive remarks of Richard Toporoski, "The Language of Worship," *Communio* Eng. ed., 4 (1977), 226–60.

19. Michael Davies, *Liturgical Revolution* III: *Pope Paul's New Mass* (New Rochelle, NY: Arlington House, 1979).

20. Victor Turner, "Passages, Margins, and Poverty: Religious Symbols of Communitas," *Worship*, 46 (1972), 390–412 and 482–94 and "Ritual: Tribal and Catholic," *Worship*, 50 (1976), 504–26.

21. Francis Schmitt, *Church Music Transgressed: Reflections on "Reform,"* (New York: Seabury Press, 1977).

22. James Hitchcock, *The Recovery of the Sacred* (New York: Seabury Press, 1974).

23. Hitchcock, *Recovery*, pp. 158–59.

24. As Pierre Jounel says:

> The dogmatic and disciplinary decrees of session 22 of the Council (September 17, 1562) constitute the point of departure for all liturgical reform (. . .) The Council should then have taken up the revision of the breviary and missal, a task which had been in preparation by a special commission for several years, but many bishops were becoming impatient to return to their dioceses. The Fathers accordingly decided, in the twenty-fifth and last session, to hand the dossier over to the pope. . . .

See "From the Council of Trent to Vatican II," *The Church at Prayer* I ed. A.-G. Martimort (New York: Desclée, 1968), pp. 41–42.

See also Klauser, *Short History*, ch. 4 "Rigid Unification in the Liturgy and Rubricism: From the Council of Trent to the Second Vatican Council," pp. 117–29 and Hubert Jedin, "Das Konzil von Trient und die Reform der liturgischen Bücher," *Ephermerides Liturgicae*, 59 (1945), 5–38.

25. See Frederick McManus, *The Congregation of Sacred Rites*, Doctoral Dissertation (Washington, Catholic U. Press, 1954), p. 24. Coll. "Canon Law Studies," 352.

26. See Pierre Batiffol, ch. 5 "The Breviary of the Council of Trent," *History of the Roman Breviary* trans. from 3rd Fr. ed. by Atwell Baylay (London: Longmans, Green & Co., 1912), pp. 177–235.

27. See Amato Frutaz, "Contributo alla storia della riforma del messale promulgato da San Pio V nel 1570," *Problemi di vita religiosa in Italia nel Cinquecento* (Padova: Editrice Antinore, 1960), pp. 187–214 and Hubert Jedin, "Das Konzil von Trient und die Reform des Römischen Messbuches," *Liturgisches Leben*, 6 (1939), 30–66.

28. Archdale King, ch. 2 "Cistercian Rite," *Liturgies of the Religious Orders* (London: Longmans, Green & Co., 1955), pp. 78 and 81.

29. William Bonniwell, *A History of the Dominican Liturgy* (New York: Joseph Wagner, 1944), p. 279.

30. See John Sullivan, "Night and Light: The Poet John of the Cross and the *Exsultet*," *Ephemerides Carmeliticae*, 30 (1979), 52–68.

31. See the Discalced petition "La Provincia delli Scalzi" dated March 18, 1586 in *Documenta Primigenia* III (Roma: Edizioni del Teresianum, 1977), p. 114. Coll. "Monumenta Historica Carmeli Teresiani," 3.

32. *Documenta Primigenia* III, pp. 137–43, especially p. 142 for the passages concerning the adoption of the Roman Rite.

33. A fundamental article on the Carmelite liturgy comes from Benedict Zimmerman, "Liturgie de l'Ordre des Carmes," *D.A.C.L.*, II (1910), cols. 2166–75. Later studies like Augustin Forcadell, "Conspectus Historicus Liturgiae Carmelitanae," *Analecta Ordinis Carmelitarum*, 10 (1938–40), 85–105; 165–79; 224–37; 294–300; 375–81; 437–45 and 11 (1942), 139–67 plus Archdale King, ch. 4 "The Carmelite Rite," *Liturgies of the Religious Orders*, pp. 235–324 acknowledge their debt to the Swiss Discalced Carmelite historian's careful study.

For new research on the rather early (1312) Ordinal of Sibert de Beka see Edmund Caruana, "The Ordinal of Sibert de Beka with Special Reference to Marian Liturgical Themes: Historical, Liturgical, Theological Investigation" (Unpublished Diss. for Licence in Liturgical Theology, Anselmianum, Roma 1976), xxxiii, 224 pp.

34. Joachim Smet, "The Revision of the Liturgy" in ch. 9 "The Spiritual and Intellectual Life of the Order," *The Carmelites: A History of the Brothers of Our Lady of Mount Carmel vol. II: The Post Tridentine Period, 1550–1600* (Darien, Ill., private publ., 1976), p. 231.

35. Smet, *The Carmelites 1550–1600*, p. 231.

36. Zimmerman, *La liturgie des Carmes*, col. 2175.

37. See *Missale Fratrum Carmelitarum Ordinis Beatae Dei Genetricis Mariae* (Romae: Ex typo. Jacobi Tornerii, 1587), p. 186:
O vere beata et mirabilis apis,
cuius nec sexum masculi violant,

> fetus non quassant,
> nec filii destruunt castitatem.
> Sed sicut sancta concepit virgo Maria,
> virgo peperit et virgo permansit.

38. Augustin Forcadell, "Ritus Carmelitarum Antiquae Observantiae," *Ephemerides Liturgicae*, 64 (1950), 48 (this fleeting reference seems to be copied by Archdale King, *Liturgies of the Religious Orders*, pp. 267–68) and Augustin Forcadell, *Conspectus Historicus*, Pt. 3 "De cultu Beatae Mariae Virginis in liturgia Carmelitana," pp. 294–300, 375–81 and 437–45.

39. See Valerius Hoppenbrouwers, *Devotio Mariana in Ordine Fratrum B. V. M. de Monte Carmelo a Medio Saeculo XVI usque ad Finem Saeculi XIX* (Roma: Institutum Carmelitanum, 1960).

40. See Herman Schmidt, "Laus Cerei," *Hebdomada Sancta* II (Roma: Herder, 1957), pp. 627–50 and Jordi Pinell, "La benedicció del ciri pascual i els sus textos," *Liturgica* II (1958), 1–119. Coll. "Scripta et Documenta," 10.

41. See Schmidt, *Hebdomada Sancta* II, pp. 640–44 for the Roman Rite version and *Ordinaire de l'Ordre de Notre-Dame du Mont-Carmel par Sibert de Beka (vers 1312)* ed. Benedict Zimmerman (Paris: Picard, 1910), p. 171 for the Carmelite usage.

   The Gelasian Sacramentary version began with the words "Deus mundi conditor, auctor luminis . . ." See *Liber Sacramentorum Romanae Aeclesiae Ordinis Anni Circuli* ed. Cunibert Mohlberg (Roma: Herder, 1960), pp. 68–70. Coll. "Rerum Ecclesiasticarum Documenta-Series Maior, Fontes," 4.

42. See Bernard Capelle, "L'Exsultet pascal oeuvre de Saint Ambroise," *Miscellanea Giovanni Mercati* I (Vatican City: 1946—"Studi e Testi," 121), p. 224. The full text of the "praise of the bees" is 28 lines long as transcribed in Schmidt, *Hebdomada Sancta* II, pp. 642–43. Schmidt indicates the passage was composed in imitation of Virgil's *Georgics*.

43. Georges Malherbe, "Les abeilles de l'*Exsultet*," *Questions liturgiques et paroissiales*, 19 (1930), 61–75.

44. Quotation taken from the *Vinea Carmeli* of Daniel of the Virgin by Augustin Forcadell, "The Carmelite Rite," *Sword*, 8 (1944), 213. The series of articles by Forcadell cited in our note 33 *supra* was translated into English for publication in the American Carmelite magazine *Sword* in an even more fragmented manner through the years 1941–1946.

45. See Valerius Hoppenbrouwers, "Virgo purissima et vita spiritualis Carmeli," *Carmelus*, 1 (1954), 255–77.

46. Hoppenbrouwers, *Virgo purissima*, pp. 264–66. In this connection it would be interesting to note that the hymn "Flos Carmeli" contains several references to virginal purity which are indicated here in italics:

> Flos Carmeli
> vitis florigera,
> splendor caeli
> *virgo puerpera*
> singularis.

Mater mitis
sed *viri nescia*
Carmelitis
esto propitia,
stella maris.

See Bartholomaeus Xiberta, "Rhythmus 'Flos Carmeli' in liturgia carmelitana," *Analecta Ordinis Carmelitarum*, 20 (1957), 156–59.

47. See *Les plus vieux textes du Carmel* ed. François de Ste. Marie (Paris: Eds. du Seuil, 1961 — 2nd ed.), pp. 111–12. One inspiration for this beautiful passage would certainly have been Cassian's *Conferences* 10, 7. Italics mine.

48. See the confirmatory reflections of Ludovico Saggi, "Santa Maria del Carmelo," *I Santi del Carmelo* ed. L. Saggi (Roma: Institutum Carmelitanum, 1972), pp. 122–29.

49. Rainero Cantalamessa, *La Pasqua nella Chiesa antica* (Torino: Soc. Editrice Internazionale, 1978), p. 163, note 9. He cites Virgil's *Georgics*, 4, 200 ff as his source for this thought.

50. As quoted in *Les plus vieux textes du Carmel*, pp. 64–65. Italics mine.

See clarifying remarks about de Vitry's description by Elias Friedman, *The Latin Hermits of Mount Carmel: A Study of Carmelite Origins* (Roma: Edizioni del Teresianum, 1979), p. 209. Coll. "Institutum Historicum Teresianum — Studia," 1.

51. The best known statement about this whole phenomenon is Alvin Toffler, *Future Shock* (New York: Random House, 1970).

52. See Part I "The Death of Permanence," Toffler, *Future Schock*, pp. 10–44.

53. *CSL*, No. 37. Italics mine.

54. E. F. Schumacher, *Small is Beautiful: Economics as if People Mattered* (New York: Harper and Row, 1973).

55. See Nathan Mitchell, ch. 1 "Useless Prayer," and Don Saliers, ch. 3 "Prayer and Emotion: Shaping and Expressing Christian Life," *Christians at Prayer* ed. John Gallen (Notre Dame, Ind.: U. of Notre Dame Press, 1977), pp. 1–25 and 46–60. Coll. "Liturgical Studies."

56. See Carl Dehne, ch. 5 "Roman Catholic Popular Devotions," *Christians at Prayer*, pp. 83–99.

57. Applied to the Divine Office this results in the distinction into "cathedral" and "monastic" style celebrations insisted upon by William Storey, ch. 4 "The Liturgy of the Hours: Cathedral versus Monastery," *Christians at Prayer*, pp. 61–82.

58. *CSL*, No. 37. Italics mine.

59. *CSL*, No. 13.